THE SCHOOLS HISTORY PROJECT
· S·H·P ·
· OFFICIAL TEXT ·

DISCOVERING THE PAST FOR GCSE

MEDICINE & HEALTH
THROUGH TIME
a development study

IAN DAWSON

IAN COULSON

Series Editor: Colin Shephard

HODDER
EDUCATION
AN HACHETTE UK COMPANY

The Schools History Project

Set up in 1972 to bring new life to history for student aged 13-16, the Schools History Project continues to play and innovatory history education. From the start, SHP aimed to show how good history has an important contribution to make to the education of a young person. It does this by creating courses and materials which both respect the importance of up-to-date, well-researched history and provide enjoyable learning experiences for students.

Since 1978 the Project has been based at Trinity and All Saints University College Leeds. It continues to support, inspire and callenge teachers through the annual conference, regional coures and website: http://www.schoolshistoryproject.org.uk. The Project is also closely involved with government bodies and awarding bodies in the planning of courses for Key Stage 3 GCSE and A level.

Note: The wording and sentence structure of some written sources have been adapted and simplified to make them accessible to all pupils, while faithfully preserving the sense of the original.

Also Available Medicine & Health through time Dynamic Learning
1) 978 0 3409 4671 8
2) 978 0 3409 4672 5

Series consultants
Terry Fiehn
Tim Lomas
Martin and Jenny Tucker

© Ian Dawson and Ian Coulson 1996

First published in 1996
by Hodder Education, an Hachette UK Company
338 Euston Road
London NW1 3BH

Reprinted 1997 (twice), 1998, 2001, 2002 (twice), 2003 (twice)
2004, 2005, 2006, 2007, 2009, 2010, 2011, 2012

Layouts by Amanda Hawkes
Artwork by Art Construction, Philip Ford, Linden Artists, Karen Donnelly and Steve Smith
Typeset in 10½ 12 Walbaum Book by Wearset, Boldon, Tyne & Wear
Printed in Dubai

A catalogue entry for this book is available from the British Library

ISBN 978-0-7195-5265-6

Acknowledgements

cover *t* & **p.134** Bridgeman Art Library, London/Royal College of Surgeons, London, *b* Science Photo Library; **p.8** *t* & *b* from *Tomb of the Eagles* by J.W. Hedges (John Murray, 1984); **p.16** *l* Hirmer Fotoarchiv, *r* Ancient Art & Architecture Collection; **p.17** *t* The Mansell Collection, *b* Christian Aid/Elain Duigenan; **p.18** Ancient Art & Architecture Collection; **p.23** *l* & *r* Wellcome Institute Library, London; **p.24** © Peter Clayton; **p.29** The Mansell Collection; **p.30** Copyright British Museum; **p.31** Copyright British Museum; **p.32** The Mansell Collection; **p.41** Ancient Art & Architecture Collection; **p.43** Wellcome Institute Library, London; **p.60** © Oxford Archaeological Unit; **p.62** *t* By permission of The British Library (MS Egerton, f.53), *b* City of Hereford Archaeology Unit/Mappa Mundi Trust; **p.63** *t* Hulton Getty Collection, *b* Mary Evans Picture Library; **p.65** Hulton Getty Collection; **p.68** Ann Ronan Picture Library; **p.69** *t* Österreichische Nationalbibliothek, Vienna, *b* The Bodleian Library, Oxford (MS Ashmole 391, part v, f.10r); **p.70** *l* By permission of The British Library (MS Sloane 1975, f.93), *r* Wellcome Institute Library, London; **p.76** Ann Ronan Picture Library; **p.77** *t* from *History of Technology, Vol II* (Clarendon Press, Oxford, 1956) reproduced by permission of Oxford University Press, *b* The Bodleian Library, Oxford (MS Ashmole 399, f.34r); **p.84** *l* Mary Evans Picture Library, *r* © The Trustee of the Wellcome Trust; **p.86** *t* The Mansell Collection, *b* Frederico Abora Mella, Milan; **p.87** The Mansell Collection; **p.88** Reproduced by kind permission of The Royal College of Physicians of London; **p.91** *t* © The Trustee of the Wellcome Trust, *b* Ann Ronan Picture Library; **p.93** *r* Wellcome Insitute Library, London; **p.94** Reproduced by kind permission of the President and Council of the Royal College of Surgeons of England; **p.95** Philadelphia Museum of Art: Purchased: SmithKline Beecham Corporation Fund; **p.96** Wellcome Institute Library, London; **p.102** Nigel Cattlin/Holt Studios; **p.106** *l* Mary Evans Picture Library, *r* Hulton Getty Collection; **p.112** © The Trustee of the Wellcome Trust; **p.115** The Mansell Collection; **p.116** Wellcome Institute Library, London; **p.117** Ann Ronan Picture Library; **p.118** *t* © The Trustee of the Wellcome Trust, *b* Copyright British Museum; **p.119** The Mansell Collection; **p.125** The Mansell Collection; **p.130** Hulton Getty Collection; **p.132** Hulton Getty Collection; **p.135** Wellcome Institute Library, London;
p.136 Ann Ronan Picture Library; **p.138** Hulton Getty Collection; **p.139** Mary Evans Picture Library; **p.140** The Mansell Collection; **p.141** Guildhall Library, Corporation of London; **p.143** Wellcome Institute Library, London; **p.144** *l* Punch, *r* Mary Evans Picture Library; **p.150** Imperial War Museum, London; **p.151** Imperial War Museum, London; **p.152** Imperial War Museum, London; **p.153** Hulton Getty Collection; **p.160** Hulton Getty Collection; **p.161** *l* The Salvation Army International Heritage Centre, *r* Camden Local Studies and Archives Centre, London; **p.163** *tl* Public Record Office, London (INF 13/140/22), *bl* Public Record Office, London (INF 13/188), *bc* Imperial War Museum, London, *br* Hulton Getty Collection; **p.164** Hulton Getty Collection; **p.165** *r* The Mansell Collection; **p.166** *l* & *r* Mirror Syndication International; **p.167** Public Record Office, London (CAM 21/2034); **p.168** © Associated Newspapers/Solo; **p.173** Manchester Evening News/News Team; **p.174** Tim Beddow/Science Photo Library; **p.177** Courtesy Gladstone Working Pottery Museum, Stoke-on-Trent; **p.178** *l* Courtesy ACTIONAID, *r* Martin Adler/Panos Pictures; **p.191** *l* Ann Ronan Picture Library, *r* The Mansell Collection; **p.192** Ancient Art & Architecture Collection; **p.194** *tl* The Mansell Collection, *tc* Reproduced by kind permission of The Royal College of Physicians of London, *tr* Mary Evans Picture Library, *bl* © Institut Pasteur, Paris, *br* The Mansell Collection; **p.197** *clockwise from tr* Mary Evans Picture Library, The Mansell Collection, Reproduced by kind permission of The Royal College of Physicians of London, Frederico Abora Mella, Milan, Ann Ronan Picture Library, Mary Evans Picture Library; **p.201** *l* Corbis/Bettmann, *tr* & *br* © The Trustee of the Wellcome Trust; **p.202** Österreichische Nationalbibliothek, Vienna; **p.203** © Sally Greenhill/Sally & Richard Greenhill; **p.204** *l* & *r* © York Archaeological Trust; **p.205** Hulton Getty Collection; **p.207** *l* Hulton Getty Collection, *r* James King-Holmes/Science Photo Library; **p.208** *t* Copyright British Museum, *b* Römisch-Germanisches Zentral Museum, Mainz; **p.209** *l* By permission of The British Library (MS Add 42130, f.61r), *r* © The Trustee of the Wellcome Trust; **p.210** *t* Wellcome Institute Library, London, *b* Geoff Tompkinson/Science Photo Library.

(*t* = top, *b* = bottom, *r* = right, *l* = left)

Contents

Health care today: has it always been like this?

Antenatal checks

Long before a baby is born its health is checked. Doctors and nurses observe it using a stethoscope and a scanner. This scanner puts a picture of the baby onto a computer screen. On the screen the nurse measures the baby's legs, arms and head to check it is developing properly.

Scientists can even test the fluid in the womb to see if the baby has any inherited diseases; their powerful equipment can spot any abnormality in a baby's GENES.

Doctors and nurses advise the mother on what to eat, drink and do during her pregnancy, for example warning her of the danger of smoking or of eating certain foods. They know that many medical problems are caused by bad diet or by smoking.

Childbirth

In childbirth the mother is helped by midwives, doctors, relations and friends. Some babies are born at home. Most are born in hospital. The mother may be offered injections as painkillers to get her through the pain of childbirth. She may also have brought her own favourite herbal REMEDIES with her to the hospital.

If there are complications the doctor can quickly arrange a Caesarian section – an operation to get the baby out of the womb – or a forceps delivery to help the baby out. A Caesarian is a major operation but surgeons nearly always perform it safely, saving the life of both the child and the mother.

Premature babies can be kept alive in an incubator.

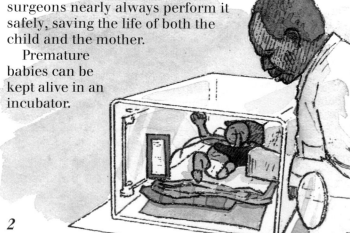

Pre-school checks

From birth onwards the health of the child is regularly checked. As soon as it is born it is weighed, its limbs are checked, its heart is listened to. Often it gets its first injection – vitamin K – when only a few minutes old.

For the next few years children have regular checks by nurses, doctors, dentists, and opticians. They are weighed, measured, have hearing tests, eye tests, blood tests and injections to protect them against diseases like whooping cough, diphtheria and tetanus.

Parents and doctors

Despite this, children still get injured or ill. Most problems are dealt with by a parent or carer at home. Ordinary people know enough about everyday health problems such as cuts, tummy aches, headaches and colds to know what to do.

Sometimes a doctor's help is needed. When the doctor sees a child he/she will look closely at the symptoms before deciding what the problem is.

1. Which of these did your doctor do when you last went to see him or her?

   - listen to your breathing
   - ask you questions
   - give you a prescription
   - give you an injection
   - take your pulse
   - test your reflexes
   - send you for more tests
   - consult a book or a computer.

2. Why do you think each of these things was helpful to the doctor?

Accident!

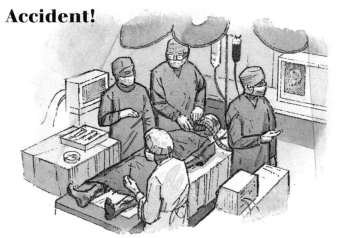

There has been a road accident. The victim has badly crushed legs and head injuries. He is rushed to hospital by ambulance. An operation is needed, and he is given a blood TRANSFUSION. He has lost so much blood that he would die without this. The victim is put to sleep by ANAESTHETIC. In a two-hour operation the surgeons set his broken legs, using a metal plate to hold the crushed bones together and repair the fracture to the skull. The surgeons are skilled – they don't have to rush the operation because under anaesthetic the patient feels no pain. The operating theatre is clean and the doctors know how to fight INFECTION in a wound after an operation so the chances are that this boy will make a complete recovery.

Later physiotherapists will help him learn to walk again.

High-tech surgery

In the same hospital another patient is receiving the latest in HIGH-TECH SURGERY to remove a small cancerous growth. Here the surgeons do not even have to put their hands inside the person's body. They send a probe called an ENDOSCOPE into the body through a small INCISION they have made. The endoscope includes a camera which projects the operation onto a computer screen. The endoscope also includes all the tools the surgeon needs to perform the operation. The surgeon guides the tools using the computer.

Doctors are performing more and more complex operations this way each year.

Old age

Health care has improved so greatly that many people live longer than they would have done 100 years ago.

This 80-year-old grandmother can remember a time when health care was very different. When she was a child her mother couldn't even afford to take her to a doctor – because in those days you had to pay for every visit. This woman has lots of medical problems. She has aches and pains in her joints from ARTHRITIS – but there are painkilling and anti-inflammatory drugs to help her. She also has to take some pills every day to control her blood pressure – otherwise she might have a heart attack. She needs an aid to help her hear and spectacles to read.

She lives on her own but once a week a health visitor comes in to check her.

■ ACTIVITY

Do you think it has always been like this?
   Work in pairs. Make two lists:

■ people involved in health care today;
■ treatments and methods used in health care today.

Use the information on this page, but also use your own knowledge of health care today.

   On each list, underline anything which you think also happened 100 years ago; underline it twice if you think it would have happened 1000 years ago.

What is a development study?

A DEVELOPMENT STUDY is a study of how things have changed over a long period of time.

Periods

In this development study you will be examining how medicine and health have changed over 5000 years. You will look at six different periods. Source 1 shows families from different periods.

Causes of illness

You will be investigating what people thought caused diseases and illness in these periods. Source 2 shows healers from different ages and some of their ideas.

Prehistory

The ancient civilisations of Egypt, Greece and Rome
The first doctors

Life expectancy: women 38; men 40

The Middle Ages (AD500–1400)
Very little medical progress

Life expectancy: women 36; men 37

The Medical Renaissance (AD1400–1700)
Many new discoveries about the body

Life expectancy: women 38; men 41

The eighteenth and nineteenth centuries
Discoveries about the true causes of disease

Life expectancy: women 49; men 45

The twentieth century
Rapid progress in preventing and curing many diseases
Life expectancy: women 78; men 72

Timeline markings:
2000
1000
BC
AD
500
1000
1400
1750
1900
2000

You are ill because you have got an evil spirit inside you.

God has made you ill because he is angry with you.

Your body contains four humours (liquids). You are ill because your humours are out of balance.

You are ill because of GERMS. They are all around you and some of them have gone inside you and your body is reacting to them. That is why you are ill.

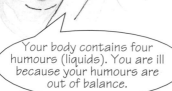

SOURCE 1

SOURCE 2

4

1. Look at the list of causes of illness in Source 2. Which of the people in Source 1 do you think might have believed in each cause? You can get a sheet from your teacher to help you.
2. Which of these ideas are still believed today?

Methods of treating illness

In this development study you are going to see how in different periods people used different methods of treating illness.

3. Look at the list of treatments in Source 3. Which of the people in Source 1 do you think might have used each method of treatment?
4. Which of these methods of treatment are still used today? Which are not?

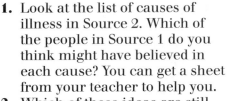

I am going to drill a hole in your head. This will let out the evil spirit which is causing your disease.

The only thing you can do is pray to God that he will take away your illness.

You are ill because the channels of your body are blocked.

Carry this charm with you wherever you go. It has magic powers and will stop you getting ill.

You are ill because this week the planet Jupiter was in conjunction with the constellation Sagittarius.

This tablet will kill the infection which is making you ill.

To get your humours back into balance I must drain some of the blood from you.

I have gathered and mixed a potion of many different herbs. You must drink it. It will heal you.

You'll only be healthy if we clear away all the awful dirt in this town.

I will cut out the infection.

You are ill because of the smells and bad air (MIASMA) which come from the rubbish in the streets.

SOURCE 3

5

Factors causing change

In this development study you will find out how different factors have affected medicine and health. Sometimes these factors hold up progress, sometimes they speed it up.

Factor	Example
Religion	Early religious leaders forbade DISSECTION of dead bodies. As a result doctors could not learn about the body.
War	The Second World War speeded up the development of PENICILLIN.
Governments	When the British government made smallpox VACCINATION compulsory in the nineteenth century, deaths from smallpox plummeted.
Individuals	Pasteur devised a famous experiment to prove that there are MICRO-ORGANISMS (called BACTERIA or germs) all around us.
Science and technology	The technology of glass making improved in the nineteenth century so that scientists had better microscopes which allowed them to study the micro-organisms which caused disease.
Improved communications	When printing was invented new medical ideas such as Vesalius's ideas about anatomy could be spread much more quickly than before.
Chance	Fleming discovered penicillin by accident when some bacteria blew in through his laboratory window.

1. On the last seven pages of your exercise book put one of these factors as a heading on each page. Write the examples from the table above onto the page. Then as you progress through this development study use these pages to record any examples you come across of this factor affecting medicine and health.

Key questions

Remember that throughout your study of the history of medicine and health you will be looking for historical explanations for change:

> **When did things change? Why?**
> **When did things stay the same? Why?**
> **When did things change very quickly? Why?**
> **When was there regression (things getting worse)? Why?**
> **Did change always mean progress?**

These are key questions which you will be asked within each period. By the end of the book you should be asking them yourself without any prompting from us.

Important terms

Medicine and health have their own specialist vocabulary. You cannot talk about medicine and health without using words like prognosis or anatomy – which you may not have come across before. We have included them in the glossary on pages 211–12, and every time an important new term appears in this book it is DISPLAYED LIKE THIS.

2. Work in groups to look up the following terms in the medical glossary on page 211 or in your own dictionary. They are all terms you will come across in Chapter 1 of this book. Look up at least two words each and write your own clear definition of what they mean.

- physician
- plague
- Asclepion
- anatomy
- embalm
- dissection
- gangrene
- rheumatism
- remedy
- sciatica
- trephining.

FROM PREHISTORY TO THE EMPIRES OF EGYPT, GREECE AND ROME 3000BC–AD500

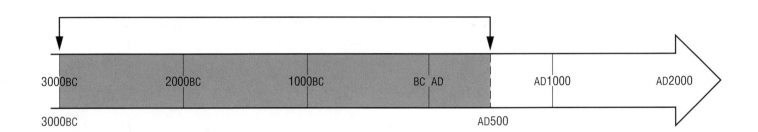

3000BC   2000BC   1000BC   BC AD   AD1000   AD2000

3000BC   AD500

This family lives in a tiny village in prehistoric Britain on the island of Orkney in 3000BC. They have a hard, but mainly peaceful life. They grow crops and gather food.

When they get ill they blame it on spirits or gods. They do not have any doctors, but they make medicines for one another out of plants and herbs, and if that doesn't work they try some magic charms or spells.

Even so, they have short lives. Many men only live to the age of 30 (if they are lucky), women to the age of 24.

This family lives 3000 years later in the Roman Empire. It is the richest and most powerful empire the world has ever known.

This family is wealthy. They have servants to do their work for them. They have fresh water piped to their house.

When members of this family become ill they can consult a doctor. Their doctor is confident he understands their illnesses. He blames illness on their 'humours' being out of balance and so he BLEEDS or purges his patients or gives them herbal medicines to get the humours back in balance.

The doctor's treatments may not sound too good to you but, even so, this family can expect to live longer than the first family: the men to age 40 and the women to age 38.

Progress?

These two families are imaginary but they are typical of what the available evidence tells us about people in each period. So the impression is that things did get better during those 3000 years. In particular, by the time of the Romans, people could expect to live longer lives.

In this chapter you will be investigating whether this is an accurate impression. The chapter begins with prehistoric Britain and then moves on to investigate how the healers of the great ancient empires of Egypt, Greece and Rome tackled illness and disease. These ancient civilisations are famous for their achievements in other areas. Was their medicine also a step forward from earlier times or not?

How healthy were people in prehistoric Britain?

The Tomb of the Eagles at Isbister, Orkney, 3000BC

On a summer evening in 1958, farmer Ronald Simison was working on the rugged clifftops that border his farm at Isbister on Orkney. He was looking for stones to help build a fence when he discovered an ancient wall buried beneath layers of turf. He began to dig and within a quarter of an hour he had unearthed a hoard of treasures which had been buried thousands of years before. They had probably been someone's most precious possessions and included a jet button and tools such as a polished stone mace-head, three stone axe-heads and a flat stone that could have been a knife.

A few days later Mr Simison dug further. He realised he was excavating some kind of room and then suddenly he found an opening. By the flame of a cigarette lighter he looked into another tiny, roofed chamber. The floor was covered with human skulls. He had discovered the 5000-year-old burial place of an Orkney tribe.

The find at Isbister caused great excitement but no one could afford to excavate further and for eighteen years the site lay unexplored. In 1976 Ronald Simison decided to do it himself. He had learnt about archaeology by reading books and watching archaeologists at work on other Orkney sites. Within two months he had excavated the whole tomb including thousands of bones (see Sources 1–2). Among the bones were the skulls and talons of eagles – and the tribe became known as the Eagles.

Professional archaeologists then took over the work. Although 16,000 human bones were found in the tomb, there were no complete skeletons. The tribe of the Eagles – like many other prehistoric people – left their dead in the open so that the flesh rotted or was eaten by birds. The remaining bones were then placed in the tomb.

However, painstaking investigations identified at least 342 individual skeletons. Using modern techniques to study the bones archaeologists have been able to build up a picture of how healthy people were at Isbister 5000 years ago. Their findings are summarised opposite. All of the information in Source 3 is adapted from the *Tomb of the Eagles* by J.W. Hedges who supervised much of the work at Isbister.

SOURCE 1 The tomb at Isbister after excavation was complete. The entrance to the tomb is at the centre

SOURCE 2 Human skulls found in the tomb

■ ACTIVITY

You are going to see how much you can learn about the health of people at Isbister from the evidence of the skeletons alone. The chart on the right gives you five questions to answer.

1. Make your own copy of the chart.
2. Use the evidence in Sources 1–3 to try to answer the questions for Isbister. You may not be able to find evidence to answer some of the questions!

		Isbister 3000BC
1	How healthy were people?	
2	What caused sickness?	
3	How did they treat illnesses and injuries?	
4	Who provided medical care?	
5	What did they think caused illness?	

Accidents rarely caused death. Only 2 per cent of the people had broken bones and most of them showed evidence of healing. Prehistoric Orkney seems to have been peaceful. No fortifications or weapons have been found.

There was a high death-rate among babies and young children, and also between the ages of 20 and 35. Very few people lived to be over 40.

Men were 160cm to 172cm tall. Their average height was 170cm. Women were from 146cm to 162cm. Their average height was 161cm.

The people had strong muscles, especially leg muscles. Some of their ankle bones were unusual, probably because they did a lot of climbing with their ankles flexed, to collect birds' eggs from the cliffs for food.

Their teeth were very healthy, although they were ground down by particles of stone which got into bread when the corn was ground. Only nine out of 1,537 teeth had decay. However, a man aged 45–50 had three abscesses on his back teeth which must have been extremely painful.

Most people suffered osteoarthritis – painful swelling of the joints. Nearly half the adults suffered from it at young ages and even children's skeletons showed signs of osteoarthritis. It may have been caused by carrying or pulling heavy loads which were fixed by a strap or rope running across the neck and under the opposite armpit. This was a common method of carrying burdens in Orkney up to recent times.

Women died younger than men. Most women died between the ages of 15 and 24. This pattern is found in almost all PRE-INDUSTRIAL societies from prehistoric times to the present. The likely reasons are the strains of pregnancy and childbirth, poor diet and the demands of heavy physical work.

SOURCE 3 Information provided by the skeletons at Isbister

		Isbister 3000BC
1	How healthy were people?	Very fit, good teeth, shorter than people today. Women died younger than men. Most people died before the age of 40.
2	What caused sickness?	Broken bones from accidents. Pregnancy very dangerous for women. Pain in joints from hard work.
3	How did they treat illnesses and injuries?	
4	Who provided medical care?	
5	What did they think caused illness?	

Your chart probably looks like this one, even if the words are slightly different. You should have been able to answer two questions but not the others. That isn't your fault! You can't answer them because the sources from Isbister – the skeletons – do not give us the evidence to answer the last three questions. To answer those questions we have to look at the other kinds of evidence which you'll find on pages 11–13. However, first of all, we will summarise what we can find out from the Tomb of the Eagles.

Short lives

The evidence from Isbister tells us that people's lives were much shorter in prehistoric Britain than they are today. Few men reached the age of 40. Even fewer women reached 40 because of the high death-rate amongst women in childbirth. The skeletons of young women and babies have often been found together.

Pain

Another difference from today was that people suffered a great deal of pain. Skeletons show that OSTEOARTHRITIS (which causes severe pain in the knees, wrists and other joints) was common, even in the young. Tooth ABSCESSES, although not so common, were agonising without painkillers or ANTIBIOTICS to kill the infection.

Fitness

Harsh though this life was, the level of fitness was higher than today because people lived outdoor, active lives. Tooth decay was rare because there was no sugar. The average height of people was little different from the average height in the 1800s.

1. Add the information in this column to your chart if you have not already done so.

What did people die from?

The high death-rate in prehistoric times was not caused by today's killers – cancer and heart-disease. Prehistoric Britons died from:

- **diseases** that could not be stopped from spreading, especially amongst babies and young children before they developed resistance to them.
- **infections** from everyday accidents such as a cut finger which easily led to blood poisoning and death. It was also difficult to stop deep cuts from **bleeding**.
- **warfare** which could result in the deaths of young men, and starvation and poverty for the defeated.
- occasional **food shortages** and **famines** that particularly weakened children and pregnant and nursing women. Over 30 per cent of the skulls from Danebury, a hillfort in Hampshire, indicated that the people did not have enough iron in the blood. RICKETS, a disease resulting in bone deformities and caused by **poor diet**, was common.

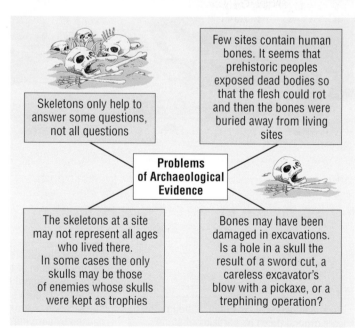

Few sites contain human bones. It seems that prehistoric peoples exposed dead bodies so that the flesh could rot and then the bones were buried away from living sites

Skeletons only help to answer some questions, not all questions

Problems of Archaeological Evidence

The skeletons at a site may not represent all ages who lived there. In some cases the only skulls may be those of enemies whose skulls were kept as trophies

Bones may have been damaged in excavations. Is a hole in a skull the result of a sword cut, a careless excavator's blow with a pickaxe, or a trephining operation?

SOURCE 4 Problems of archaeological evidence

2. Look at Source 4. Which of these problems apply to the excavations at Isbister?

Can we learn about prehistoric medicine from people living today?

Does anyone today still live in the same way that their prehistoric ancestors did? It sounds unlikely, but in parts of Australia there are Aborigines whose beliefs and way of life have not changed for centuries. This might sound like an insult but it isn't. The Aborigines' way of life did not need to change because it was ideally suited to their environment and their needs.

They had enough food and could live happily. They hunted animals when they needed meat and they collected fruits and other foods growing around them. The same has been true for many other peoples. Their way of life remained unchanged for centuries until the arrival of outsiders forced them to change. Maybe this is the secret to discovering more about prehistoric medicine. If we find out how Aborigines approached medicine and health until they were changed by outside influences, then we can get some clues about how prehistoric people, such as those at Isbister, might have treated the sick, or what they thought were the causes of disease.

The role of spirits

Spirits were at the heart of the Aborigines' world. They believed that spirits had created the world and that every person had his own spirit. These spirits explained why people became sick. If your spirit left your body then you fell ill. You could also become ill if an evil spirit found its way into your body while you were asleep.

The medicine man

If an Aborigine believed that a spirit was causing sickness then he or she visited the 'medicine man' who knew how to deal with spirits. The sick person lay down. The medicine man began to sing and chant so that the patient fell into a trance. Then the healing could begin. The medicine man bent over the sick body and massaged the sore or sick place. He asked the evil spirit to come out. It did! The medicine man held up a quartz crystal containing the evil spirit for everyone to see.

The patient came out of the trance. He or she heard that the evil spirit had gone. The patient was delighted, relieved and felt better. The relief was so great that the patient might well recover.

Charms

The Aborigines believed that spirits were always a danger. Therefore they wore charms to ward off the evil spirits that could cause disease. The charm might be made from the seeds of a plant or from parts of a human body. They also took care to bury their cast-off hair or nails and their excrement. This may have been to stop evil spirits or an enemy using them to cast a spell on them. Even if this was not the reason it was good hygiene and must have prevented the spread of diseases.

Herbs

Although Aborigines believed in spirits and medicine men they also used other methods to treat medical problems, particularly if the problem had an obvious cause – a cut or a broken leg perhaps. They used herbs and plants to treat sickness. Each generation passed down to the next their knowledge of the herbs that helped treat particular illnesses. The Aborigines were not the only people to do this as you can see from Source 5.

> **SOURCE 5** S.M.Barrett (ed.), *Geronimo: His Own Story*, 1974. Geronimo was a chief of a North American Indian tribe
>
> 66 *The Indians knew what herbs to use for medicine, how to prepare them and how to give the medicine. This they had been taught in the beginning, and each generation had men who were skilled in the art of healing, in gathering herbs, in preparing them, and in administering the medicine. As much faith was placed in prayer as in the actual effect of the medicine. (Prayers were made at the same time as giving the medicine.)* 99

A cut is treated with a herbal remedy

People wear charms to keep away evil spirits

The medicine man casts out an evil spirit

An Aboriginal woman gathers herbs

SOURCE 6 Features of Aboriginal medicine

Evidence from peoples such as the Aborigines gives us clues about the medicine of prehistoric peoples. This adds to other types of evidence, in addition to archaeology, shown in Source 7. If we use all this evidence together we can answer the questions we could not complete just by looking at the skeletons from the Tomb of the Eagles.

1. Use the information on this page to complete your Isbister chart.

How did they treat illnesses and injuries?

Herbs and plants were used to treat illnesses. The evidence is:

■ Herbs and plants were used in Roman Britain immediately after the prehistoric period. It is therefore very likely that they were used in Britain before the Romans arrived.

■ There is evidence from all over the world that farming peoples used herbs and plants before modern medicines were available.

■ Herbs and plants, which were later used as medicines, have been found at prehistoric sites. Examples include chickweed leaves (used to treat open sores called ULCERS or as an ointment for skin problems) and violets (used as an ANTISEPTIC and as the basis for cough medicines).

Remedies had to be remembered because there was no writing and so no books.

Surgery was used. Broken bones were set, often successfully, but the most startling surgical treatment was TREPHINING, which meant cutting a hole in the skull and removing a piece of bone. This dangerous operation was sometimes carried out successfully! Skulls have been found that show evidence of healing after trephining.

Trephining may have been used because of severe headaches or to ease the pressure of swelling after skull injuries. Another possible reason for this dramatic operation was to let out evil spirits that were causing pain and illness. However, there is no written evidence to prove this idea correct.

Who provided medical care?

There were probably two kinds of healers:

1. **Medicine men** who were very powerful and important members of a tribe because they could understand and deal with the spirits.

2. **Women**, who were closely involved in treating illness as mothers and wives. Written evidence from the Roman period onwards shows that women were responsible for day-to-day health care. They knew about the healing powers of herbs.

What did they think caused illnesses?

Unless the cause was obvious (a broken bone for example) prehistoric people probably believed that spirits were the cause of illnesses. We know from Roman writers that the Celts (who lived in Britain when the Romans came) worshipped a wide range of gods connected with nature, such as water spirits. If they believed in such spirits they probably believed they caused some illnesses.

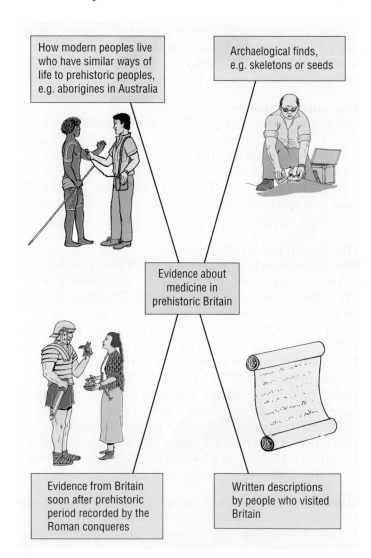

How modern peoples live who have similar ways of life to prehistoric peoples, e.g. aborigines in Australia

Archaelogical finds, e.g. skeletons or seeds

Evidence about medicine in prehistoric Britain

Evidence from Britain soon after prehistoric period recorded by the Roman conqueres

Written descriptions by people who visited Britain

SOURCE 7 Types of evidence about medicine in prehistoric Britain

■ ACTIVITY

Get a blank copy of this chart from your teacher.
Some of the statements in column A are correct.
Some need altering to make them correct.

1. Take each of the statements in column A in turn.
   Write them in your own chart, correcting them if
   they are wrong.
2. In column B write down the evidence which best
   supports the statement. The types of evidence to
   choose from are listed in the box on the right. If
   you think there is other useful evidence for the
   statement add it to column C. Give specific
   examples if you can.
3. Repeat for each of the other statements.

Types of evidence

- skeletons and other archaeological evidence
- later people who lived similar lives to people in prehistoric Britain
- written evidence from people who lived at the same time, e.g. the Romans
- how people later behaved in Britain

A Copy out and/or correct these statements.	B Choose the appropriate evidence from the box above.	C Note other evidence you have come across.
	The best type of evidence to support this statement comes from:	Other evidence to support the statement in column A is:
1. Most people lived short lives in prehistoric Britain.		
2. Many people suffered frequent pain.		
3. Herbs and plants were used to treat illnesses.		
4. Medicine men provided medical care.		
5. No operations were performed inside the body.		
6. Prehistoric Britons believed that spirits caused illness.		
7. Skeletons provide the best evidence about prehistoric medicine.		

1. If you had lived at Isbister and you had a bad headache
   a) What would you have thought caused the headache?
   b) Who could you have gone to see about the headache?
   c) How would the headache have been treated?
   d) Would the treatment have helped you?
2. Schoolbooks on the history of medicine contain a lot of information about the medical ideas of the Aborigines. Is this a useful way to learn about prehistoric medicine?

3. Could healers in prehistoric times help people who were sick?
   Write an answer to this question, organising your answer under the following topics:

   ■ Different kinds of healers
   ■ What they understood about the causes of sickness
   ■ Different ways of treating sickness
   ■ Problems of pain
   ■ Can we answer the question for certain?

Egypt, Greece and Rome: the great empires

OVER THE NEXT 3000 years life in Britain changed very little. This was still the prehistoric period (see Source 1). However, in the lands around the Mediterranean, great changes were taking place.

While the people of Isbister were laying the bones of the dead in the Tomb of the Eagles, far away in **Egypt** skilled builders were erecting massive pyramids to house their dead rulers.

While the early Britons had still not learned to write, the **Greeks** were building cities with universities and libraries.

While Britons were still living in isolated hillforts, the **Romans** were building roads, aqueducts and sewers across their great empire.

You are now going to investigate the health and medical skills of people in the great empires of Egypt, Greece and Rome.

Before you start, use your own knowledge and the information in Sources 2–4 to suggest answers to the questions below. Don't worry if you are not sure about the answers. These are only first ideas and you will have a chance to improve them or even change your mind once you start looking in detail at Egypt, Greece and Rome.

1. What important new kind of evidence is available about this period?
2. What questions will it help us to answer which we could not answer about prehistoric Britain?
3. Prehistoric Britons did not understand the causes of disease. Do you think that the Egyptians, Greeks and Romans understood them better?
4. Do you expect to find that healers in Egypt, Greece and Rome were more successful than those in prehistoric Britain?

SOURCE 1 What does prehistoric mean?

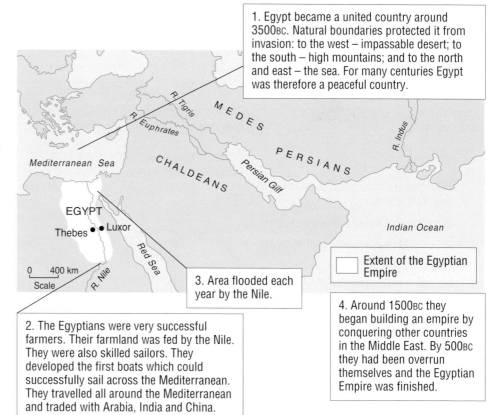

1. Egypt became a united country around 3500BC. Natural boundaries protected it from invasion: to the west – impassable desert; to the south – high mountains; and to the north and east – the sea. For many centuries Egypt was therefore a peaceful country.

2. The Egyptians were very successful farmers. Their farmland was fed by the Nile. They were also skilled sailors. They developed the first boats which could successfully sail across the Mediterranean. They travelled all around the Mediterranean and traded with Arabia, India and China.

3. Area flooded each year by the Nile.

4. Around 1500BC they began building an empire by conquering other countries in the Middle East. By 500BC they had been overrun themselves and the Egyptian Empire was finished.

SOURCE 2 The Egyptian Empire 3000BC

BRITAIN	Isbister tomb		Stonehenge		
EGYPTIAN EMPIRE	The Pyramids				
GREEK EMPIRE					
ROMAN EMPIRE					
	3000BC			2000BC	

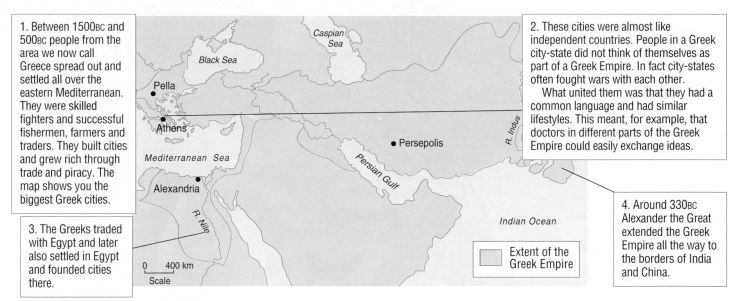

1. Between 1500BC and 500BC people from the area we now call Greece spread out and settled all over the eastern Mediterranean. They were skilled fighters and successful fishermen, farmers and traders. They built cities and grew rich through trade and piracy. The map shows you the biggest Greek cities.

2. These cities were almost like independent countries. People in a Greek city-state did not think of themselves as part of a Greek Empire. In fact city-states often fought wars with each other.
What united them was that they had a common language and had similar lifestyles. This meant, for example, that doctors in different parts of the Greek Empire could easily exchange ideas.

3. The Greeks traded with Egypt and later also settled in Egypt and founded cities there.

4. Around 330BC Alexander the Great extended the Greek Empire all the way to the borders of India and China.

Extent of the Greek Empire

SOURCE 3 The Greek Empire 334BC

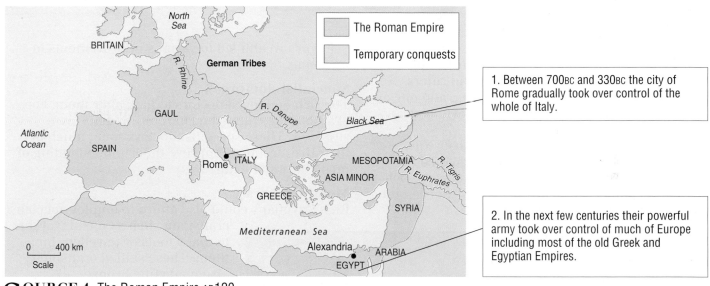

The Roman Empire

Temporary conquests

1. Between 700BC and 330BC the city of Rome gradually took over control of the whole of Italy.

2. In the next few centuries their powerful army took over control of much of Europe including most of the old Greek and Egyptian Empires.

SOURCE 4 The Roman Empire AD120

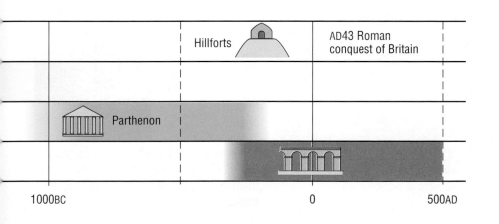

SOURCE 5 Timeline of the great empires

How did life in Egypt affect medicine?

ACTIVITY

1. Use the information and sources on this page to make notes around your own copy of the picture on the right. Your notes should explain how the following features of Egyptian life affected Egyptian medicine:

   - wealth
   - trade
   - improved writing
   - religion
   - the Nile and farming.

2. Choose one of these features which you think was particularly important and write a paragraph to explain your choice.

A wealthy country

Egypt was very different from prehistoric Isbister. It was a wealthy country, with powerful rulers, international trade, large cities, writing, and one of the most advanced civilisations the world had known.

Egypt's wealth was based on the River Nile. When the river flooded every year it covered the surrounding land with fertile soil which gave rich harvests of good crops. Farming was so successful that landowners in Egypt became rich.

Egypt's wealth led to various improvements in medicine.

Specialist doctors

The rich employed doctors to look after them. For example, the ruler (the Pharaoh) had his own PHYSICIAN. These specialist doctors spent much of their lives trying to improve their understanding of medicine and health.

Metal workers

Rich Egyptians could also afford to employ specialist craftsmen such as metal workers to make tools or jewellery for them. These skilled craftsmen also made fine bronze instruments for the doctors, so Egyptian doctors worked with better medical instruments than healers in prehistoric times.

SOURCE 1 A tomb painting showing Egyptian farmers at work

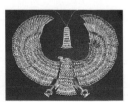

SOURCE 2 'Vulture Collar' necklace made for the Egyptian pharaoh, Tutankhamun.
The outlines of all the feathers, the head and limbs were made of gold. The feathers themselves were encrusted with precious stones

Trade

Egypt had widespread trade links. Ships and merchants arrived from India, China and parts of Africa, bringing new herbs and plants with them. Many of these herbs and plants were recommended as medicines, so Egyptian healers built up a wide knowledge of herbal medicines.

Improved writing

The Egyptians also developed PAPYRUS (a kind of paper made from reeds) and a simpler, quicker form of writing, which together made writing easier and more convenient than before.

Doctors benefited from these developments. Treatments and remedies could be written down and passed on accurately to other healers.

Religion

Religion helped to increase medical knowledge. Egyptians believed that people had a life after death and that they would need their bodies in the afterlife. Therefore, the bodies of important people were EMBALMED ready for the afterlife. Parts of the body, such as the liver, were taken out and preserved. The rest of the body was embalmed, which involved treating it with spices and wrapping it in bandages to make a mummy.

The Nile and farming

Egyptian doctors began to think hard about the reasons why people became ill. They got some of their ideas from the River Nile itself. The Nile was so important to the health of their farmland. The irrigation channels dug by the farmers brought life to the farmland. Egyptian doctors began to think of the body as having many channels inside it which, if they became blocked, could cause a person to be unhealthy.

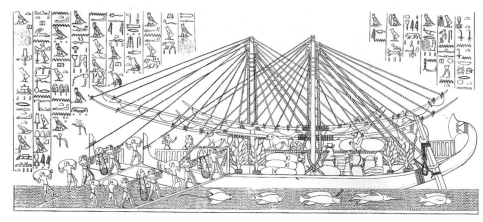

SOURCE 3 A wall carving showing Egyptians loading a trading ship for a voyage to Arabia. The Egyptians greatly improved the design of their ships so they could sail long distances across the Mediterranean

SOURCE 4 A modern African farmer opens an irrigation channel to let water flow onto his crops. This same method of irrigation was used by ancient Egyptian farmers around the River Nile

---

Summary

River Nile $\longrightarrow$ rich crops $\longrightarrow$ wealthy people

specialist craftsmen: metalworkers and doctors

trade: new herbs and plants

writing

Who treated the sick in ancient Egypt?

YOU HAVE ALREADY found that the Egyptians had specialist doctors. They were not the only people who healed the sick in ancient Egypt. Sources 1–5 tell you more about the doctors, and provide clues about some of the other healers.

SOURCE 1 An Egyptian poem written around 1500BC

  ❝ *It is seven days from yesterday since I saw my love,*
And sickness has crept over me,
My limbs have become heavy,
I cannot feel my own body.
If the master-physicians come to me
I gain no comfort from their remedies.
And the priest-magicians have no cures,
My sickness is not diagnosed.
My love is better by far for me than any remedies.
She is more important than all the books of medicine. ❞

SOURCE 3 The goddess Sekhmet, goddess of war. Egyptians believed that she also caused and cured epidemics. Some of her priests were also doctors

---

SOURCE 2 Redrawing of a carved panel showing Irj, doctor to the Pharaoh, with his medical equipment, c.1500BC. In his funeral inscription Irj is described as 'Palace doctor, Superintendent of the court physicians, Palace eye physician, Palace physician of the belly, One understanding internal fluids, Guardian of the anus'

SOURCE 4 The funeral inscription of one of Sekhmet's priests

  ❝ *I was a priest of Sekhmet strong and skilful in the Art: One who put his hands upon the sick and so found out; One who is skilful with his eye.* ❞

SOURCE 5 From J. Worth Estes, *The Medical Skills of Ancient Egypt*, 1989

  ❝ *Perhaps the most surprising amongst the known [healing priests] is a woman named Peseshet who lived during the Old Kingdom [2649–2150BC]. She was Lady Overseer of Lady Physicians ... The only other woman among the [129] known physicians of Ancient Egypt [was] named Tawe ...* ❞

---

1. List the kinds of healers mentioned in Sources 1–5.
2. What evidence is there that Egyptian doctors were specialists?
3. According to Source 1 how did Egyptian doctors pass on their knowledge to each other?
4. There is no evidence here that mothers and wives acted as healers. Does that prove that they did not act as healers?

What did Egyptian healers know about the body and causes of disease?

The Egyptians knew about the heart, the pulse, liver, brain, lungs and the blood. However, they did not understand the proper roles of these parts of the body.

Egyptians believed that the heart was the most important organ in the body. They described how blood flowed through over 40 channels from the heart to every part of the body. The blood carried air and water that were essential for life. Healthy channels were vital for good health. Everyday greetings included 'May your channels be sound'!

In Egypt when someone died the body was embalmed (see page 17). Many of the organs were taken out (only the heart was left inside) and the body was then preserved with spices. Egyptians learned a little about ANATOMY (the parts of the body) from this but embalming was carried out quickly for religious reasons and because of the heat. Egyptians also believed that people would need their bodies in the afterlife so dissection of other parts of the body was forbidden.

5. If Egyptian doctors wanted to learn more about parts of the body how did embalming:
  a) help them
  b) hinder them?
6. Irrigation was important to Egyptian farmers. If the channels from the River Nile were blocked the crops would die in the great heat. How do you think the River Nile influenced their ideas about the causes of disease? You may need to refer back to page 17.
7. What other factors might have helped Egyptians arrive at the explanation of disease in Source 6? For example, why might they think that rotting food in the bowel lets off gases?

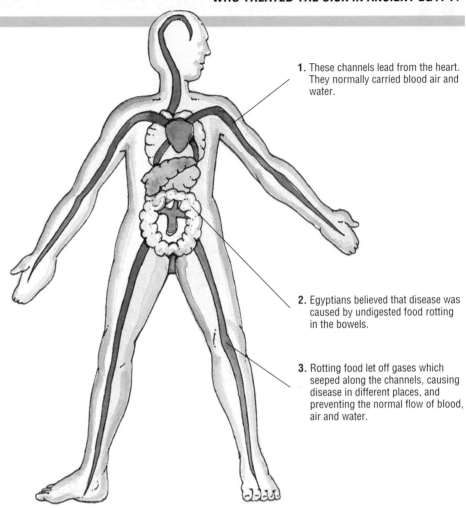

1. These channels lead from the heart. They normally carried blood air and water.

2. Egyptians believed that disease was caused by undigested food rotting in the bowels.

3. Rotting food let off gases which seeped along the channels, causing disease in different places, and preventing the normal flow of blood, air and water.

SOURCE 6 Egyptian ideas about the causes of disease

■ ACTIVITY

Here are the beginnings of a chart summarising Egyptian medicine. Use the information on these two pages to complete the first three sections. You can complete the final section from the information and sources on the next two pages.

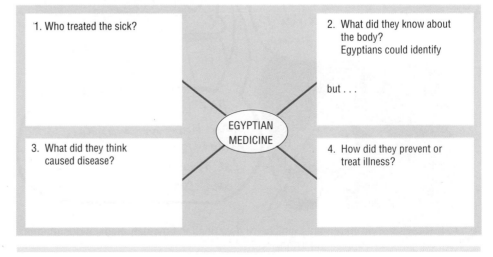

1. Who treated the sick?

2. What did they know about the body? Egyptians could identify

  but . . .

3. What did they think caused disease?

EGYPTIAN MEDICINE

4. How did they prevent or treat illness?

How did the Egyptians treat illnesses and injuries?

1. Sort Sources 1–7 into the following categories:

   - the use of herbs
   - the use of surgery
   - the use of magic or charms
   - other treatments (list them).

2. Which of these kinds of treatment were also used in prehistoric times? (See pages 11–13.)

3. Egyptian doctors were developing rational cures like that in Source 3. Why do you think they still used the treatments described in Source 4?

4. Use this information to complete your chart from the previous page.

SOURCE 1 The Greek historian Herodotus visited Egypt around 450BC and recorded this information

Each Egyptian has a net. He uses it to fish by day, but at night spreads it over his bed to keep off mosquitoes.

SOURCE 2 From the Ebers Papyrus

For a diseased eye
To clear up the PUS: *honey, balm from Mecca and gum ammoniac.* To treat its discharge: *frankincense, myrrh, yellow ochre.* To treat the growth: *red ochre, malachite, honey.*

For diseases of the bladder
Bread in a rotten condition. The doctor must use it to fight the sickness – not to avoid the sickness.

SOURCE 3 From the Edwin Smith Papyrus, a collection of Egyptian medical documents written around 1600BC. The papyrus lists 48 cases of surgery, each with a careful description of examination, symptoms, diagnosis and treatment

Instructions for treating a broken nose
Examination
If you examine a man whose nose is disfigured – part of it squashed in, the other part swollen and both his nostrils are bleeding.
Diagnosis
Then you should say 'You have a broken nose and this is an AILMENT which I can treat'.
Treatment
You should clean his nose with two plugs of linen and then insert two plugs soaked in grease into his nostrils. You should make him rest until the swelling has gone down, you should bandage his nose with stiff rolls of linen and treat him with lint every day until he recovers.

SOURCE 5 Some ceremonies of ancient Egypt in around 750–300BC described by J. Worth Estes in *The Medical Skills of Ancient Egypt*, 1989

… some temples were also associated with healing … The sick could bathe in water that had been sanctified, perhaps in the temple's sacred lake, so that they would be healed … another procedure … required the sick person to spend a night in the SANATORIUM with the expectation that the god would cause him to dream his cure.

This charm will protect you against evil spirits. It is made from evil smelling herbs and garlic and from honey which is sweet for people but horrible for spirits, from a fishtail and a rag and a backbone of a perch.

This is certain to make your hair grow again. It mixes fat of lion, fat of cat, fat of crocodile, fat of ibex and fat of serpent.

SOURCE 4 Two treatments which are described in Egyptian medical documents written between 1900BC and 1500BC

20

SOURCE 6 Written by the Greek historian, Herodotus, in the fifth century BC

❝ For three successive days every month they [the Egyptians] purge themselves … for they think that all diseases stem from the foods they eat… they drink from cups of bronze which they clean daily. They are careful to wear newly washed linen clothing. They practise circumcision for the sake of cleanliness. Their priests shave their whole body every third day so no lice may infect them while they are serving the gods. Twice a day and every night they wash in cold water. ❞

SOURCE 7 From J. Worth Estes, *The Medical Skills of Ancient Egypt*, 1989

❝ Skinned whole mice have been found in the stomachs of children buried in an [ancient Egyptian] cemetery, perhaps administered as a treatment of last resort. Mouse fat is recommended in the Ebers Papyrus 'to relax stiffness' and a mouse head to remedy earaches. A rotten mouse is the chief ingredient of a Hearst Papyrus ointment that would keep the hair from turning white. During the reign of Nero (AD54–68), the Greek physician Dioscorides noted that whole mice would dry children's saliva, and that chopped mice were useful for scorpion bites. Two thousand years later, in 1924, skinned whole mice were being used for the treatment of both urinary incontinence and whooping cough in rural England. ❞

5. Why might the cure for a diseased eye in Source 2 have worked? Use Source 9 to help you.
6. Choose either Source 1 or Source 6 and explain why the measures it describes might help prevent disease.
7. Source 7 describes a cure which has been used for a long period. Why might such a cure be used over so many centuries?

■ ACTIVITY

Choose one of the treatments or remedies mentioned on this page and write an advertisement for it. Your advertisement should try to attract people to use your kind of treatment. It should therefore say:

■ what the treatment involves
■ who will provide it and where
■ what the effects will be on the patient.

Did the Egyptian treatments work?

Some of these treatments might seem quite sensible to you, others might look no use at all. But just because a treatment is different from those we use today does not mean to say it would not work.

SOURCE 8 The most commonly used ingredients in Egyptian medicines as recorded in the Ebers Papyrus

Honey	*30.3%*
Djaret	*14.6%*
Frankincense	*14.1%*
Salt	*10.4%*
Dates	*9.6%*

[Historians are not sure what 'djaret' was. Many other ingredients were used, including juniper and figs.]

SOURCE 9 Scientists have analysed and tested some of the ancient Egyptian remedies. This cartoon is based on information in *The Medical Skills of Ancient Egypt*, written by J. Worth Estes, 1989

Egyptian medicine: a summary

Change

Medical knowledge and methods changed when people began to live in cities and became richer.

Their world was very different from that of prehistoric hunter-gatherers. They had specialist craftsmen, including doctors. Trade increased the range of herbs available for use as medicines. They developed writing and they began to learn about anatomy.

They also tried to work out a logical reason why people became ill. Learning from the waters of the Nile, they blamed blocked channels for causing illness.

> **Summary: what was new?**
> - There were doctors as well as medicine men.
> - Doctors looked for logical causes of disease.
> - Doctors could identify some parts of the body.
> - New herbs were used as medicines.
> - Metal instruments were used for surgery.

Continuity

However, not everything was new. Egyptians used many herbs in the same ways as their ancestors. They still did not understand the function of important parts of the body, such as the liver, and how they kept people healthy.

Nor did the Egyptians understand the real causes of disease despite efforts to find a logical cause. Without that understanding they were often helpless when sickness spread. That was why Egyptians still believed in evil spirits and protected themselves with AMULETS.

> **Summary: what stayed the same?**
> - People still believed in gods and spirits.
> - Herbs were still used as medicines.
> - People still did not understand how the body worked.
> - People still did not understand what caused diseases.

■ TASK

You are going to write an essay on the topic 'Was Egyptian medicine an important step forward?'

Use each of these questions as the basis for one paragraph of your essay.

1. Which old ideas or methods did the Egyptians continue to use?
2. What new ideas or methods did the Egyptians use?
3. Were the changes more important than the continuities?

You can get a sheet from your teacher to help you.

1. Which of the speakers in the cartoon below do you most agree with? Use the evidence on pages 8–21 to explain your answer.

Were there medical developments in other places?

Egypt was not the only early society to have doctors and new medical ideas as you can see from Sources 1–5.

SOURCE 1 An inscription on a doctor's seal from Mesopotamia, 2000BC

66 O God Edinmugi, Servant of the God Gir, you who help animal mothers to give birth, Urlugaledina the doctor is your servant. 99

SOURCE 2 A herbal remedy written in an Indian medical book. The remedy was used by 1000BC and probably earlier. Takman, the disease being treated, was probably malaria

66 Kushta the most healing of plants, you are born in the mountains. Come down O Kushta, destroy Takman, drive Takman away from here. Aches in the head, inflammation on the eye, pains in the body, all these the Kushta plant heals. 99

SOURCE 3 From the *Laws of Hammurabi*, Babylon, around 2000BC

66 If a doctor opens a spot in a man's eye with a bronze instrument and so heals the man's eye he is to be paid ten shekels of silver for his work. If the doctor destroys the man's eye, his hands are to be cut off. 99

SOURCE 4 Sewers, water pipes and baths were built in the city of Mohenjo Daro in India around 1500BC. Cities like this needed to bring in fresh water supplies and to get rid of huge quantities of sewage. If they did not have a good PUBLIC HEALTH system then diseases spread quickly in crowded cities. This photo shows the remains of the sewers which can still be seen today

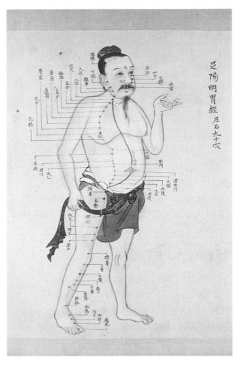

SOURCE 5 An illustration showing acupuncture points. Acupuncture was used in China well before 1000BC. Chinese doctors stopped pain by pressing on certain points of the body. At first they used sharp flints and later metal needles

■ ACTIVITY

Your teacher will give you a copy of Source 6. On your own map fill in the empty rectangles to show or describe each of the developments in the sources on this page.

Include in your description whether these are features which were also present in prehistoric Britain or in ancient Egypt.

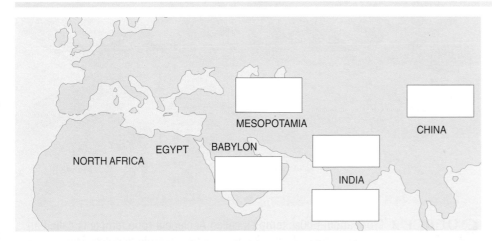

MESOPOTAMIA

CHINA

EGYPT BABYLON

NORTH AFRICA

INDIA

SOURCE 6 Map showing the places mentioned in Sources 1–5

Greek medicine: what happened at an Asclepion?

YOU ARE NOW going to leave ancient Egypt and move on to study ancient Greece.

The Greeks play a very important part in this story of medicine and health – even more important than the ancient Egyptians. The Greeks had many new ideas about causes of disease and methods of treatment, and these ideas remained important for centuries to come. Over the next twelve pages you are going to find out about some of these new ideas. But you are going to start with one which is not so new – the gods.

As you have seen, one of the oldest medical beliefs was that gods could cause and cure disease. Did the Greeks believe that gods affected people's health?

Greek gods

The Greeks had many gods. They had a god of wisdom; a god of wine; even a god of laughing. They believed that gods caused events such as earthquakes or thunderstorms. If there was a rich harvest they said that the gods were pleased. If someone was a great soldier they said it was the gods that favoured him. With all these gods it is no surprise therefore that they also had a god of healing. His name was Asclepius (which is also sometimes written Asklepios).

1. Look at Source 1. Asclepius had two daughters. Which English words come from the names of his daughters?
2. Both these words have a medical meaning today. What do they mean?
3. Look at Source 2. The ASCLEPION at Epidaurus was surrounded by other buildings which were useful in health care. How might each part have helped make a visiting patient healthier?
4. Why would an Asclepion be built in a quiet place?

SOURCE 1 A relief of Asclepius, the Greek god of healing. He was helped by his daughters, Panacea and Hygeia. People believed that if they went to sleep in the Asclepion at night, the god and his daughters would come to heal them

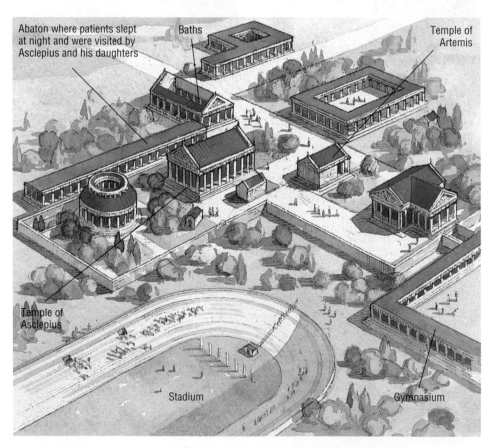

Abaton where patients slept at night and were visited by Asclepius and his daughters

Baths

Temple of Artemis

Temple of Asclepius

Stadium

Gymnasium

SOURCE 2 From about 600BC temples called Asclepeia (one temple is called an Asclepion) were built in quiet places. Some were very simple temples. This reconstruction drawing shows the Asclepion at Epidaurus. This was the most important Asclepion. It was built around 400BC

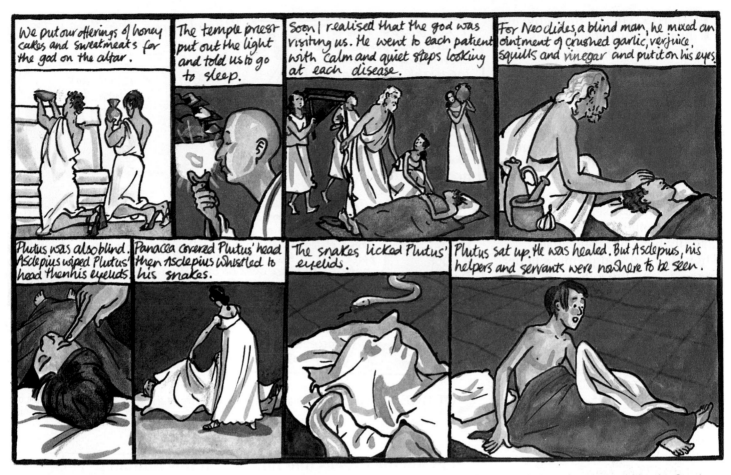

We put our offerings of honey cakes and sweatmeats for the god on the altar.

The temple priest put out the light and told us to go to sleep.

Soon I realised that the god was visiting us. He went to each patient with calm and quiet steps looking at each disease.

For Neoclides, a blind man, he mixed an ointment of crushed garlic, verjuice, squills and vinegar and put it on his eyes.

Plutus was also blind. Asclepius wiped Plutus' head then his eyelids.

Panacea covered Plutus' head then Asclepius whistled to his snakes.

The snakes licked Plutus' eyelids.

Plutus sat up. He was healed. But Asclepius, his helpers and servants were nowhere to be seen.

SOURCE 4 An inscription from the Asclepion at Epidaurus in Greece. Grateful visitors paid for and left inscriptions on stone columns at the temple. Four of these columns have been found during excavations

66 *A man with an abscess within his abdomen. When asleep in the Temple [of Asclepius] he had a dream. It seemed to him that the god ordered the servants who accompanied him to grip him and hold him tightly so that he could cut open his abdomen. The man tried to get away, but they gripped him and bound him … Asclepius cut his belly open, removed the abscess and, after having stitched him up again, released him from his bonds. Whereupon he walked out sound, but the floor … was covered in blood.* 99

SOURCE 3 A visit to an Asclepion. The story is based on one told by the Greek writer Aristophanes around 400BC. It comes from a play, but Aristophanes was a careful observer of people's attitudes and behaviour and he put a lot of realistic description into his plays

■ **ACTIVITY**

Many people who visited the Asclepion believed that the gods cured them. They went home excited, determined to tell their friends about the wonderful cure.

Your task is to write a letter about your healing at an Asclepion. Your friend is suffering from the same medical problem as you. Tell your friend the story of your visit, and how you were healed. Try to persuade him or her to go to be cured.

You need to include:

■ a description of your medical problem
■ what the Asclepion is like
■ what happened at the temple
■ who you saw and how you were cured
■ what you did when you left.

Use Sources 1–4 to help you write your letter.

Why did the Greeks have new ideas about medicine?

THE HISTORY of medicine and health is full of surprises. The Greeks are one of them. Many Greeks sought Asclepius' help and believed that he had healed them. Yet at the same time as people were flocking to Asclepeia other Greeks were gradually developing new theories about disease and treatment. Their ideas suggested that gods such as Asclepius had nothing at all to do with health or disease. They began to believe that diseases actually have natural causes. They claimed that people's belief in magic and the gods prevented effective medical treatment.

What was this new idea?

The theory of the four humours: the Greeks' greatest idea

Greek thinkers believed that the body contained four important liquids which they called humours. They were

- phlegm
- blood
- yellow bile
- black bile

If these humours stayed in balance then a person would remain healthy, but if the humours became unbalanced (if there was too much of one humour, not enough of another) this could make a person ill (see Source 1).

It is important to understand this theory because:

- it was the basis for many Greek treatments
- doctors continued to believe in the theory of the four humours for well over 1000 years and so it affected the way people were treated throughout that time.

SOURCE 1 Hippocrates explains the Greek theory of the four humours

How did the Greeks find time for all this thinking?
Like the Egyptian Empire, the Greek Empire was rich. Its wealth came from farming and trade and from the hard work done by slaves and the poor. This allowed the wealthy classes to spend their time becoming educated and discussing new ideas. Trade also helped, bringing knowledge and methods from other civilisations.

Why did the Greeks develop the theory of the four humours?

The Greeks had enquiring minds. They did not just have ideas about medicine – they had theories about everything! Many Greeks went on believing in the old ideas about gods or spirits controlling everything, but a small number of Greeks were interested in finding more rational explanations. They wanted to understand how and why things worked. Greek thinkers investigated mathematics, geometry, science, astronomy, philosophy and politics, as well as medicine.

Observation

Greek thinkers and doctors tried to understand what caused disease through careful observation of people who were ill. They saw that when someone was ill there was usually a liquid coming out of the body, for example, phlegm from the nose or vomit from the stomach. They decided that these liquids (which they called humours) must somehow be the causes of illness. The liquid or humour must be coming out of the body because there was too much of it. The humours had got out of balance with each other.

How did the theory of the four humours fit in with the Greeks' other ideas?

The theory of the four humours grew directly out of the theory of the four **elements**.

The Greeks believed that everything in the world was made up from four elements – which were air, water, earth and fire. They said that each of these elements had different qualities – which they could observe from the world around them. Water was cold and moist, for example. Source 2 shows the qualities they associated with the other elements.

Source 3 shows you how the Greeks also linked the four **seasons** with the four elements. Greek thinkers looked carefully at the world around them. They knew that each season was different and they could see how the elements could explain that. Water was cold and moist and so, too, was winter. Therefore in winter, water must be the dominant element.

Greek doctors observed their patients carefully. In winter they noted that people were often ill with sneezing and runny noses. Clearly they had too much phlegm, the humour most like the element water, which was cold and moist. This linked phlegm to water and to the cold, moist season of winter – which was exactly when people did have too much phlegm. The whole argument fitted together perfectly as you can see from Source 3! Doctors could now see the humours that were causing illness. This was such a good theory that it stayed in use for over 1000 years and changed the way illnesses were treated, as you will see from pages 30–31.

SOURCE 2 The four elements

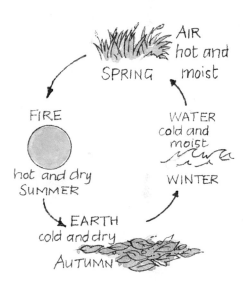

SOURCE 3 How the four seasons were linked to the four elements

■ ACTIVITY

In pairs think of five quiz questions to ask the rest of the class about the information on these two pages. Try to include a couple of easy questions and a couple of difficult ones.

Write your five questions on one side of a piece of card and the correct answers on the other.

S OURCE 4 How a Greek doctor could link the theories of the four elements and
the four humours

Elements	Qualities	Season	Humour	Illness/Symptoms
Water	cold and moist	Winter	phlegm	sneezing/colds
Air	hot and moist	Spring	blood	DYSENTERY/nose bleeds
Fire	hot and dry	Summer	yellow bile	fevers, vomiting, yellow skin
Earth	cold and dry	Autumn	black bile	dry skin, vomiting

S OURCE 5 Chart showing the links between the different Greek theories

Was it a step forward?

It is easy to laugh at ancient ideas about illness. Rotting food sending gases round the channels – mad! The body's humours are out of balance – ridiculous! Or is it? This idea led the Greeks to do everything in moderation – not eating too much; not exercising too much – and so it did help to make them more healthy.

It's also important for another reason – in those far-off times people had started to search for the causes of illness, instead of simply saying 'It's the gods. We must pray to them.'

While people still believed that natural events like disease were caused by gods or spirits they would never find the real causes. However, if they looked closely at what they saw, as the Greeks were doing (and as the Egyptians had done with their idea of blocked channels), and tried to explain it rationally and logically then eventually they might find the real causes.

The theory of the four humours was a far cry from blaming illness on evil spirits. Hippocrates, the most famous Greek doctor, who developed the theory of the four humours, told his students that all diseases could be treated without using any magic. He said that all they had to do was to discover the nature of each disease. Then they would be able to treat it. You can find out about the treatments they came up with on page 30.

Who treated the sick in ancient Greece?

THE IDEA OF the four humours made doctors in ancient Greece much more important than they were before. Because people thought doctors now really knew what caused disease they were more prepared to trust them and pay for their treatments.

However, doctors were not the only healers in ancient Greece. You have already come across some other healers. Yet the bulk of medical care was probably still handled by women – wives and mothers – at home, using herbs, and remedies which had been handed down by their ancestors. This was particularly true among the poor, who could not afford to consult a doctor.

■ TASK

Types of healer	Prehistoric period	Ancient Egypt	Ancient Greece Did they have them?	Ancient Greece Example
Mothers and wives	✓	✓		
Medicine men/priests	✓	✓		
Trained male doctors		✓		
Trained women doctors		✓		

Draw your own copy of the chart above.

From Sources 1–3 and from what you have so far found out about Greek medicine, complete the chart. In the third column put a tick if they had that kind of healer in ancient Greece. In the fourth column note down an example of such a healer.

1. What evidence is there in Source 2 that Greek doctors took their work seriously?
2. There is no written evidence that mothers and wives treated everyday health problems in the home. Why do you think historians are so sure that they did?
3. As you saw on pages 26–28 Greek doctors had developed logical explanations of disease. Why do you think people still went to priests and visited Asclepeia for healing?

SOURCE 1 Hippocrates, the most famous Greek doctor. He is thought to have been born in Cos around 460BC. He wrote a number of medical books, advising doctors how to treat their patients. However, we cannot be certain about the details of his life. This bust, produced long after his death, may not even be very like him! You can find out more about him on pages 32–33

SOURCE 2 From the HIPPOCRATIC OATH which was created by Hippocrates to give people confidence in doctors

66 *I will swear by Apollo, Asclepius and by all the gods that I will carry out this oath. I will use treatment to help the sick according to my ability and judgement but never with a view to injury or wrongdoing. I will not give poison to anybody ... whatever I see or hear professionally or in my private life which ought not to be told I will keep secret.* 99

SOURCE 3 Adapted from the works of Hyginus, a Greek writer

66 *The ancient [Greeks] had no midwives ... for the Athenians had decided that no slave or woman should learn the science of medicine. A certain girl, Hagnodice, as a young woman desired to learn the science of medicine. Because of this desire, she cut her hair, put on male clothing, and entrusted herself to a certain Herophilus for training. After learning this science, when she heard that a woman was having labour-pains, she would go to her. And when the woman refused to entrust herself [to Hagnodice], thinking she was a man, Hagnodice lifted her undergarment and revealed that she was a woman. In this way she used to cure women.* 99

[Herophilus (c. 320–250BC) was one of the most learned Greek doctors. Hagnodice became so successful that she was accused of seducing her female patients and this forced her to admit that she was a woman. However, Hagnodice's female patients gave her so much support that 'the Athenians amended the law so that free-born women (not slaves) could learn the science of medicine'.]

How did Greek doctors prevent and treat illnesses?

Observation

Greek doctors were trained to diagnose illnesses carefully. They observed symptoms and recorded each stage of an illness. Sometimes they wrote up what doctors today would call a case-history of the patient.

SOURCE 1 A patient's case-history which is included in a book called *On Epidemics,* part of the Hippocratic Collection (see page 32)

66 *Silenus began with pains in his abdomen, heavy head and stiff neck.*

First day: he vomited, his urine was black, he was thirsty, his tongue dry and he did not sleep.

Second day: slightly delirious.

Sixth day: slight perspiration about the head, head and feet cold, no discharge from the bowels, no urine.

Eighth day: cold sweat all over, red rashes, severe DIARRHOEA.

Eleventh day: he died – breathing slow and heavy. He was aged about twenty. 99

1. Read Source 1. List which of the following techniques of observation the doctor probably used:

   - inspecting urine
   - inspecting FAECES
   - feeling temperature
   - listening to breathing
   - asking the patient questions.

2. Why would such a case-history be written down in a book?

Advice

Silenus, the patient in Source 1, may have died, but by their observation doctors knew that many diseases cleared up on their own without any help from a doctor. So a lot of the time they simply gave advice to patients on how their disease might develop (a PROGNOSIS). This was based on their knowledge of earlier patients whom they had treated with similar symptoms.

They also offered advice on avoiding illness altogether. They instructed their patients on what they should eat, on taking exercise, and on keeping clean.

Treatments

Once they had established how the patient's humours were unbalanced the main task of the Greek doctor was to try to help nature restore the proper balance – by making them vomit, purging their bowels, or BLEEDING them.

They also knew there were some illnesses they could not cure. In these cases they could see nothing wrong with a visit to an Asclepion – miracles might happen!

3. The treatments and advice on preventing disease in Sources 2–4 are all based on the theory of the four humours. Explain how each one would help restore the balance of the humours.

SOURCE 2 From a book in the Hippocratic Collection, *On the Treatment of Acute Diseases,* 400–200BC

66 *If the pain is under the diaphragm, clear the bowels with a medicine made from black hellebore, cumin or other fragrant herbs.*

A bath will help PNEUMONIA as it soothes pain and brings up phlegm. 99

SOURCE 4 From *A Programme for Health,* one of the books in the Hippocratic Collection of medical books

66 *In winter, people should eat as much as possible and drink as little as possible – unwatered wine, bread, roast meat and few vegetables. This will keep the body hot and dry. In summer they should drink more and eat less – watered wine, barley cakes and boiled meat so that the body will stay cold and moist. Walking should be fast in winter and slow in summer.* 99

SOURCE 5 Adapted from a book by a Greek doctor, Diocles of Carystus, who lived in Athens c.390BC

66 *After awakening he should not arise at once but should wait until the heaviness of sleep has gone. After arising he should rub the whole body with oil. Then he should wash face and eyes using pure water. He should rub his teeth inside and outside with the fingers using fine peppermint powder and cleaning the teeth of remnants of food. He should anoint nose and ears inside, preferably with well-perfumed oil. He should rub and anoint his head every day but wash it and comb it only at intervals. Long walks before meals clear out the body, prepare it for receiving food and give it more power for digesting.* 99

SOURCE 3 A bleeding cup, used to draw blood from a patient. It was heated and placed over a scratch. The warmth drew blood to the surface of the skin and out through the scratch. Doctors used bleeding in the spring and summer when it was thought that people had too much blood because they often became hot and red

4. Read Source 5. List the ways in which this advice would help someone stay healthy.
5. Do you think that all Greeks would be able to follow the advice in Sources 4 and 5?
6. Are there any treatments on the opposite page that you know were practised:

   ■ in prehistoric times
   ■ in ancient Egypt?

7. Hippocrates and his followers used methods that are still used today. What are they?

Surgery

From around 1200BC the use of iron and steel gave doctors stronger and sharper instruments. Greek surgeons developed good techniques for setting broken bones and also, in extreme cases, AMPUTATION (the cutting off of a leg or an arm). However, very few operations were done inside the body. One of the exceptions was the draining of the lungs – performed if a patient had pneumonia. This operation was frequently and successfully undertaken, thanks to doctors' careful observation of the symptoms and pattern of the illness.

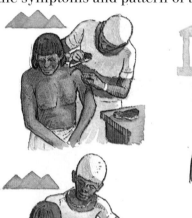

Egypt   Greece

SOURCE 6 An extract from the *Iliad* Book 11, written by the Greek poet, Homer. The *Iliad* is the story of the Greek war against the Trojans

❝ *'My lord,' replied the wounded man, … 'I want you to cut out this arrow from my thigh, wash off the blood with warm water and spread soothing ointment on the wound. They say you have some excellent prescriptions… I cannot get help from our surgeons for one of them is lying wounded in our camp while the other is fighting the Trojans in the battle …'* ❞

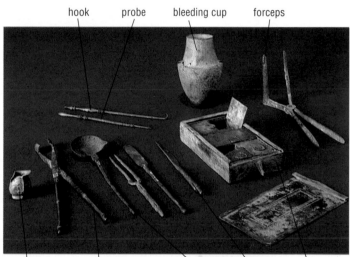

hook   probe   bleeding cup   forceps

mixing container   small shears   measuring spoon   scalpel   medicine container

SOURCE 7 A set of Greek surgical instruments

SOURCE 8 Adapted from H. von Staden, *Herophilus, The Art of Medicine in Early Alexandria*, 1989

❝ *The three most common 'non-magical' Egyptian techniques of wound care – putting a slab of fresh meat on a wound; applying a SALVE of honey and animal fat; applying adhesive linen tape – are not among the techniques that dominate Greek wound care.*

The Greeks instead washed the wound with wine or vinegar – a basic antiseptic procedure apparently ignored in Egypt. Sometimes they bandaged wounds with linen soaked in wine. ❞

8. What technological improvement helped Greek surgeons?
9. Read Source 6. How might war have helped Greek doctors improve their skills and knowledge?
10. Read Source 8. What new treatment did the Greeks use which the Egyptians had not used?
11. Was this treatment likely to be successful?

Hippocrates – the greatest doctor of them all?

IN THE LAST few pages you have read a good deal about Hippocrates. He is an important figure in the story of medicine and health. These two pages summarise some of the reasons why.

1. Which parts of Hippocrates' work and ideas helped to:
a) improve his patients' health
b) improve medical knowledge?
2. What was new about Hippocrates' work?
3. For all his skills, Hippocrates did not understand the true causes of diseases. Why not?
4. Why is Hippocrates important in the history of medicine?

The Hippocratic Oath
The oath (see Source 2 on page 29) is still used today. It makes clear that doctors are not magicians. They have to keep high standards of treatment and behaviour and to work for the benefit of patients rather than to make themselves rich.

Why was Hippocrates important?

Books
The Hippocratic Collection contains books which doctors used for centuries. Hippocrates may not have written all of these books and historians simply cannot tell who did write them.

However, this collection is important because it is the first detailed list of symptoms and treatments. Doctors continued to use the theories of Hippocrates as the basis of their own work for hundreds of years.

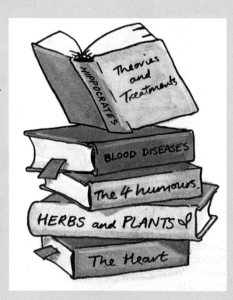

Observing and recording

Hippocrates showed how important it was to observe and record carefully the symptoms and development of diseases.

This had two advantages. Doctors were more likely to choose the right cure if they took care to find the cause of the problem. These notes could also be used to help with the diagnosis and treatment of future patients.

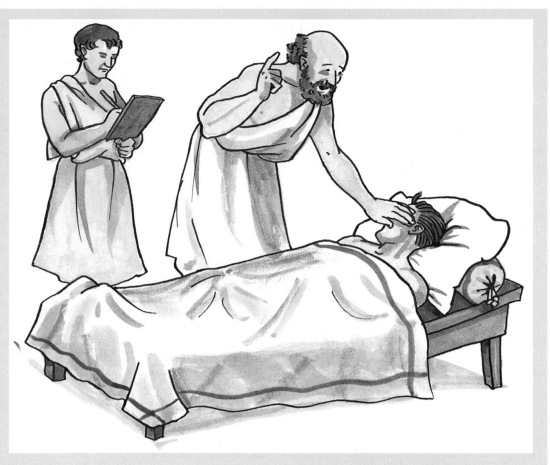

Diseases have natural causes. The body's humours become unbalanced and this causes illness. We can see this when a patient sweats or vomits when ill. This is the body trying to get rid of the excess humours in a natural way.

There is no need to look for magical cures because illness is not caused by magic. We must use natural treatments, for example, rest and change in your diet and then perhaps when you are feeling stronger some more regular exercise. If this does not work then we can bleed or purge to remove excess humours.

Causes of disease

Hippocrates developed the theory of humours to explain the causes of disease. We now know that this theory was wrong but it dominated medical treatments for many centuries.

Natural treatments

Hippocrates encouraged people to look for natural treatments for illnesses rather than going to the gods for help.

Greek and Egyptian medicine: a summary comparison

	EGYPT	GREECE
WHO TREATED THE SICK?	Priests and doctors Family members, especially women	Priests and doctors Family members, especially women
WHAT DID THEY KNOW ABOUT THE BODY?	They could identify some parts of the body but they did not understand what they did.	They could identify some parts of the body and began to understand some of its workings, e.g. that the brain controlled the body.
HOW DID THEY TREAT AND PREVENT ILLNESS?	Herbal remedies Simple surgery Charms and spells Personal hygiene	Careful observation Herbal remedies Charms and spells Rest Diet and exercise Personal hygiene Bleeding
WHAT DID THEY THINK CAUSED DISEASE?	Gods Food rotting in the channels of the body	Gods The humours in the body getting out of balance
HOW HEALTHY WERE PEOPLE?	In both societies the wealthy probably lived longer than the poor because they ate more and lived in cleaner conditions. This meant, for example, that women in wealthier families were likely to have stronger babies that were less vulnerable to infection. People in Egypt and Greece had similar life expectancy.	

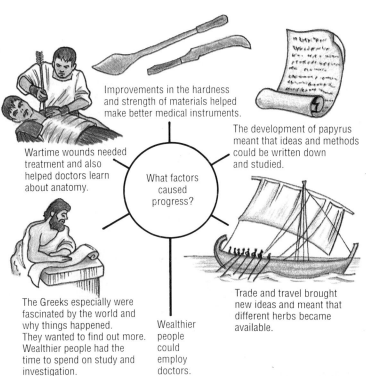

Improvements in the hardness and strength of materials helped make better medical instruments.

Wartime wounds needed treatment and also helped doctors learn about anatomy.

The development of papyrus meant that ideas and methods could be written down and studied.

The Greeks especially were fascinated by the world and why things happened. They wanted to find out more. Wealthier people had the time to spend on study and investigation.

Wealthier people could employ doctors.

Trade and travel brought new ideas and meant that different herbs became available.

What factors caused progress?

SOURCE 1 Reasons for the increase in medical knowledge

■ TASK 1

It is 400BC. Here are some possible changes which might in the future improve people's health:
a) more trained doctors
b) better herbal remedies
c) improved knowledge of the body
d) discovering the true causes of disease.

1. Choose one which you think would be most helpful.
2. Write a paragraph to explain your choice.
3. Write a second paragraph to explain whether you think a Greek doctor such as Hippocrates would agree with your choice.

■ TASK 2

1. Look at Source 1. Which factors were most important in increasing medical knowledge in:
a) ancient Egypt
b) ancient Greece?
2. Draw a second diagram to show 'factors which held up progress in medical knowledge'.

Why was Alexandria so important?

ALTHOUGH THEY WERE curious about the world around them, Greek doctors very rarely dissected dead bodies. They were not aware of how much they could have learned through dissection. Also they thought that dissecting the dead was wrong.

One of the first Greek doctors to carry out dissections was Herophilus who lived around 250BC. His most important discovery, thanks to his careful dissections, was that the brain controls the body. Herophilus made other vital discoveries too. He showed that there was a difference between ARTERIES and nerves and he identified parts of the stomach, such as the duodenum, and the prostate.

Alexandria: the centre of all medical knowledge

Herophilus was successful partly because of his hard work and his genius. However, another reason was that he was working in Alexandria. If he had been in Greece he would not have been able to perform dissections – in Alexandria he could. Alexandria had become a centre of medical knowledge after the Greeks built a university and a library there. The library collected together writings not only from Greek writers such as Hippocrates, but also from doctors in India, China, Egypt and Mesopotamia. It was said that eventually there were 700,000 different items in the library.

Herophilus was not the only great doctor working in Alexandria. Another was Erasistratus who almost made an even greater discovery. Erasistratus was busy dissecting a heart when he noticed it had four one-way valves. Why? What did this mean? He made the link to a new invention – the pump. Perhaps the heart was a kind of pump?

Unfortunately no one developed this idea. Erasistratus cannot have been popular. He was one of the few Greeks who did not believe in the theory of the four humours. It was to be another 1800 years before his idea was finally proved to be correct – that the heart was indeed a pump, sending blood around the body (see pages 88–89).

The influence of Alexandria

Alexandria was the centre of new medical ideas and knowledge. Eager medical students from around the Mediterranean travelled to Alexandria to learn from this knowledge. One was a young man called Galen who became the most famous doctor in the Roman Empire.

■ ACTIVITY

You are a doctor in ancient Greece. You are sending a letter to the library at Alexandria reporting on medicine and health in ancient Greece.

Write a letter which sums up:
a) the theory of the four humours
b) the range of treatments you use based on it
c) the influence of Hippocrates
d) why Greek medicine is better than anything that has gone before it.

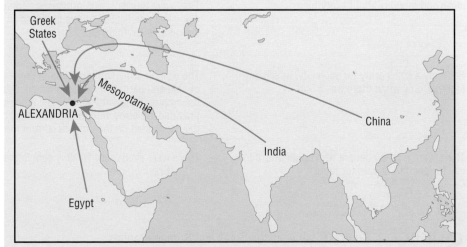

Egypt was conquered by the Greeks in the fourth century BC.
The Greek leader, Alexander the Great founded the city of Alexandria in 331BC.
Medical writings were brought to the library from India, China, Mesopotamia, Egypt and Greece.

SOURCE 1 The flow of medical knowledge into Alexandria. The library continued to attract medical students for another 500 years until it was burned down in AD391

Was the Roman Empire different from the Greek Empire?

FROM AROUND 300BC the Greek Empire was growing weaker. At the same time, the new Roman Empire was steadily growing stronger. By AD120 Rome controlled most of the Mediterranean lands and western Europe (see Source 4 on page 15).

The Romans took over almost all the Greeks' old empire, and as you might expect, the two empires were very closely connected (see Source 1). These connections affected Roman medicine. However, there were also important differences between the two empires (see Source 2) which affected medicine too.

Some people say that the Romans simply borrowed all the Greeks' ideas about medicine. In the rest of this chapter you are going to investigate whether that really was the case or did the Romans produce new ideas of their own?

1. Study Source 2. How might each of these features affect Roman medicine?
2. What do you expect? Do you expect that Roman medicine will show:
a) continuity from Greek ideas
b) change from Greek ideas?

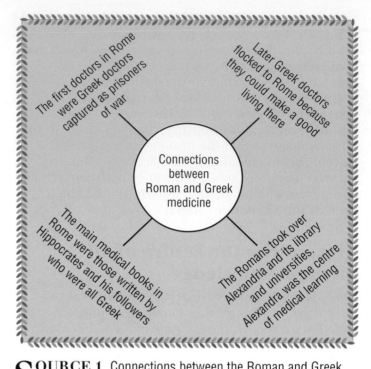

SOURCE 1 Connections between the Roman and Greek Empires

Connections between Roman and Greek medicine

- The first doctors in Rome were Greek doctors captured as prisoners of war
- Later Greek doctors flocked to Rome because they could make a good living there
- The main medical books in Rome were those written by Hippocrates and his followers who were all Greek
- The Romans took over Alexandria and its library and universities. Alexandra was the centre of medical learning

Greek Empire	Roman Empire	
Mostly small cities – less than 20,000 people – which did not pose health problems.	Large cities – Rome itself had a million people. Many people living cramped together posed health problems.	
Not very centralised. Each city was independent. Ideas spread slowly.	Very centralised with strong government. Quick communication around the empire. New ideas and treatments spread quickly. So too could diseases.	
Greek philosophers were famous for having ideas and theories about everything.	Romans were less interested in theories. They were efficient, well-organised people who liked practical solutions to illness as well as to everything else.	
Had only a small army for each city, which got together only when there was a war.	The Roman army had hundreds of thousands of soldiers, permanently stationed all over the empire. Frequently at war. The government provided the army with the best medical care as they depended on the army to control the empire.	
There were wealthy people who could afford to pay for doctors to care for them.	There were even more wealthy people than in the Greek Empire.	

SOURCE 2 Contrasts between the Greek and Roman Empires

A Roman army hospital

'Best amputate, whilst he has some strength.'

Historical novels can be a very good way of learning about the past simply because reading novels doesn't feel like hard work. History can be fun! However, you only learn about the past if the story is accurate, and describes the real ideas, clothes or houses of that period. *The Silver Pigs* is a carefully researched novel. The author has worked hard to ensure that her historical detail is as accurate as possible. This extract is about medicine

The story is set in AD70 and it is told by Marcus Didius Falco, a 'private informer' employed by the Emperor Vespasian to uncover details of a plot to smuggle silver from Britain to Rome. Falco goes to Britain ('the province out beyond civilization') but, working undercover as a slave in a silver mine, he breaks his leg and several ribs and has to be rescued …

1. Read Source 1. Describe the impression it gives of Roman surgery. You could use some of these words: skilful, hygienic, gentle, painful, dirty, brutal.
2. What actually happened to Marcus?

■ ACTIVITY

1. On the copy of Source 1 provided by your teacher underline each phrase referring to medicine, medical methods or doctors.
2. Look at the sources on pages 38–39. If a source provides evidence to support anything which you underlined about Roman medicine then write the source number in the margin next to the phrase.

SOURCE 1 From *The Silver Pigs* by Lindsey Davis (reproduced with permission from Pan Books)

❝ I was lying on a high, hard bed in a small, square room at a legionary hospital. Unhurried footsteps sometimes paced the long corridor round the courtyard at the back of the administration block. I recognized the evil reek of antiseptic turpentine. I felt the reassuring pressure of neat, firm bandaging. I was warm. I was clean. I was resting in tranquillity in a quiet, caring place …

Their opium had ebbed away. When I moved pain shot back. A red tunic, brooched on one shoulder with the medical snake and staff, loomed over me, then sheered off again when I stared him in the eye. I recognized the complete absence of bedside manner: must be the chief (medical) orderly. Pupils stretched their necks behind him like awestruck ducklings jostling their mother duck.

'Tell me the truth, Hippocrates!' I jested. They never tell you the truth.

He tickled me up and down my ribs like a moneychanger on an abacus. I yelped, though not because his hands were cold.

'Still in discomfort – that will last several months. He can expect a great deal of pain. No real problems if he avoids getting pneumonia …' He sounded disappointed at the thought that I might. 'Emaciated specimen; he's vulnerable to GANGRENE in this leg.' My heart sank. 'Best amputate, whilst he has some strength.' I glared at him with a heartbreak that brightened him up. 'We can give him something!' he consoled his listeners. Did you know, the main part of a surgeon's training is how to ignore the screams? …

The surgeon was called Simplex … Simplex had spent fourteen years in the army. He could calm a sixteen-year-old soldier with an arrow shot into his head. He could seal blisters, dose dysentery, bathe eyes, even deliver babies from the wives the legionaries were not supposed to have. He was bored with all that. I was his favourite patient now. Among his set of spatulas, scalpels, probes, shears, and forceps, he owned a shiny great mallet big enough to bash in fencing stakes. Its use in surgery was for amputations, driving home his chisel through soldiers' joints. He had the chisel and the saw too: a complete toolbag, all laid out on a table by my bed.

They drugged me, but not enough. Flavius Hilaris wished me luck, then slipped out of the room. I don't blame him. If I hadn't been strapped down to the bed with four six-foot set-faced cavalrymen grappling my shoulders and feet, I would have shot straight out after him …

'Stop it at once!' cried Helena Justina. I had no idea when she came in. I had not realized she was there. 'There's no gangrene!' stormed the senator's daughter. She seemed to lose her temper wherever she was. 'I would expect an army surgeon to know – gangrene has its own distinctive smell. Didius Falco's feet may be cheesy, but they're not that bad!' Wonderful woman; an informer in trouble could always count on her. 'He has chilblains. In Britain that's nothing to wonder at – all he needs for those is a hot turnip mash! Pull his leg as straight as you can, then leave him alone; the poor man has suffered enough!'

I passed out with relief. ❞

1. Some references to medicine in Source 1 are not supported by Sources 2–8. Do you think that they are likely to be based on other sources? Explain your answer.
2. Is Source 1 an accurate description of medical treatments in Roman Britain? Explain your answer.
3. Do you think that historical novels are a better way of learning history than lessons or textbooks in school?

SOURCE 4 A tombstone found at Housesteads, one of the major forts on Hadrian's Wall. It reads 'To the spirits of the departed [and] to Anicius Ingenuus, medical orderly of the First Cohort of the Tungrians: he lived 25 years'

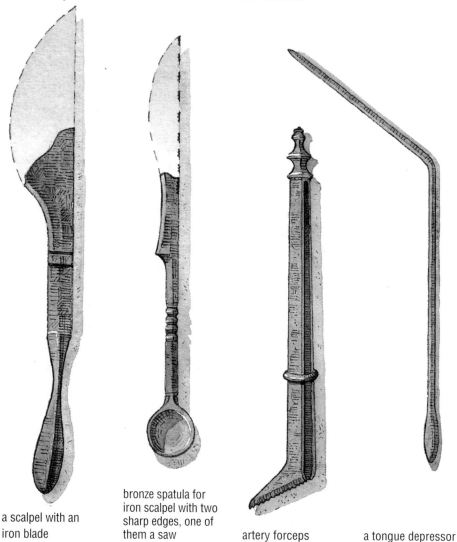

a scalpel with an iron blade

bronze spatula for iron scalpel with two sharp edges, one of them a saw

artery forceps

a tongue depressor

SOURCE 2 A Roman doctor's surgical instruments found in Britain. The dotted lines show reconstruction

SOURCE 3 Celsus, *De Medicina*, Book V. Celsus was a Roman doctor. This gives instructions for making opium, a sedative used in surgery

  ... take a good handful of wild poppy-heads when just ripe for collecting the juice and put into a vessel and boil with water sufficient to cover it. When this handful has been well boiled there, after being squeezed out it is thrown away; and with its juice is mixed an equal quantity of raisin wine and heated ... when the mixture has cooled, pills are formed ... they procure sleep.

SOURCE 5 From *De Medicina*, Book VII, part of an encyclopaedia compiled by the Roman writer, Celsus in the first century AD.

  When gangrene has developed ... the limb ... must be amputated. But even that involves very great risk; for patients often die under the operation ... It does not matter, however, whether the remedy is safe enough, since it is the only one. Therefore between the sound and the diseased part, the flesh is cut through with a scalpel down to the bone, but this must not be done actually over a joint, and it is better that some of the sound part should be cut away than that any diseased part should be left behind ... the bone is then to be cut through with a small saw ...

SOURCE 6 Celsus, *De Medicina*, Book VII concerning the training of surgeons

" … a surgeon should be youthful or at any rate nearer youth than age; with a strong and steady hand which never trembles, and ready to use the left hand as well as the right; with vision sharp and clear, and spirit undaunted; filled with pity, so that he wishes to cure the patient, yet is not moved by his cries, to go too fast, or cut less than is necessary; but he does everything just as if the cries of pain cause him no emotion. "

SOURCE 7 Pliny the Elder, *Natural History*, Book XX, written in the first century AD

" A hot application of [turnips] cures chilblains, besides preventing the feet from being chilled. A hot decoction of it is good even for gout, and raw turnip, pounded and mixed with salt, for every ailment of the feet. "

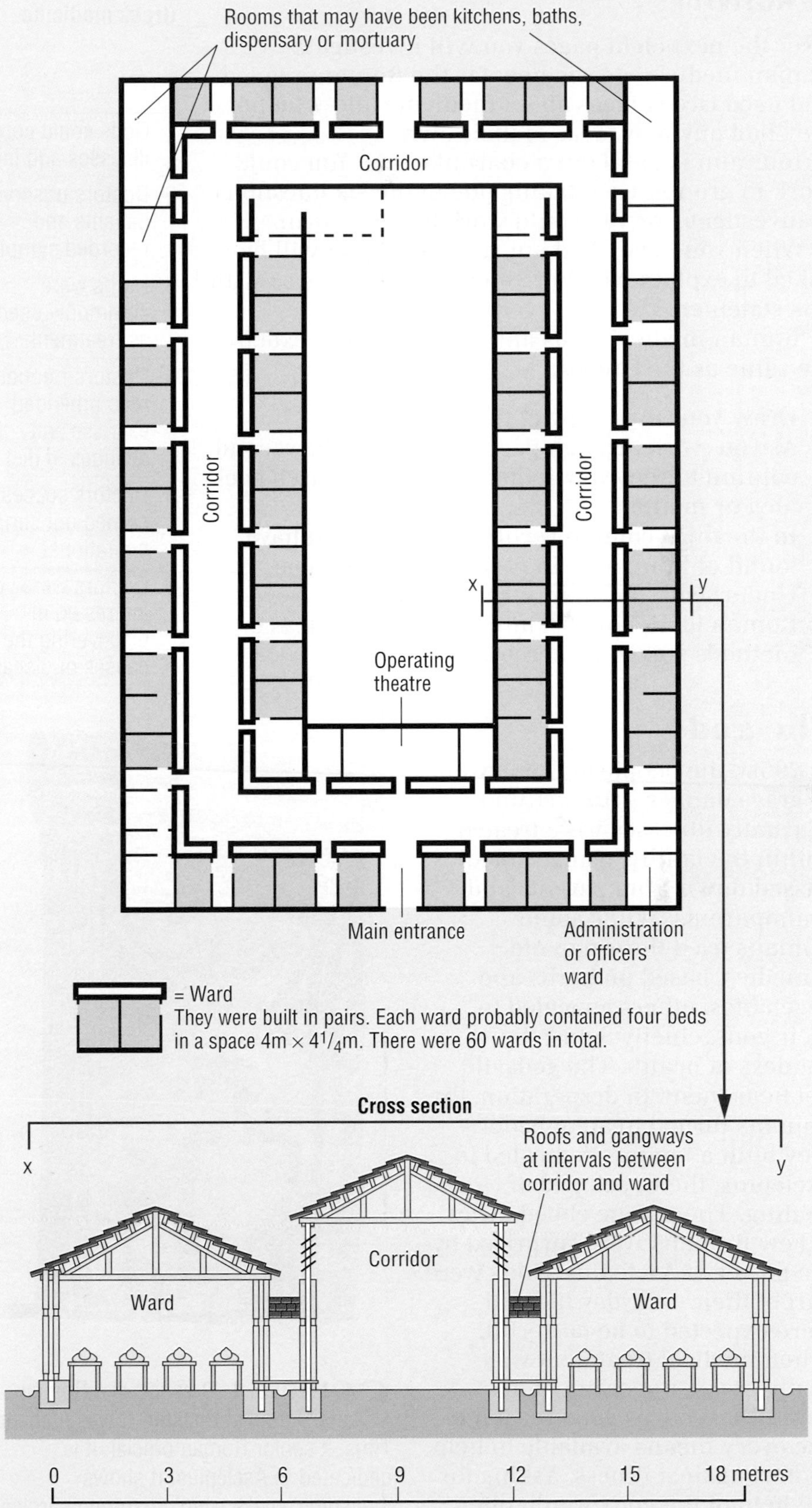

Rooms that may have been kitchens, baths, dispensary or mortuary

Corridor

Corridor

Corridor

Operating theatre

x | y

Main entrance

Administration or officers' ward

= Ward
They were built in pairs. Each ward probably contained four beds in a space 4m × 4¼m. There were 60 wards in total.

Cross section

x

Roofs and gangways at intervals between corridor and ward

y

Corridor

Ward

Ward

0   3   6   9   12   15   18 metres

SOURCE 8 A plan of the hospital at the Roman fort of Inchtuthil, Perthshire, which was excavated in the 1950s. There were separate roofs over the outer row of wards, the corridor and the inner wards

Were Roman medical ideas the same as those of the Greeks?

■ ACTIVITY

Over the next eight pages you will investigate Roman medicine to see how far the Romans copied and used Greek ideas about medicine and whether they had any new ideas of their own.

Your aim is to fill out a chart like this. You could work in groups, each taking one of the six questions to investigate, or you could work on your own.

When you have filled out your chart you will be asked to explain whether you agree or disagree with this statement:

'Roman medical ideas and methods were exactly the same as the Greeks.'

1. Draw your own copy of this chart.
2. As you work through pages 40–47 use the second column to record whether the Romans used each idea or method.
3. In the third column record examples you have found of Romans using that idea or method.
4. Underneath the chart write the heading 'New Roman ideas' and list any new Roman ideas or methods you come across.

Aspects of Greek medicine	Did the Romans use this idea or method – a lot – a little – not at all	Example
1. Gods could cure illnesses and injuries.		
2. Doctors observed patients and recorded symptoms.		
3. Herbs were commonly used as treatments.		
4. Doctors frequently recommended exercise and changes in diet.		
5. Doctors successfully carried out simple operations.		
6. Doctors were very interested in discovering the causes of disease.		

The gods

In 295BC the people of Rome were in grave danger – from PLAGUE. Normally illnesses were treated within the family, using remedies passed down from parents and grandparents. While some Romans tried these age-old remedies, based on herbs and vegetables, others appealed to their gods, chiefly Salus, the goddess of health. The gods did not hear them. In desperation, the Romans turned to an outsider – they built a temple, dedicated to Asclepius, the Greek god of healing. The plague ebbed away.

Few Romans were surprised by the power of Asclepius. Gods were part of their everyday life and were expected to be powerful. When medical treatment was costly, risky, uncertain and painful there was good reason to use every means available to help protect against illness. Asking for the help of the gods would often have been a first, not a last resort.

SOURCE 1 Drawing of a Roman altar found at Chester. It was made for Titus, a senior Roman official. It is dedicated to Asclepius. It shows Asclepius' snake winding around surgical instruments

SOURCE 2 Inscriptions from altars found at Overborough in Lancashire, Chester and Binchester in County Durham

    66 *To the Holy God Asclepius and to Hygeia, Julius Saturninus [set this up].*

    To the mighty Saviour gods I, Hermogenes, a doctor, set up this altar.

    To Asclepius and Salus for the welfare of the Cavalry regiment. **99**

1. Which Greek god did the Romans pray to?
2. Why do you think the Romans used both Roman and Greek ideas?
3. Fill in the first row of your chart.

Doctors

Doctors were employed in many Roman cities to give free treatment to the poor. Some were women, mostly specialising in treating women's illnesses. One woman doctor, Antiochus, was so successful that her home town allowed her to erect a statue to herself, 'in recognition of her skill as a medical practitioner', which probably included discovering medicines for treating RHEUMATISM and SCIATICA. Women in general played a vital role in treating illnesses. 'The science of [charms and herbs] is the one outstanding skill of women' admitted the writer, Pliny the Elder.

How were doctors trained?

Some medical students learned by reading the Hippocratic Collection but only the wealthiest owned copies because books were very expensive. Others read them in the great libraries of Rome or Alexandria but more often students became apprentices to experienced doctors, watching, then copying, their methods. This was not always popular! One writer complained: 'I was sickening; but you at once attended me, Symmachus, with a train of a hundred apprentices. A hundred hands frosted by the north wind have pawed me. I had no fever before, Symmachus, now I have!' This writer did not realise how lucky he was. Medical training was not compulsory for doctors. Anyone could call him – or herself – a doctor!

SOURCE 3 This drawing of a second-century carving shows a midwife and her assistant delivering a baby. Soranus, a Roman medical writer, said that 'we call a midwife faultless if she merely carries out her medical task; whereas we call her the best midwife if she goes further and in addition to her management of cases is well versed in theory [and] … is trained in all branches of THERAPY …'

The most famous Roman doctor of all was Galen whom you can read about on pages 43–45. He savagely criticised other Roman doctors who did not reach his high standards. He said they 'talk any nonsense that comes to their tongues – stupid, insane language.' One Roman writer, Pliny, described Greek doctors in Rome as profiteers, simply trying to get rich.

1. According to this page what roles did women play in healing the sick?
2. Do you think these are the only roles they played?
3. The text and sources mention various ways of training doctors. Which do you think would be most effective?
4. How important were doctors to the Roman army?
5. Read the information on the next page, then fill out row 2 of your chart.

SOURCE 4 A carved scene from Trajan's column which celebrated his victories over the Dacians. This probably shows medical orderlies at work pouring ointment on a war wound. Each legion had a doctor and medical orderlies but they rarely held high rank. The military writer, Vegetius, noted that 'generals believe that daily exercise is better for soldiers than treatment by physicians.' Prevention was better than cure, especially when doctors often had very little chance of saving the sick

Treatments

Like the Greeks, Roman doctors used three main methods of helping their patients. They recommended more exercise, changes in diet or prescribed herbal medicines as 'opposites' (see page 44).

Most Romans agreed with Hippocrates that people should take daily exercise to stay fit. Many took exercise with trainers at public baths or the gymnasium. Celsus wrote: 'He who has been engaged in the day, whether in domestic or on public affairs, ought to keep some portion of the day for the care of the body. The primary care … is exercise, which … ought to come to an end with sweating.'

Roman families used herbs and vegetables in medical treatments. Roman doctors used opium as a weak anaesthetic. Turpentine and pitch were used as antiseptics. Around AD64 Dioscorides, a former army doctor, wrote a huge book listing 600 herbal remedies. Modern doctors have calculated that 20 per cent of these remedies would have been effective. Amidst the good remedies there were many others like the one in Source 5 recorded by Pliny the Elder.

Theories about disease

The most common surgical treatment was bleeding. Roman surgical instruments as you can see from Source 2 on page 38 were very similar to those of the Greeks. Internal operations were still rare because they were so risky without effective antiseptics, anaesthetics or more detailed anatomical knowledge. However, there were amputations; trephining was used to relieve pain in the head and cataracts were removed from eyes using fine needles. The greatest danger in eye operations came from the patient moving.

Despite the influence and ideas of Greek doctors in Rome, there was a major difference between the two empires in their attitude to medicine. The Romans were not as interested as the Greeks in developing theories about the causes of disease. Galen suggested that 'seeds of disease' floated in the air. However, he knew that this idea did not help cure illnesses and so he spent little time on it, preferring to collect more practical knowledge.

SOURCE 5

   The best of all safeguards against serpents is the saliva of a fasting human being, but our daily experience may teach us yet other values of its use. We spit on epileptics in a fit, that is, we throw back infection. In a similar way we ward off WITCHCRAFT and the bad luck that follows meeting a person lame in the right leg. "

SOURCE 6 An engraving of a third-century Roman coin which shows various stages of a treatment associated with the goddess Salus

1. Look at Source 6. Identify these stages in the treatment:

   ■ an offering is made on an altar
   ■ healing water flows from the goddess's pitcher
   ■ a slave boy collects the water
   ■ a man drinks the water
   ■ the man thanks the goddess for healing.

2. What was the treatment of opposites?
3. Why did Galen use the treatment of 'opposites'?
4. Use the information on this page to fill out the last four rows of your chart.

What made Galen famous?

THE PIG SQUIRMED on the table. Galen cut into its neck and found the nerves. The pig squealed. 'Watch,' said Galen to his audience, 'I will cut this nerve but the pig will keep on squealing.'

He cut. The pig kept squealing. Galen cut another nerve. Again the pig squealed.

'Now,' said Galen, 'I will cut another nerve which controls the pig's voice. It will not squeal.'

Galen cut the nerve. The room was silent.

Galen had just arrived in Rome. He wanted to win fame and a fortune. His public experiments were his way of attracting attention from other doctors. In this experiment Galen proved that the brain controlled the body, not the heart.

Where did Galen come from?

Galen was born in AD129 in Greece. He began studying medicine at the age of sixteen and spent twelve years travelling to improve his knowledge, including a visit to the famous medical school at Alexandria in Egypt (see page 35).

He gained practical experience as a surgeon at a gladiators' school. Gladiators were trained to fight with other gladiators and with wild animals in amphitheatres around the Roman Empire. They suffered stab wounds, broken bones, and other major injuries yet they were usually very healthy and fit young men. It was an ideal place for a young ambitious surgeon to learn his craft.

In AD162 he travelled to Rome. He soon became famous as doctor to the Roman emperor and teacher of other doctors.

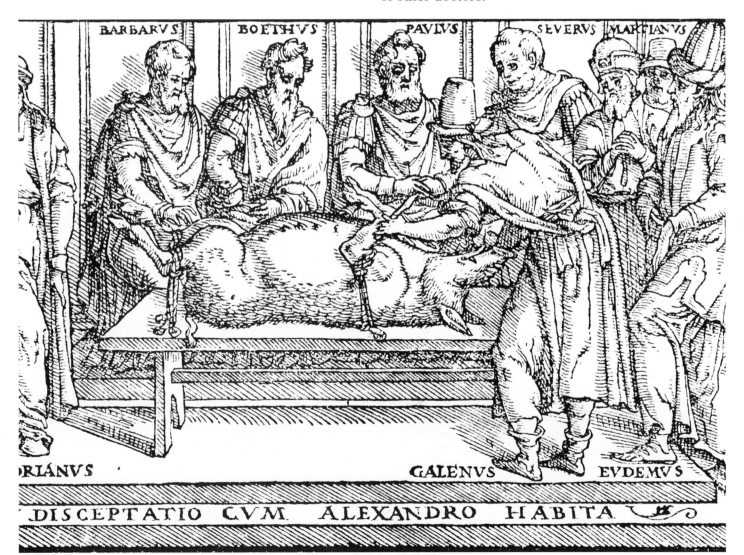

SOURCE 1 A medieval illustration showing Galen's famous experiment

What were Galen's ideas and methods?

Observation
Galen emphasised the importance of Hippocrates' methods. He told doctors to observe, record and use their experience of past cases to decide how to treat an illness.

The four humours
Like Hippocrates he believed in the theory of the four humours and that treatments should restore the balance of the humours. However, Galen did not just copy Hippocrates.

Galen believed in using 'opposites' to balance the humours. If the symptom was too much phlegm then the patient's problem was caused by cold. Galen recommended an opposite treatment – a hot treatment such as taking pepper.

Galen also followed Greek ideas in telling people who were weak to take physical exercise.

Dissection
Galen dissected human bodies in Alexandria to increase his knowledge of the body. In Rome, however, he usually had to make do with animals for his experiments. This meant that some of the detail of his work was wrong. However, much of it was very precise. He proved that the brain, not the heart, controlled speech and that arteries as well as veins carried blood. Although he used animals for dissection he proved that animals' anatomy is different from that of humans, and he told his students that they should dissect human corpses whenever possible.

SOURCE 3 From Galen's *On Anatomy*, AD190

66 *Human bones are the subject which you should first get to know. At Alexandria this is very easy, since the physicians in that country let their students inspect human bodies for themselves. Try to get to Alexandria. But if you can't manage this it is not impossible to get to see human bones. I have often had the chance to do this where tombs have been broken. Once I examined the skeleton of a robber lying on a mountain-side. If you don't have the luck to see anything like this, you can still dissect an ape. For this you should choose apes which most resemble men. In the apes which walk and run on two legs you will also find other parts as in man.* 99

Writing

What really made Galen famous were the 60 books he wrote. They combined Greek ideas, with what he had learned from his own work in Alexandria and Rome and presented it all so convincingly that they became the basis for medical teaching and learning for the next 1500 years. For most of that time nobody dared to say that Galen was wrong!

Careful observation

The four humours
• Hippocrates' ideas
• His own ideas about 'opposites'

Dissection and surgery
Knowledge of anatomy

Galen wrote 60 books on medicine. They were the main books used by medical students for over 1500 years

SOURCE 4 Galen's work

Design

Galen tried to show his students how different parts of the body all fitted together into a well-designed whole. This idea was particularly important in later centuries because the Christian Church saw that Galen's explanations of the body fitted in with the Christian belief that God created human beings.

■ ACTIVITY

Galen is applying for a job as the Roman emperor's doctor. Write a CV for him. Your teacher can give you a sheet to get you started.

What was the Romans' big idea?

Public health

Public health means action taken by governments to improve the health of their people.

Even though the Romans were not so interested in theories about the causes of illness, their practical skills produced the best public health schemes yet seen anywhere in the world. These did much to protect people against disease.

In the crowded city of Rome sewers were essential if the city was to be fit to live in. But the Romans didn't limit their schemes to Rome. Throughout the Empire fresh water was supplied to major towns along aqueducts and brick conduits. Sewers were built to take away sewage from private houses and public toilets. Even small towns had public baths, open to anyone for a quadrans, the smallest Roman coin. The baths helped rid people of fleas which spread disease. Public toilets were also built in towns. Up to twenty people could be seated at once around three sides of the room. Individual cubicles were rare. Other public health measures included rules about burying the dead, and preventing fires.

Engineers took great care over the siting of towns, forts and villas. In his book on country life Marcus Varro wrote:

SOURCE 1

66 When building a house or farm especial care should be taken to place it at the foot of a wooded hill where it is exposed to health-giving winds. Care should be taken when there are swamps in the neighbourhood because certain tiny creatures which cannot be seen by the eyes breed there. These float through the air and enter the body through the mouth and nose and cause serious diseases. 99

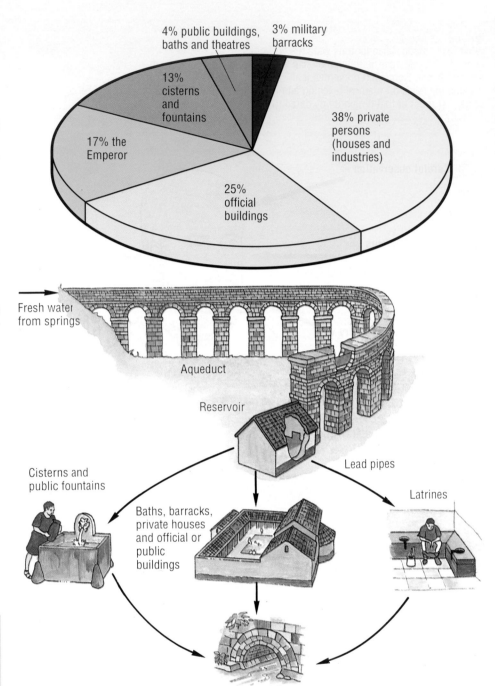

- 4% public buildings, baths and theatres
- 3% military barracks
- 13% cisterns and fountains
- 38% private persons (houses and industries)
- 17% the Emperor
- 25% official buildings

Fresh water from springs

Aqueduct

Reservoir

Lead pipes

Cisterns and public fountains

Baths, barracks, private houses and official or public buildings

Latrines

Sewers emptying into River Tiber

SOURCE 2
Water supply and sewage system in ancient Rome. Not everyone had equal access to clean water. Even in homes which had a water supply it could not reach the upper floors. The pie chart shows how the water supply was shared out

■ ACTIVITY

You have been asked to make a leaflet promoting the Romans' public health schemes. It should summarise the main measures taken, the reasons for them, and the effects they have had.

Use evidence from Sources 1–5 to draw up your leaflet.

In Rome water commissioners were appointed to ensure good supplies of clean water. One of them, Sextus Julius Frontinus (who held the post in AD97), wrote of the improved health of the city:

SOURCE 3

❝ ... as a result of the increase in the number of works, reservoirs, fountains, and water-basins ... the air is purer; and the causes of the unwholesome atmosphere, which gave the air of the City so bad a name ... are now removed ... With such an array of indispensable structures carrying so many waters, compare, if you will, the idle Pyramids or the useless, though famous, works of the Greeks. ❞

Frontinus exaggerated. Toilets were still built in kitchens, and sewage pits dug near wells. There was no clear understanding of how dirt caused disease. However, the improvements did help, especially in the Roman army.

To help the legionaries stay fit, each fort had a bath house with drains and fresh water and also a hospital carefully sited in the quietest part of the camp. The military writer, Vegetius, added:

SOURCE 4

❝ Soldiers must not remain for too long near unhealthy marshes. A soldier who must face the cold without proper clothing is not in a state to have good health or to march. He must not drink swamp water. ❞

SOURCE 5 K. Branigan, *Roman Britain: Life in an Imperial Province*, 1980

*❝ **The baths**
In Britain, in towns like Chichester, Leicester and Wroxeter in Shropshire, probably as many as 500 people a day used the [public baths], even if they only visited them once a week. One of the finest suites of public baths in Britain was at Wroxeter, which also included an outdoor swimming pool and a massive exercise hall.*

***Water supply**
... Water in most large towns in Britain was supplied by aqueduct – contoured channels dug in the ground and perhaps lined with clay. The most impressive surviving example is the one running into Dorchester; an eight-mile [13km] channel, 5 ft [1.6m] wide and more than 3 ft [1m] deep.*

The aqueduct at Wroxeter could deliver two million gallons of water each day, distributed through the town by a complex system of timber and lead pipes. Mains ran along the principal streets to side channels from which sluices diverted the water into individual buildings.

If, during a drought, the level of water in the mains dropped below 7 in. [18cm], then the supply to private houses was automatically cut off. Householders often supplemented their needs with wells, lined with stone or with old topless and bottomless barrels.

***Drains and sewers**
Timber-lined drains were constructed in many towns, and substantial stone-built sewers have been found beneath the streets of Roman Colchester and York...*

Main sewers collected water from the public baths, and recycled it to flush the latrines. These were usually built within the bath-house, though at Wroxeter a very large public latrine next to the baths was flushed by water that had already coursed through another lavatory in the market hall. The original source was rainwater collected from the roof of the market... ❞

1. Read Source 1. What did Varro think was the cause of disease?
2. Was this an intelligent explanation?
3. Read Source 3. Why did some Romans feel superior to the Greeks?
4. How did public health schemes help the Roman army?

■ ACTIVITY

Divide into groups of three. One of you is a wealthy Roman living in Rome, one a soldier serving in Wroxeter, and the other a poor person living in Rome.

Each of you work out (from the information and sources on these two pages) what public health facilities you have available.

Compare your facilities with the others in your group and decide who has the best facilities.

■ TASK

Look back to your completed chart from page 40. Write an essay explaining whether you agree or disagree with this statement: 'Roman medical ideas were the same as the Greeks.' You can get a sheet from your teacher to help you.

So ... did the Romans have new ideas?

■ TASK

Study the summary chart below. You can get a copy of it from your teacher.

1. On your own copy mark which of these features show change from the ideas of the Greeks and which show continuity (lack of change).

2. Find examples from pages 36–47 of how each of the following factors helped either to bring about change or prevent change:

■ war/the army
■ governments
■ religion
■ technological developments
■ individuals.

Change and continuity in Roman Britain

IN AD43 the Romans began the conquest of Britain and kept control of most of Britain for nearly 400 years. There is no doubt that the medical skills and ideas of Roman doctors were more advanced than those of the Celtic people they conquered. Did Britons benefit from the medical skills and knowledge of the Romans?

Changes

At the time of the Roman conquest Britain was a prosperous country. Its agricultural wealth and trade had been a major reason for the Roman invasion. Its farms supplied Rome with food and paid for the baths and water supplies in villas and towns. Undoubtedly the climate played an important part in this prosperity. Warmer temperatures, together with moderate rainfall, ensured good harvests. These in turn provided a plentiful diet that made people more resistant to disease. As a result, the population grew, perhaps as high as six million people.

Changes took place in medical care. There were trained army doctors and army hospitals in the largest towns, and legionary doctors probably treated local people. Some doctors may also have settled in Britain after they left the army. A wider range of drugs (based on plants and herbs) was used, adding to British knowledge, and in some cases proving more effective. Perhaps the greatest change was in the provision of fresh water supplies and public baths in major towns (see Source 5 on page 47).

Some people did benefit from these changes. Legionaries had the best medical attention and were assured a good diet and a high level of physical fitness. Wealthy town dwellers also benefited. Life expectancy for the rich probably increased, although less for women than for men, because these changes did nothing to solve the biggest medical problem faced by women – the complications of childbirth.

Few of the poor benefited although some slaves who served in villas of the rich, who were able to use baths and were spared hard physical labour, would have been fit and healthy well past 50.

Summary: changes
- good harvests, better houses, more food
- trained doctors in the army and towns
- wider range of herbal medicines
- fresh water supplies, sewers and baths.

Continuities

Despite these changes a great deal stayed the same. A high proportion of children still died in infancy. Men still lived longer than women.

Life expectancy of the poor was far lower than that of the wealthy. It would have been very unusual for an agricultural labourer to reach 50 and they suffered while alive. Over 80 per cent of the skeletons unearthed at Cirencester had painful osteoarthritis in their joints – the result of digging, carrying and other basic toil.

The danger of disease was as great as ever. Diseases struck without warning and there was little protection against them. There were serious plagues in AD166–67 and in the 250s (brought back from Asia by the army). The greatest, in the fifth century devastated the population, helping to cause a long-term population decline. Here, the impact of the Roman Empire was positively harmful. Plagues spread more rapidly, due to improved communications and trade.

The poor saw little of the public health improvements. Their smoky homes led to much coughing, a sure way of spreading some diseases quickly. For most people medical care continued to be provided by family members. Childbirth was overseen by older women in the village. Few had access to doctors, either because they did not live in towns or because they could not afford fees. Medical treatments were still based on remedies passed down through families.

Summary: continuities
- most people died young
- many suffered pain from hard work
- diseases could not be stopped from spreading
- women treated most health problems, often using herbal remedies
- the poor (especially in the country) did not benefit from the public health schemes.

1. On a scale of 1 to 5 say how significant each of the following were for the health of **wealthy people** in Roman Britain:
   a) Galen
   b) the Roman army
   c) herbal remedies
   d) women as healers.
2. Repeat question 1 for **poor people** in Roman Britain.

Would you survive in ancient Rome?

THIS IS A game – but a game with a purpose. By playing it you can revise or learn about some of the main features of Roman medicine.

Your objective is to survive by finding a cure for your illness! This is how you play.

1. Get into pairs. You will each need a counter – a rubber or a coin will do as long as it is different from your opponent's.
2. Choose one of the **people** from Box A; one of the **ailments** from Box B; and one of the **healers** in Box C.
3. On the board opposite start by putting your counter on the number your healer instruction tells you to.
4. Take turns following the instructions in your square. At each turn note down what happened to you, using the sheet you can get from your teacher.
5. If you die (or recover) before your partner, try the game again either as a different person, or using a different healer.

Good luck!

Box A: People

Marcus Decimus a wealthy Roman senator and his wife Helen Rubina.

Julius Camillus and Silvia Priscilla, shopkeepers.

Gaius Fabius and Julia Claudia, who scratch a living as best they can. When they are ill, they cannot afford to stop working to rest.

Box B: Ailments

1. You have a sharp headache that has lasted for several days. It is stopping you sleeping.
2. You have been vomiting all day and you cannot eat without being sick again.
3. You have a pain in your side that hurts more as you walk. In fact you can hardly stand because of the pain. It has lasted for a couple of days.

Box C: Healers

The temple of Asclepius. If you choose this option start at square 11.

Trebonius, a well-qualified and wealthy doctor. You will need to pay him a high fee. If you choose this option start at square 9.

Brutus, a retired legionary doctor. He is now the town doctor and will treat you without charging a fee. If you choose this option start at square 13.

Buying a potion from a local shop. If you choose this option start at square 21.

You could simply stay at home to be treated by your own family. If you choose this option go to square 19.

1

The remedy contains opium and eases the pain. You feel more relaxed lying down at home. Go to 16.

2

Purging. If you have a headache, the purging makes you feel weaker. Go to 24. If you have a pain in your side or you are vomiting, the purging makes you feel worse. Go to 22.

3

You wake up feeling better. The vomiting has stopped. Your stomach feels more settled. Go to 16.

4

Trephining. The doctor drills carefully into your skull. Was this a good idea? Toss a coin. Heads go to 12. Tails go to 23.

5

The visit to the temple has relaxed you, but you need more rest. If you can afford time off work, then go for a walk, get some fresh air and go to 16. If not, choose another healer so that you can get back to work and earn some money quickly.

6

If you are vomiting, the doctor offers you a herbal remedy. If you take it, go to 10. If not, go to 17. For a side-pain the doctor recommends rest and then exercise. If you agree, go to 14. If not, go to 17. For a headache the doctor suggests trephining. If you agree, go to 4. If not, go to 17.

7

Sadly you have just died.

8

You wake up feeling even worse. Your arm is swollen where the blood was taken and you feel feverish. You feel sicker and sicker. Go to 7.

9

You can only see this doctor if you are the senator or his wife. If you are, go to 6. If you are not, choose another healer.

10

Herbal remedy. If you have a side-pain the remedy has no effect. Go to 17. If you are vomiting, take the remedy, then go home and fall asleep. Go to 3.

11

At the temple you get a good night's rest. You feel better but a few hours later the problem returns. If you have a headache, go to 5. If you are vomiting or have a side-pain, go to 17.

12

The trephining seems to have worked. You feel better and the small hole gradually heals. Go to 16.

13

For a headache the doctor suggests trephining. If you agree, go to 4. If you do not, go to 17. For vomiting the doctor suggests bleeding or purging. If you decide on bleeding, go to 18. If purging, go to 2. If neither go to 17. For a side-pain the doctor suggests a herbal remedy. If you agree, go to 10. If not, go to 17.

14

Rest, fresh air, exercise and a better diet. If you have a headache, you feel better after a few days. Go to 16. If you have a side-pain the treatment does not help. Go to 17.

15

This quack remedy has weakened your body and made the problem worse. Go to 7.

16

The symptoms have disappeared and you have recovered.

17

Either you do not like the treatment or the cure you chose has not worked. Choose again.

18

Bleeding. This makes you feel weaker. Go home and sleep. Toss a coin. Heads go to 20. Tails go to 8.

19

At home you take a herbal remedy that your family has used for years. It contains honey, rhubarb and lots of other ingredients. Then lie down to sleep. If you have a headache, go to 1. If you are vomiting, go to 3. If you have a side-pain, go to 22.

20

You wake feeling better. Perhaps rest was all that was needed. Go to 16.

21

At the shop you buy Plautus' Remedy for All Ailments. Sounds good! It will certainly purge your bowels. Go to 2.

22

This wasn't the right treatment. It might have worked for another illness, but you feel worse – and worse. Go to 7.

23

You feel better for a day but then a fever begins. Perhaps the instruments were not clean. Go to 7.

24

The purging has made you feel weaker but at least it hasn't made the headache worse. You're still alive. Go to 17.

From prehistory to the Romans: how much change?

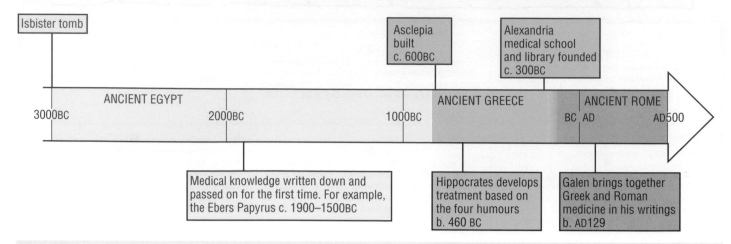

■ TASK

1. Which of the developments shown in the timeline was the most important in improving medicine and health? Explain the reasons for your answer.
2. Your teacher will give you a copy of the chart below. Complete your own summary of medical developments by filling in the empty boxes and adding to the details already there.

3. Explain which of these statements you most agree with:
   a) There were very few changes in medical treatments and ideas in this period.
   b) There were a few important changes in medical treatments and ideas but they mostly stayed the same.
   c) There were many important changes in medical treatments and ideas in this period.

	Prehistory	Egypt	Greece	Rome
Medical problems	Pain, infection, disease, bleeding	Pain, infection, disease, bleeding	Pain, infection, disease, bleeding	Pain, bleeding. Infection and disease became greater problems
Who treated illnesses?	Medicine men, family, particularly women	?	Trained doctors, priests at Asclepeia, women in families	Trained doctors, priests at temples, women in families
What did they think caused illnesses?	?	Gods. Another explanation was that food rotting in the body caused disease	Gods, the humours in the body becoming unbalanced	Some believed in gods. The humours in the body becoming unbalanced
How did they prevent and treat illness?	Herbal remedies, charms, setting broken bones	Herbal remedies, simple surgery, charms	?	Herbs, simple operations, treatment by opposites, advice on exercise, public health schemes
Was life expectancy improving?	Nearly everyone died before the age of 40	Some of the wealthy probably lived a little longer	Some of the wealthy lived into their 60s	?

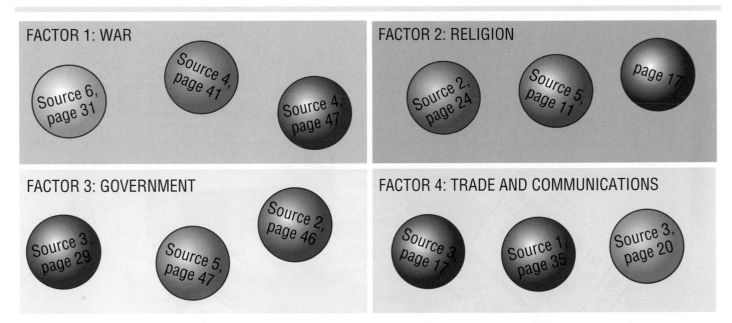

FACTOR 1: WAR	FACTOR 2: RELIGION
Source 6, page 31	Source 2, page 24
Source 4, page 41	Source 5, page 11
Source 4, page 47	page 17

FACTOR 3: GOVERNMENT	FACTOR 4: TRADE AND COMMUNICATIONS
Source 3, page 29	Source 3, page 17
Source 5, page 47	Source 1, page 35
Source 2, page 46	Source 3, page 20

■ TASK 1

Each square tells you about one factor which has affected the history of medicine. You just have to look up the page and source references on the balls.

1. Look up each example and add it to your 'factor' list at the back of your book.

2. For each example explain whether this factor helped to change medical ideas and treatments or helped to keep them the same.
3. Of the four factors here, which factor do you think did most to change ideas and treatments?
4. Which factor did most to keep them the same?
5. Were other factors such as technology or individuals, more or less important than these four in causing change?

■ TASK 2

Choose one of the following essay writing tasks:

A. Explain whether you agree or disagree with this statement: 'Women played a more important role than men in the early history of medicine.'

B. Did ancient healers and medicines help the sick? Whichever you choose you can get a sheet from your teacher to help you in your answer.

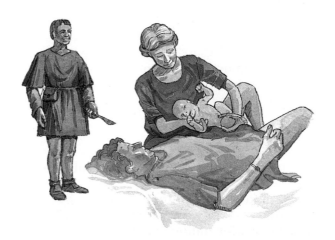

THE FOUR HUMOURS MUST BE KEPT IN BALANCE TO AVOID DISEASE

The health jigsaw AD200

This is a picture of Galen. The drawing is trying to show how far healers had succeeded in solving the problem they have all struggled with – how to improve the health of their patients and to give them a longer life. The pieces show the ideas and skills that Galen and his contemporaries had available to finish the jigsaw.

1. Why can Galen not complete this jigsaw? Take each jigsaw piece in turn and explain why it was important to a Roman doctor.
2. Looking ahead, do you expect that a doctor 1000 years later will be able to do more of this jigsaw than Galen?

■ ACTIVITY

Galen and Hippocrates are two of the most influential people you have studied in this chapter.

Write an obituary for each of them explaining when they lived, what they did and why they are famous. You can start with pages 32–33 and 43–45. You can also get a further information sheet from your teacher to help you.

chapter 2

MEDICINE AND HEALTH AD500–1400

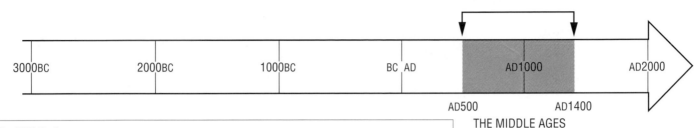

3000BC · 2000BC · 1000BC · BC AD · AD1000 · AD2000

AD500 · AD1400

THE MIDDLE AGES

The Middle Ages
A word of warning! In the history of medicine the Middle Ages is used to describe the whole period between the collapse of the Roman Empire (around AD500) and the Medical Renaissance (around 1400). You may have used the term in different ways before, particularly in your study of 'Medieval Realms'. So don't be caught out!

Did medicine grow worse in the Middle Ages?

THE LEGIONARIES WERE going home. All over Europe, centurions shouted orders and looked at maps. Legionaries packed their kits, said goodbye to their unofficial wives and families and began to march. Rome was in danger and the legions had been recalled to defend the city.

It was all in vain. In AD410 tribes called the Goths pillaged Rome and by AD500 the Roman Empire had disintegrated in western Europe. Instead there was a mass of small kingdoms with ever-changing borders.

What has all this to do with medicine and health? Remember that the Roman army had played a very important part in spreading medical knowledge and providing practical skills. Now it was gone. In the largest towns there were collections of medical books filled with effective herbal remedies, advice on diet and fitness, instructions on diagnosing and treating illnesses but the tribes who followed the Romans could not read them.

This chapter investigates what happened to medical ideas and knowledge after the collapse of the Roman Empire. Did the legionaries take their knowledge home with them, leaving people such as the Britons helpless if they fell ill or broke a leg? Was Roman medical knowledge and understanding destroyed when Rome was attacked? Did medicine and health in the Middle Ages take a step backwards?

■ TASK

Before you start to tackle this chapter look at these three graphs. From what you already know about the Middle Ages from your earlier study of history, explain which you would expect to be the most accurate description.

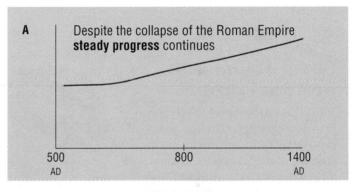

A Despite the collapse of the Roman Empire **steady progress** continues

500 AD · 800 · 1400 AD

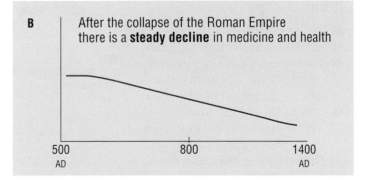

B After the collapse of the Roman Empire there is a **steady decline** in medicine and health

500 AD · 800 · 1400 AD

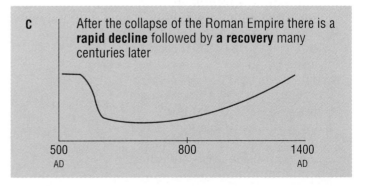

C After the collapse of the Roman Empire there is a **rapid decline** followed by **a recovery** many centuries later

500 AD · 800 · 1400 AD

Why were they still reading Galen in 1400?

ROMAN DOCTORS USED the books of Galen. They believed that his ideas were correct and that it was nearly impossible to improve on his work.

Follow the timeline arrow across the page to the thirteenth century and you can see that 900 years later Galen is still the unchallenged authority on medicine! This spread explains why.

We have divided the period into three phases, although the phases obviously overlap with each other.

Phase 2: The growing power of the Christian Church

Christianity was the religion of the Roman Empire. Surprisingly it did not decline when the Roman Empire fell apart. Instead it grew stronger. The Church sent missionaries all around Europe converting the pagan tribes to Christianity. Within a few centuries there were thousands of churches and monasteries all over Europe.

The Christian Church was the only strong, centralised organisation to survive the collapse of the Roman Empire. It was very powerful throughout the Middle Ages.

Phase 1: Chaos in western Europe

With the collapse of the Roman Empire western Europe was gradually split into many much smaller countries and tribes. The following factors affected the development of medicine and health.

- These countries and tribes were often at war with each other.
- Wars destroyed the Roman public health systems. It also destroyed medical libraries.
- The rulers of the small kingdoms built up defences and armies rather than improving medical skills or public health.
- War disrupted trade so countries became poorer.
- Travel became more dangerous thus reducing communication between doctors.
- Education and the development of technology was disrupted.
- In Europe the training of doctors was abandoned. Copies of Galen's books were either lost, or hidden away for safety.

War
War destroyed many of the Romans' achievements.

Government
Central government collapsed. Small kingdoms fought with each other.

Trade
Trade and travel decreased.

Churches
Each village had its church and priest who told people what to believe and how to behave.

Conservatism
The Pope and his bishops were afraid that new ideas would challenge the power of the Church. Every new idea was checked to make sure it did not challenge the Bible.

Education
Monasteries controlled education. Priests and monks were often the only people who learned to read in this period.

The monasteries also controlled what people read. The only libraries were in monasteries. The Church sometimes banned books which they did not want people to read.

SUPERSTITION
The ancient Greeks had looked for rational explanations. The Church taught the opposite – that there were supernatural explanations for everything. People believed that God, the Devil, or the planets controlled their lives.

Phase 3: Things start to change in the late Middle Ages

After about 1000 Europe had begun to recover from the period of chaos:

- harvests improved
- trade increased
- scholars travelled more freely
- there was more money around
- the Church also became richer.

By the 1300s:

- the Church had set up universities where doctors could be trained
- armies took trained doctors to war with them where they gained experience as surgeons on the battlefields
- rulers were again taking measures to clean up towns
- merchants and scholars were once again travelling around Europe, spreading ideas.

■ TASK

The illustrations and information on these two pages explain some of the factors which influenced medicine and health through the Middle Ages.

1. Explain how each of the following factors helped to cause change or prevent change in the Middle Ages:

   - war
   - government
   - religion
   - poor communications
   - education.

2. Which factor do you think was the most important in explaining why doctors in 1400 were still reading Galen?

Galen rediscovered!

In Europe Galen's ideas were rediscovered. Church leaders looked carefully at Galen's works and decided that they fitted in with Christian ideas after all. His books became accepted. In fact, the Church put a great deal of effort into defending Galen.

Doctors in 1400 still read the books of Galen. They believed that his ideas were correct and that it was nearly impossible to improve on his work.

Did health decline in the Middle Ages? A case study of York

WOULD YOU EXPECT the changes described on pages 56–57 to affect people's health? You are going to investigate this question through a case study of the English city of York.

York is a good place for such a case study because it was an important town throughout most of the Middle Ages, and archaeologists and historians have unearthed a lot of evidence about the period from Roman times to 1400.

■ TASK

1. Across the middle of a page draw a timeline from 400 to 1400 – two centimetres per century is ideal. Mark on it the periods covered in this case study.
2. Above the line put notes about how healthy people were in each period.
3. Below the line put notes about how factors such as religion, war and government affected people in York in each period.

At the end of the case study you will be asked to write an essay using these findings.

Roman York – Eboracum

Roman York had been a legionary headquarters. The soldiers had a bath building and latrines flushed by sewers. Fresh water was brought to York by an aqueduct and lead pipes carried it to individual buildings. The civilian population also had stone buildings which were heated, drained by sewers and supplied with water from wells and pipes. Skeletons show no evidence of rickets or other diseases caused by poor diets. The Roman citizens of York were well supplied with wheat, beef and other foods including imported figs, olives and grapes. Despite this, many of them still died at an early age because it was impossible to protect people, especially the newborn and young, from infectious diseases.

Saxon York – Eoforwic: AD400–800

Most of York was probably abandoned after the Roman legions left, although the stone buildings stood for centuries as reminders of the Roman past. Then in the 600s York gradually grew once more, becoming an important centre for the Church. The middle of the city became densely populated but, within a few hundred metres, there was rough grassland and patches of woodland.

One of York's most famous citizens was Alcuin, a scholar renowned throughout Europe. Alcuin lived from around 732 to 804 and spent nearly all his life in York. He wrote the description of the city in Source 1.

SOURCE 1 Alcuin's description of York

❝ *The city is watered by the fish-rich Ouse*
Which flows past flowery plains on every side;
And hills and forests beautify the earth
And make a lovely dwelling-place, whose health
And richness soon will fill it full of men ... ❞

Pleasant though this sounds, the living conditions in York at this time were not healthy. M.L. Cameron, author of *Anglo-Saxon Medicine*, summed up the evidence for Saxon life as revealing 'a fairly short life expectancy, a high infant mortality, women dying young, particularly in childbirth, and a fairly high incidence of bone and joint diseases, such as rheumatism, arthritis and rickets. The Anglo-Saxon population cannot have been particularly healthy.'

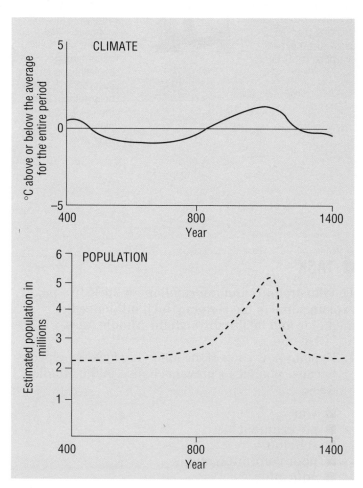

SOURCE 2 Climatic and population changes in Britain 400–1400. There were similar important changes in weather conditions in the Middle Ages all over Europe. How would these changes have affected the health of people in Saxon York?

SOURCE 3

A reconstruction of an Anglo-Saxon house, based on archaeological evidence. Most dwellings were small, dark, dank and smoky. They had just one room and were also draughty.

Water was collected from a nearby stream or well

Waste matter was taken away from the house to a cesspit

SOURCE 4

Life expectancy of ordinary people in Anglo-Saxon times. This table shows the average life span of the skeletons found at six Anglo-Saxon cemeteries. Recent findings say that only 10–15 per cent of Anglo-Saxon women who reached the age of twenty went on to live beyond the age of 50. Excavations also show that at least a third of people died before they were eighteen.

	Men	Women
Norton	28.4	28.5
Jarrow	41.5	40.7
Monkwearmouth	37.5	36.0
Kingsworthy	37.0	39.4
North Elmham	38.2	35.8
Thetford	38.1	30.4

SOURCE 5

Life expectancy of the rich in Anglo-Saxon times. Details taken from R. Fletcher, *Who's Who in Roman Britain and Anglo-Saxon England*, 1989

66 *The average age at death of seventeen famous Anglo-Saxon church leaders – 72 years*
The average age at death of thirteen Anglo-Saxon kings – 46 years. 99

[All these died of natural causes.]

1. Compare Sources 4 and 5 with life expectancy in Roman times (refer to page 47). Has there been improvement or decline?

Viking York – Jorvik: AD800–1066

York once again became a major town in the ninth and tenth centuries. It filled with Viking settlers, trading with their homelands in Scandinavia and even further afield.

Viking York was a town of tightly-packed streets and houses. Pigs, chickens and other animals roamed freely. As the city grew, rubbish and dung was at first put in wicker-lined pits but the city grew so fast that soon there was no control. Rotting fish bones, human faeces, animal dung and food waste mixed underfoot in the streets. Water for drinking and cooking was collected from the river, on roofs and in pits, but the pits were often next to CESSPITS. Rats, mice and flies infested the town; hawks, falcons and ravens scavenged amongst the rubbish. One archaeologist has described York as 'a town composed of rotting wooden buildings, covered by decaying vegetation, surrounded by streets and yards filled by pits and middens [piles] of even fouler organic waste'.

Despite this the diet of many citizens was varied and nutritious. They ate plenty of fish, oysters and other shellfish, beef, chickens, cereals, fruits (including apples, plums, bilberries and raspberries) and vegetables. Unfortunately most people also suffered from WORMS and other PARASITES, thanks to the way water was collected from pits dug near cesspits. Some of these worms may have measured 30 centimetres in length. In such conditions health did not improve and neither did life expectancy!

Norman York: 1066–1400

Around 1066 York had a population of around 9000, many of whom suffered from the upheaval of the Norman Conquest. Around one-sixth of the houses were destroyed to make way for the two Norman castles. After a rebellion in 1069 there was even more destruction, but perhaps this destruction had some beneficial effects. From the 1060s there were increasing numbers of stone houses in the city. Between 1000 and 1200 improved harvests were helping to make York a healthier city. By the 1200s many houses had at least stone foundations, and fired-clay roofing tiles were also common instead of thatch.

By then York was beginning to return to Roman standards of cleanliness. In the 1300s cesspits were lined with stone or brick and were emptied instead of simply being left when they were full. The abbey of St Mary's had a stone-built sewer and other complicated arrangements for clean water supplies.

SOURCE 7 A Norman sewer similar to one found in York. The original sewer had a wooden cover which has now rotted away

SOURCE 6 A house in the thirteenth century. Most of the thirteenth-century houses investigated by archaeologists were 8–15 metres long and 4 or 5 metres wide. During the twelfth and thirteenth centuries there were important improvements to houses. Stone foundations were added in some areas. In others, flint walls were built. Houses were not 'home-made' but were built by professional carpenters. Doors were hung on iron hinges and had iron locks and keys. Houses were also thoroughly swept – archaeologists have found the hollows made by the owners' brooms!

ACTIVITY

Work in pairs. Write a comparative report on the houses in Sources 3 and 6. Report on:

- size
- construction: what the houses are made of
- accommodation: what rooms/features they have
- hygiene: are they easy to keep clean?

Like other towns, York did have a problem removing waste. People knew that their streets ought to be kept clean but it was a near impossible task without better technology. As a result, York received this letter from Edward III in 1332.

SOURCE 8

66 *To the mayor and bailiffs of York.*
The king, detesting the abominable smell abounding in the said city more than in any other city of the realm from dung and manure and other filth and dirt wherewith the streets and lanes are filled and obstructed, and wishing to provide for the protection of the health of the inhabitants and of those coming to the present parliament, orders them to cause all the streets and lanes of the city to be cleansed from such filth … and to be kept clean … 99

Edward knew York well, visiting the city several times when leading his armies to wars with Scotland. He also married Queen Philippa in York Minster.

The evidence suggests that in the late 1300s people in York were better fed, better housed and wealthier than in earlier periods. However, there was no great increase in life expectancy for ordinary people (see Sources 9 and 10) because they had no real answer to the problems of infection.

Four cemeteries have been excavated in York from this period. They show that over 25 per cent of people died before the age of fifteen. In fact one baby in every three or four may have died before the age of one. Women still had a lower life expectancy than men because of the dangers of childbirth. Fewer than 10 per cent of the population lived to be 60.

However, York was not a violent place. Of more than 1000 skeletons examined at St Helen's in York, only eighteen had wounds, thirteen of them to the skull. Four were sword cuts but two had healed completely and the others had partially healed.

SOURCE 9
Life expectancy of the rich. Details taken from M.A. Hicks, *Who's Who in Later Medieval England*, 1991

66 *The average age at death of thirty-two bishops and abbots who died between 1300 and 1500 – 68 years*

The average age at death of twenty-five noblemen who died between 1300 and 1500 – 61 years

The average age at death of thirteen noblewomen who died between 1300 and 1500 – 62 years 99

[All these died of natural causes.]

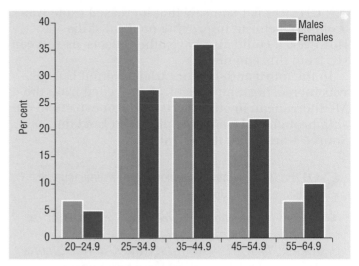

SOURCE 10
Life expectancy for ordinary people. This graph shows the age at death of those who were buried at St Helen's, York who survived past the age of twenty. Most of them were dead before the age of 45

SOURCE 11
Archaeological evidence suggests diet in York improved in this period. This pie chart shows the proportions of different foods in a good diet eaten by harvest workers in 1300

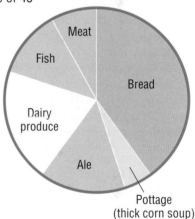

1. Compare Sources 9 and 10 with Sources 4 and 5. Has there been any improvement?

■ TASK

Using the information about York which you have gathered on your timeline, write an essay 'Did health decline in the Middle Ages?' Your essay should explain:

■ why a case study of York provides good evidence to answer this question
■ whether people in York were healthy or not in each period of the Middle Ages
■ what factors most affected their health in each period.

Finally you should reach your own judgement on the original question whether health declined in the Middle Ages or not. Your teacher can give you a sheet to help you further if you want it.

The Black Death: a case study in medieval medicine

IN CHAPTER 1 you saw that increased trade was often a factor in improving medical skills. However, it could also have other effects, as you can see from this enquiry.

In the fourteenth century trade around Europe was increasing. Ships regularly travelled from the Mediterranean to other parts of Europe. In 1348 one ship brought a devastating plague to England. Source 1 describes its arrival.

SOURCE 1 Written by a monk from Malmesbury in Wiltshire, in the 1350s

" In 1348, at about the feast of the Translation of St Thomas the martyr [7 July] the cruel pestilence, hateful to all future ages, arrived from countries across the sea on the south coast of England at the port called Melcombe in Dorset. Travelling all over the south country it wretchedly killed innumerable people in Dorset, Devon and Somerset … Next it came to Bristol, where very few were left alive, and then travelled northwards, leaving not a city, a town, a village, or even, except rarely, a house, without killing most or all of the people there so that over England as a whole a fifth of the men, women and children were carried to burial. As a result, there was such a shortage of people that there were hardly enough living to look after the sick and bury the dead… "

SOURCE 2 King Death, an illustration in a French book of prayers

According to modern historians Source 1 underestimates the effects of the BLACK DEATH. It is now estimated that over 40 per cent of the people in England died. Towns and ports were hardest hit. Villages and farms high in the hills were safest. Further outbreaks of plague came in 1361, 1369, 1374 and 1390. It killed the rich and poor alike, and it killed quickly and painfully.

We now know that the Black Death included two kinds of pestilence.

- **Bubonic plague** made people suddenly feel very cold and tired. Painful swellings (buboes) appeared in their armpits and groin and small blisters all over their bodies. This was followed by high fever and severe headaches. Many lingered, unconscious for several days before death. This form of the Black Death was spread by fleas.
- **Pneumonic plague** attacked the victim's lungs, causing breathing problems. Victims began to cough up blood and died more rapidly than those who had bubonic plague. This form of Black Death was spread by people breathing or coughing germs onto one another.

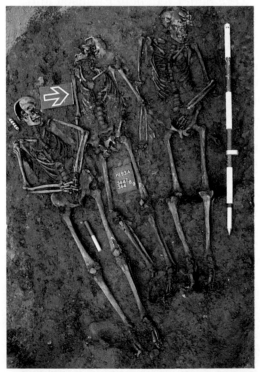

SOURCE 3 Black Death graves at Hereford cathedral, recently excavated. In many places new burial grounds were opened and in London, according to one chronicler, 'they dug broad, deep pits and buried the bodies together and, reducing everyone to the same level, threw them into the ground – treating everyone alike except the more eminent'

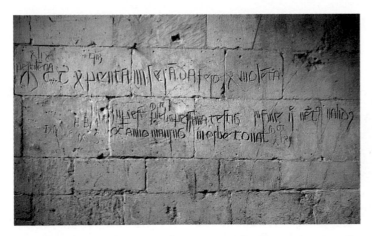

SOURCE 4 These words were scratched on a church wall in Ashwell, Hertfordshire: '1349 the pestilence. 1350, pitiless, wild, violent, the dregs of the people live to tell the tale.'

How did people react? Panic? Horror? Shock? Anger? Probably in all these ways and more. Most simply waited, hoping against hope, that they and their families would survive. However, others took action.

The king and his bishops sent out orders for churchmen to lead processions, pleading with God to end the pestilence. Some people made candles their own height and lit them in church as an offering to God. In Barcelona the citizens tried to protect themselves by making a candle seven kilometres long – enough to encircle the city.

A Londoner called Robert Avesbury describes in Source 5 how a group of men, called the Flagellants, responded.

SOURCE 5 The group Robert Avesbury is describing had recently come from Flanders, to London

66 *They went barefoot in procession twice a day in the sight of the people … their bodies naked except for a linen cloth from loins to ankle. Each wore a hood painted with a red cross at front and back and carried in his right hand a whip with three thongs. Each thong had a knot in it, with something sharp, like a needle stuck through the middle of the knot … and as they walked one after the other they struck themselves with these whips … three times in each procession they would all prostrate themselves on the ground, with their arms outstretched in the shape of a cross.* 99

1. Look at Source 3. Why did people bury Black Death victims in this way?
2. Read Source 5. Why do you think the Flagellants behaved as they did?

SOURCE 6 Advice written by John of Burgundy in 1365, on how to avoid the plague. His was one of the first books to be written about the plague

66 *First you should avoid too much eating and drinking and also avoid baths which open the pores, for the pores are the doorways through which poisonous air can enter the body.*

In cold or rainy weather you should light fires in your room, and in foggy or windy weather you should inhale perfumes every morning before leaving home.

If however the epidemic occurs during hot weather you must eat cold things rather than hot and also drink more than you eat. Be sparing with hot substances such as pepper, garlic, onions and everything else that generates excessive heat and use cucumbers, fennel and spinach. 99

SOURCE 7 A nineteenth-century engraving showing medieval knights greeting the king with the customary 'kiss of obedience'. During an outbreak of plague in 1439 English noblemen were told not to greet King Henry VI this way because of the danger of spreading the disease

3. What evidence is there in Source 6 that John of Burgundy knew the works of Galen?
4. Do Sources 1–7 suggest that people understood what caused the plague or how it spread?

What did they think caused the Black Death?

■ ACTIVITY

Amidst the chaos and fear caused by the Black Death some people tried to explain why the pestilence had come.

This diagram shows the most common medieval explanations for the Black Death. These explanations also appear in some of Sources 8–16.

1. Read through each source to decide if it matches one of the explanations in the diagram.

2. a) On your own copy of the diagram write the number of the source which matches each explanation.
   b) If the source adds anything further to the explanation summarise it by adding notes around the diagram.

3. Some of Sources 8–16 give additional explanations for the Black Death. On your own copy of the diagram, add your own drawings or notes to summarise them.

4. Use these notes to write your own account of the explanations of the Black Death. You should include the following details:

   ■ what the main explanations were
   ■ whether similar explanations were also used to explain disease in earlier times
   ■ whether any of the explanations were accurate (see page 62)
   ■ why people believed in these explanations if they were not accurate.

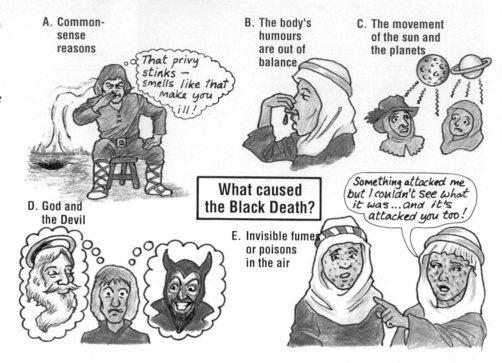

A. Common-sense reasons

That privy stinks – smells like that make you ill!

B. The body's humours are out of balance

C. The movement of the sun and the planets

D. God and the Devil

What caused the Black Death?

Something attacked me but I couldn't see what it was...and it's attacked you too!

E. Invisible fumes or poisons in the air

SOURCE 8 From an account by a fifteenth-century Swedish bishop who based his studies on a work written in the 1360s by John Jacobus, a royal doctor and Chancellor of Montpellier University, which had a renowned school of medicine

❝ Sometimes [the pestilence] comes from … a privy [toilet] next to a chamber or any other particular thing which corrupts the air in substance and quality … sometimes it comes of dead carrion or the corruption of standing waters in ditches … ❞

SOURCE 9 Part of a letter from the Prior of the abbey of Christchurch, Canterbury, to the Bishop of London, 28 September 1348

❝ Terrible is God towards the sons of men … He often allows plagues, miserable famines, conflicts, wars and other forms of suffering to arise, and uses them to terrify and torment men and so drive out their sins. And thus, indeed, the realm of England, because of the growing pride and corruption of its subjects, and their numberless sins … is to be oppressed by the pestilences … ❞

SOURCE 10 From an account of the pestilence written by a French doctor in 1349

❝ This epidemic … kills almost instantly, as soon as the airy spirit leaving the eyes of the sick man has struck the eye of a healthy bystander looking at him, for then the poisonous nature passes from one eye to the other. ❞

SOURCE 11 From the writings of John of Burgundy, who wrote one of the earliest books about the Black Death in 1365

Many people have been killed, especially those stuffed full of evil humours. As Galen says in his book on fevers, the body does not become sick unless it already contains evil humours. The pestilential air does no harm to cleansed bodies from which evil humours have been purged.

SOURCE 12 Guy de Chauliac, one of the most famous doctors in the 1300s

... whatever the people said, the truth is that there were two causes, one general, one particular. The general cause was the close position of the three great planets, Saturn, Jupiter and Mars. This had taken place in 1345 on 24 March in the 14th degree of Aquarius. Such a coming together of planets is always a sign of wonderful, terrible or violent things to come. The particular cause of the disease in each person was the state of the body – bad digestion, weakness and blockage, and for this reason people died.

SOURCE 13 A German woodcut showing the burning of Jews in Germany. The Jews were blamed for the Black Death by some people. This is what one German friar wrote in 1348–49: 'Some say that it was brought about by the corruption of the air; others that the Jews planned to wipe out all the Christians with poison and had poisoned wells and springs everywhere. And many Jews confessed as much under torture ... men say that bags full of poison were found in many wells and springs ...'

SOURCE 14 From a chronicle written by a monk at Westminster

1344 ... the English have been madly following outlandish ways, changing their grotesque fashions of clothing yearly. They have abandoned the old, decent style of long, full garments for clothes which are short, tight, impractical, slashed, every part laced, strapped or buttoned up, with the sleeves of the gowns and the tippets of the hoods hanging down to absurd lengths, so that, if truth be told, their clothes and footwear make them look more like torturers, or even demons, than men ... The sin of pride must surely bring misfortune in the future.

SOURCE 15 From an account of the causes of the pestilence by an unknown German author, written c. 1350–80

It is a matter of scientific fact that earthquakes are caused by the exhalation of fumes enclosed in the bowels of the earth ... I say that it is the vapour and corrupted air which has been vented ... in the earthquake on St Paul's day 1347 ... which has infected the air above the earth and killed people in various parts of the earth ...

SOURCE 16 Written by an unknown churchman in the early 1360s. The pestilence in 1361 had a severe impact on children and young people

If your father and mother come to want and mischief by age or misfortune you are bound to help them both with your body and help with your possessions ... And if they are dead you are obliged to pray night and day to God to deliver them from pain ... it is vengeance of this sin of dishonouring and despising fathers and mothers that God is slaying children by pestilence.

What did they do about public health in fourteenth-century London?

Descriptions

1. Butchers were put in the pillory for selling 'PUTRID, rotten, stinking and abominable meat'. The meat was burnt in front of them.
2. 1301 – four women butchers were caught throwing rotten blood and offal into the street.
3. 1343 – butchers were ordered to use a segregated area for butchering animals.
4. Wide streets had two gutters, one at each side. Narrow streets had one gutter in the middle.
5. By the 1370s there were at least twelve teams of rakers with horses and carts, removing dung from the streets.
6. In 1345 the fine for throwing litter in the street was increased to two shillings. In 1372 anyone who had filth outside their house could be fined four shillings. Anyone throwing water from a window was fined two shillings.
7. There were open sewers carrying refuse to the river.
8. By the 1380s there were at least thirteen common privies (public conveniences) in the city. One on Temple Bridge was built over the Thames.
9. Houseowners living next to streams built latrines over the streams.
10. Houses away from streams sometimes had their own latrines. In 1391 a latrine built in a house cost £4. The mason dug the pit, and used stone, tiles and cement to line it.
11. Butchers carried waste through the streets, loaded it onto boats and threw it into the middle of the river at ebb tide.
12. Wells for fetching water and cesspools for dumping sewage were often close together. Regulations said that cesspools had to be built two and a half feet (76 centimetres) from a neighbour's soil if walled with stone, three and a half (1 metre, 6 centimetres) if walled with earth.
13. 1364 – Two women were arrested for throwing rubbish in the street.
14. 1307 – Thomas Scott was fined for assaulting two citizens who complained when he urinated in a lane instead of using the common privy.

1. What evidence is there here of governments taking measures to make London healthier?
2. What evidence is there of ordinary people trying to make London healthier?
3. Explain whether the measures shown here would help prevent the spread of the Black Death.
4. Does the evidence in this picture suggest that people understood
   a) what caused disease
   b) how to make London a healthier place?

■ ACTIVITY

This illustration shows London in the fourteenth century. Can you match the descriptions 1–14 with events shown in the picture? Each description is based on a real event, recorded in London.

What did a doctor need to know in the Middle Ages?

AS YOU SAW from the case study of York, in many places, the late Middle Ages was a period of increasing wealth in Europe. With the wealth came a new demand for doctors and an increased interest in developing the medical skills of doctors.

How were doctors trained?

In AD900 the first university medical school in Europe was set up. Others followed. Old manuscripts by Galen and other ancient writers were rediscovered and translated. By the late Middle Ages anyone who wanted to be a doctor had to train at one of the medical schools. (These trained doctors were usually known as physicians. PHYSIC means the art of healing.) Sources 1–5 show some of the skills and knowledge a medieval doctor would be taught at a medical school.

■ ACTIVITY

Imagine that you are a teacher in a medieval medical school. Use Sources 1–5 to help you list the topics you will teach to your students while they are training to be doctors.

Your course must sound interesting and relevant to your pupils, so you must be sure that it contains all the important topics.

Then write a prospectus for your course describing the most important topics on the list, and explaining why doctors need to study them.

SOURCE 1 A teacher presiding over dissection at a medical school. The oldest medical school in Europe was founded at Salerno around 900. By the 1200s Montpellier in France was the most famous but there were a number of others. At these schools students listened to lectures where the teacher read out passages from the work of Galen and other ancient writers. At Montpellier, after 1340, the students were allowed to use one corpse a year for dissection, but the dissection was done by the teacher's assistant, not by the student

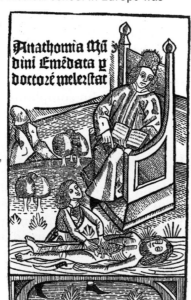

SOURCE 2 From the writings of Guy de Chauliac, a French doctor who lived c. 1300–80

Knowledge of anatomy is gained in two ways. One is by books. This is useful but it is not enough to discover all that can be learned by observation. The second way is by dissecting dead bodies, namely, of those who have been recently beheaded or hanged. By this we learn the anatomy of the internal organs, the muscles, skin, veins and SINEWS.

Mondino of Bologna, who wrote about this, made dissections many times, and my master did the same, placing the dead body on the table and dealing with it in four lectures.

[In his books he made over 3200 references to other medical texts that he had consulted. The writer he mentioned most frequently was Galen (890 quotations), followed by the Arabic writers Avicenna and Rhazes. There were 120 references to Hippocrates.]

SOURCE 3 Adapted from codes of behaviour for doctors that developed throughout Europe in the period after AD1000

A doctor should be willing to learn, be sober and modest, charming, hard-working and intelligent. Anyone wishing to become a good doctor must be able to study for long periods, so that his judgement and understanding improve by constant reading of different books. He should not be greedy. He should take care of the rich and poor quite impartially, for medicine is needed by all classes of people. If payment is offered, he should accept rather than refuse it. But if it is not offered, it should not be demanded. Whatever you hear in the course of your treatment, unless it is something that ought to be reported and judged, keep it secret.

A medieval doctor might believe in many of the explanations of disease on pages 64–65; some might also blame worms (see page 80). A doctor would be trained to base his treatments on the theory of the four humours. He would examine the patient's urine and check its colour against a chart (such as Source 5) to help diagnose the illness. He may also have used ASTROLOGY to work out the position of the planets before deciding the best treatment. A table of the positions of the planets would be used by every doctor. The moon, in particular, was believed to have a great effect on the humours in the body and so the doctor had to know the moon's position before, for example, bleeding the patient.

Bleeding was one of the most common treatments because doctors believed wholeheartedly in the importance of keeping the body's humours in balance. One medical handbook claimed that blood-letting:

SOURCE 4

66 ... clears the mind, strengthens the memory, cleanses the guts, dries up the brain, warms the marrow, sharpens the hearing, curbs tears, ... promotes digestion, produces a musical voice, dispels sleepiness, drives away anxiety, feeds the bloods, rids it of poisonous matter and gives long life ... it cures pains, fevers and various sicknesses and makes urine clear and clean. 99

Given this list of effects it is not surprising that bleeding was common. Monastery records suggest that monks were bled between seven and twelve times a year. The bleeding continued until the patient was on the verge of unconsciousness which means that he had lost three or four pints of blood!

A range of techniques were used for bleeding. Sometimes the bleeding cup (as used by the Greeks, see Source 5 on page 30) was employed. LEECHES, which suck blood from human beings, were also used.

There were strict rules for blood-letting. One doctor in Paris had to show his skills by bleeding twenty people. He also paid for the meals and wine of his examiners. They still failed him!

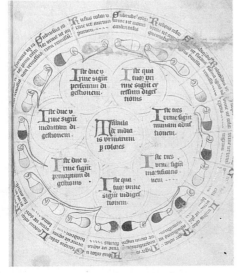

SOURCE 5
A urine chart. This was one of the basic tools which doctors used to diagnose illnesses. Wealthy families regularly sent urine samples to their doctors so that the doctors could look for signs of illness developing. The text around the outside of the chart describes the colour and the quality of the urine (whether it is cloudy or clear). The text in the middle groups the samples together according to what they tell the doctor about the patient's digestion. The best digestion is bottom left. Death (mortification) is bottom right (black urine)

Could women become doctors in the Middle Ages?

Women were not allowed to go to universities, so although women still carried out much of the everyday medical care in towns and villages they could not train to become physicians. The effect was to devalue the skills of women healers. The Church which oversaw the training of doctors was particularly suspicious of the WISE WOMEN in villages. However, women continued to act as midwives, and they could still become surgeons.

SOURCE 6
Midwives attending a birth. Doctors did not get involved in childbirth in the Middle Ages. By the 1400s midwives in France and Germany had to gain licences, follow apprenticeships and had to keep to rules of behaviour

■ TASK

Some of the statements below are true and some are false.

Rewrite each statement, correcting it if necessary, and then explain what evidence in Sources 1–6 proves that your new statement is correct. You may wish to add to the statements and make them longer.

Statements
a) Both men and women could become qualified doctors.
b) More illnesses were treated by women than by men.
c) Doctors were poorly trained and educated.
d) The ideas of Galen and Hippocrates had been forgotten.
e) It was important for doctors to understand astrology.

Was surgery improving in the Middle Ages?

Surgery was not usually taught in the universities. People became surgeons by being apprenticed to another surgeon, watching his or her work and copying it. There were guilds of surgeons who controlled entrance to the profession. Master surgeons needed to have licenses and sometimes had to pass lengthy tests. Women could become surgeons and a number did.

1. According to Sources 7–10 how did surgeons cope with the problems of:
   a) pain during an operation
   b) infection after an operation?
2. Look at Source 7. Why is it an advantage for surgeons to become specialists as John of Arderne did?
3. Surgery is one area of medicine that is often helped by war. Is there evidence that this happened in the Middle Ages?
4. Would you say that medieval surgery was more advanced that the methods used in the Roman legionary hospital (see page 37). Explain your answer.

SOURCE 7 An operation on the rectum, from a medieval medical book. Such operations were the speciality of John of Arderne. He was one of the most famous surgeons in medieval England. He served as an army surgeon in wars between England and France in the early 1300s, then returned to England and worked as a surgeon in London. His methods were based on careful study of anatomy and on practice. He used methods that are still in use today.

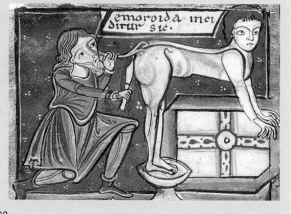

SOURCE 8 From the writings of Theodoric of Lucca, a thirteenth-century surgeon. His father, Hugh, who was also a famous surgeon in Italy, had travelled to Egypt with a Christian army to fight against Muslims

❝ … every day we see new instruments and new methods being invented by clever and ingenious surgeons. ❞

❝ Ancient surgeons and their disciples teach (and almost all modern surgeons follow them) that pus should be generated in wounds. There could be no greater error than this. For pus hinders the work of nature, prolongs the disease, prevents healing and the closing up of wounds … My father used to heal almost every kind of wound with wine alone and he produced the most beautiful healing without any ointments. ❞

[The idea of 'praiseworthy pus' was preached and used by the Greeks, by Galen and by the Arabs. Theodoric's ideas went against Galen. They did not win much support .]

SOURCE 9 A recipe for an anaesthetic from the late Middle Ages

❝ To make a drink that men call dwale to make a man sleep while men carve him: Take three spoonfuls of the gall of a boar, three spoonfuls of hemlock juice, three spoonfuls of wild nept, three spoonfuls of lettuce, three spoonfuls of poppy, three spoonfuls of henbane and three spoonfuls of vinegar and mix them all together and boil them a little … and put thereof three spoonfuls into half a gallon of good wine and mix it well together … let him that shall be carved sit against a good fire and make him drink until he falls asleep and then you may safely carve him … ❞

[This mixture of hemlock, henbane and wine would certainly have sent patients to sleep and, if the dose was too strong, they may never have woken up.]

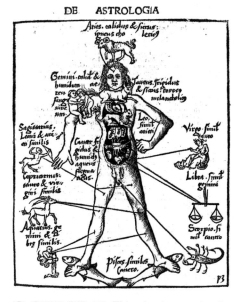

SOURCE 10 This chart gave details about when each part of the body was affected by the planets and stars. If the stars told the surgeon not to open wounds or bleed the patient in that area then he would not do so for fear of causing death. Such charts were in common use. It is popularly called a Zodiac Man

Were herbal remedies useful?

Whatever people believed were the causes of disease, most illness was treated with herbal potions. Doctors used them, and women healers in villages and towns possessed a large store of knowledge about the use of herbs to treat everyday illness.

Many locally grown plants were used, although foreign herbs became increasingly popular. Sugar was believed to be particularly effective and was imported in large quantities by the 1400s.

Were these remedies useful? Medical historians who have studied many of them say yes. Plaintain was an ingredient in 48 remedies in the Anglo-Saxon *Leechbooks*. It was recommended for boils in the ear, dog-bites, cuts and wounds. Modern analysis shows that plantain is an antibiotic and in 25 of the 48 remedies would have helped to stop infection. The diagram below shows how the remedy in Source 11 might work. Source 11 comes from *Bald's Leechbook*. This Anglo-Saxon book contained herbal remedies with sensible advice from Greek and Roman medicine. It included remedies designed to balance the body's humours.

SOURCE 11 From Bald's *Leechbook*

66 *Make an eye-salve for a* STYE: *take onion and garlic, equal amounts of both, pound well together, take wine and bull's gall, equal amounts of both, mix with the onion and garlic, then put in a brass vessel, let stand for nine nights in the brass vessel, strain through a cloth and clear well, put in a horn and about night-time put on the stye with a feather.* 99

■ ACTIVITY

Look back to your prospectus from page 68. Add another paragraph to it explaining why doctors should be trained in the use of herbal remedies.

SOURCE 12 The preparation of herbal remedies improved in the late Middle Ages, but for a surprising reason. Many scholars of the time were interested in 'alchemy' – they were trying to find methods to turn cheap metals into gold. Not surprisingly, they did not succeed. However, in the process they did develop new equipment and new technology for extracting chemicals, refining liquids and mixing potions, which later became useful in preparing more complicated herbal remedies. This shows some of their new equipment

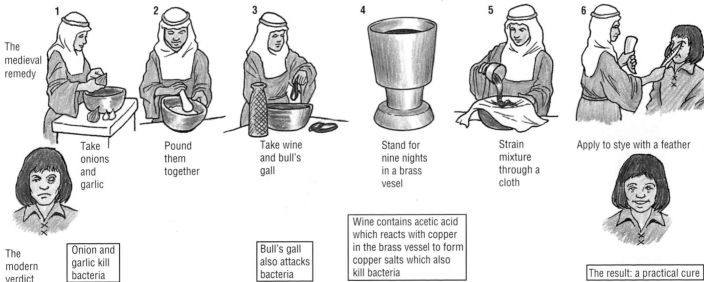

The medieval remedy

1. Take onions and garlic
2. Pound them together
3. Take wine and bull's gall
4. Stand for nine nights in a brass vesel
5. Strain mixture through a cloth
6. Apply to stye with a feather

The modern verdict

Onion and garlic kill bacteria

Bull's gall also attacks bacteria

Wine contains acetic acid which reacts with copper in the brass vessel to form copper salts which also kill bacteria

The result: a practical cure

Did medieval hospitals help the sick?

THE CHRISTIAN CHURCH taught that it was part of people's religious duty to care for the sick, but it was not until the 1100s that it actually took many practical measures to encourage this teaching. You have already seen that in the eleventh century the Church started to open up medical schools where the ideas of Galen were taught. It also began to set up hospitals run by nuns and monks.

These were not hospitals as we would understand them today. Nearly 1200 places called hospitals have been identified in medieval England and Wales but, as Source 1 shows, only 10 per cent of them actually cared for the sick. The others were called hospitals because they provided 'hospitality' for visitors.

Most of the hospitals in England and Wales which did care for the sick were founded in the 1100s and 1200s, a time of increasing wealth and prosperity. Some of them were large. St Leonard's, York, had space for over 200 patients. St Mary Without Bishopgate in London had 180 beds. Others had only five or six beds.

Some hospitals specialised in certain kinds of patients. At least four took in only MATERNITY cases. Richard Whittington, three times Lord Mayor of London, paid for the building of an eight-bed chamber at St Thomas's hospital, London, especially for unmarried pregnant women. In Stamford one hospital cared for the blind, deaf and mute. In Chester, there was a hospital set up to look after 'poor and silly persons', as did St Mary of Bethlehem in London, or Bedlam as it became known.

Although hospitals were new in Britain in the twelfth century they were much more common in other parts of the world. Hospitals existed in Sri Lanka in 500BC and in India in 250BC. Ancient Rome had hospitals for civilians as well as legionaries. In the Middle Ages the most famous hospitals were in the Middle East. The city of Baghdad alone had 60 hospitals in the 1100s when Londoners were marvelling at their first.

In Cairo, the Al-Mansur hospital was founded in 1283 and was one of the scientific wonders of the age. It had separate departments for patients with different diseases, a library and lecture halls for students training to be doctors. There was also a kitchen that prepared special diets for patients and wards where convalescent patients could stay as long as they wished. When they went home they were given money. Helping the poor and needy was and is a central part of Islamic faith.

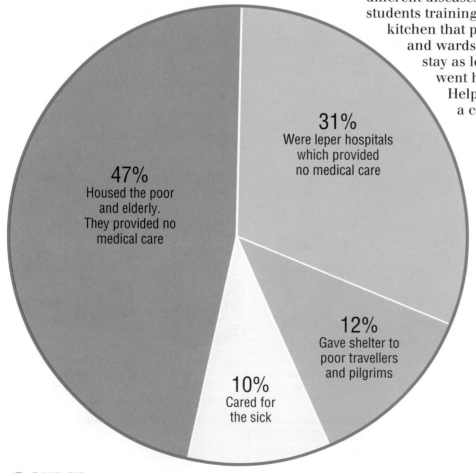

47%
Housed the poor and elderly. They provided no medical care

31%
Were leper hospitals which provided no medical care

12%
Gave shelter to poor travellers and pilgrims

10%
Cared for the sick

SOURCE 1

SOURCE 2 The Hotel Dieu in Paris. This is one of the few pictures of the inside of a medieval hospital. Hotel Dieu was not a typical hospital – the king's doctors worked there. It opened in 1452. The main hall measured 72 metres by 14 metres

How did hospitals treat their patients?

Imagine that you are standing at the hospital gate.

The first person you meet is the warden. He looks you up and down. Do you look respectable? How much money do you have? Why do you need help? Do you have any infectious or serious illnesses? He certainly will not let you into the hospital if you are infectious because you would spread sickness.

The warden decides you can be admitted. He opens the gate and you enter a courtyard. There are monks scurrying to a service but they pay you no attention. Their work is to pray for your soul, not look after your body. A servant leads you into the hall, so large it is like a church but full of beds. At the end of the hall is a series of chapels where priests say mass every day. Patients can watch or join in. Above each bed is a lamp and there's a cutaway space in the wall for belongings. The servant helps you into bed alongside another patient. You are old and frail. You fall asleep.

Next day you awake. No need to worry about the doctor – there is no doctor. Doctors treat kings and nobles and wealthy merchants, not ordinary old folk in hospitals. You are cared for by the nuns and their helpers. They keep you warm, clean, rested and fed. Do you have any aches, pains? Do you feel queasy? They have some excellent herbal remedies, learned from the nuns who worked in the hospital before them. They also have books full of remedies in the monastery library.

All you have to do is rest and pray for the soul of the merchant who paid for the upkeep of your bed. Your prayers will speed his soul to heaven. Sleep, warmth, food and the nuns' herbal potions will make your old bones comfortable – that is what hospitals are for.

■ **ACTIVITY**

Get a copy of Source 2 from your teacher and use the text to label as many features of the hospital as you can.

SOURCE 3 From the rules of the hospital of St John, Bridgwater, 1219

66 *No LEPERS, LUNATICS, or persons having the falling sickness or other contagious disease, and no pregnant women, or sucking infants, and no intolerable persons, even though they be poor and infirm, are to be admitted in the house; and if any such be admitted by mistake, they are to be expelled as soon as possible. And when the other poor and infirm persons have recovered they are to be let out without delay.* 99

SOURCE 4 From the rules to the medieval Hospital of St John, Cambridge

66 *We strictly ordain … that sick and weak people should be admitted kindly and mercifully, except for pregnant women, lepers, the wounded, cripples and the insane.* 99

1. If you had the Black Death would you have been let into a hospital?
2. Why do you think hospitals made the rules described in Sources 3 and 4?
4. What were the differences between Christian and Islamic hospitals?
5. Why do you think there were differences between Christian and Islamic hospitals? You may need to refer to pages 74–75.

Was Arab medicine more advanced than European medicine?

WHILE WESTERN EUROPE collapsed into disorder with the decline of the Roman Empire, a new civilisation based on the Islamic faith was growing in the Middle East. Islamic scholars picked up and developed the ideas of the ancient Greeks whom they greatly admired.

In this chapter you have already come across a number of references to Islamic or Arab medicine. Look at these references to remind yourself of what they say about Arabic medical writers (page 70) and Arabic hospitals (page 72). These references suggest that medical skills and understanding may have been more advanced in Arab countries than in western Europe. Was this really the case?

Source 1 was written by an eyewitness to the work of both Arab and European doctors – Usamah Ibn Menquidh. He was a wealthy Muslim nobleman who lived from 1095 to 1188. Usamah knew Saladin, the great Muslim leader, and he also travelled among the towns and castles of the Crusaders. Some of them, who had been long-settled in Palestine, were his friends. In old age Usamah wrote the story of his life. Here are two of his stories. 'The Franks' are the Europeans.

1. What suggests that Usamah may be providing reliable evidence about Arab and European medicine? Refer to the information above.
2. Do any aspects of the stories make you think that Usamah may be an unreliable witness?
3. Usamah's stories prove that Arab medicine was more advanced than European medicine. Do you agree with this? Explain your reasons.

SOURCE 1

66 Among the curiosities of medicine among the Franks, I will tell how the governor of Al-Mounaitira wrote to my uncle to ask him to send him a doctor who would look after some urgent cases. My uncle chose a Christian doctor called Thabit. [All Arabs were not Muslims. Some were Christians, like this doctor.] He was absent only ten days and then returned to us. There was a general exclamation – 'How rapidly you cured your patients!' Thabit replied 'They brought before me a knight with an abscess in his leg and a woman wasting away with fever. I treated the knight with a herbal medicine which I put on the abscess. His abscess opened and took a turn for the better. I forbade the woman certain food and her condition improved.

It was at this point that a Frankish doctor came up and said 'This man will not cure them'. Then he said to the knight 'Do you wish to live with one leg or die with two?' The knight answered 'I would rather have one leg and live'. 'Bring a strong knight', said the doctor, 'and a sharp hatchet.'

I was present at the scene. The doctor stretched the patient's leg on a block of wood and then said to the knight 'Strike off his leg!' The knight aimed a violent blow but did not cut off his leg. He aimed another blow, as a result of which the marrow came out of the poor man's leg and he died instantly.

As for the woman, the doctor examined her and said, 'She is possessed by the Devil! Shave off her hair.' This was done and she was allowed to eat what she wished, including garlic and mustard. Her CONSUMPTION became worse. The doctor believed that this was because the Devil had entered her head. Taking a razor, he cut open her head in the shape of a cross, scraping away the skin so that the bone was showing. He then rubbed the head with salt. The woman died instantly…

I was also present on one occasion when the medical skills of the Franks were seen in an entirely different light. A horse had kicked the leg of one of their knights, one of their most detestable and criminal characters called Bernard. His foot was very painful. They made incisions in fourteen places but as soon as the wounds healed in one place they opened in another. I made vows for the death of this godless man. But he was visited by a Frankish doctor who began to wash the wounds in a very acid vinegar. His wounds healed up.

He returned to health and rose up like a demon. 99

Why had Arab medicine become famous in the Middle Ages?

The Koran, the holiest book of Islam containing the words of Muhammad, tells Muslims that taking care of the sick and needy is a vital part of the Muslim faith. This helps to explain why large hospitals were built in Baghdad, Cairo and other cities. Muslims also admired educated people. A nobleman like Usamah had a large library at a time when very few English or French knights could read. This interest in learning led Arab scholars to collect and study manuscripts containing the work of Hippocrates, Galen and other classical medical writers. These books were translated into Arabic and were read by medical students.

The result of these developments was that Arab doctors, whether they were Muslims or Christians like Thabit, were very knowledgeable.

Ibn Sinna (980–1037) was a Muslim who lived in Spain. He wrote a million-word textbook covering all aspects of medicine. In Europe he was known as Avicenna. Other Arab doctors also made important discoveries. Rhazes (852–925) wrote the first accurate descriptions of measles and smallpox. Ibn Nafis dared to disagree with Galen about how blood flows around the body.

However, in other ways Islam did not encourage new developments. Islamic law forbade the dissection of human bodies. Muslims also believed that the Koran contained all important knowledge so there was no point in trying to make new discoveries. Their attitude to the Koran also meant that they were unwilling to criticise other ancient books, such as the writings of Galen. Many influential Arab doctors believed that understanding theory was more important than practical experience. Even great doctors like Rhazes and Ibn Sinna thought that doctors should not dabble in surgery. In these ways Arab ideas were little different from European attitudes – and they could not stop the Black Death either!

4. In what ways was Arab medicine better than European medicine?
5. In what ways was Arab medicine similar to European medicine?
6. How did Arab medicine affect European medicine?

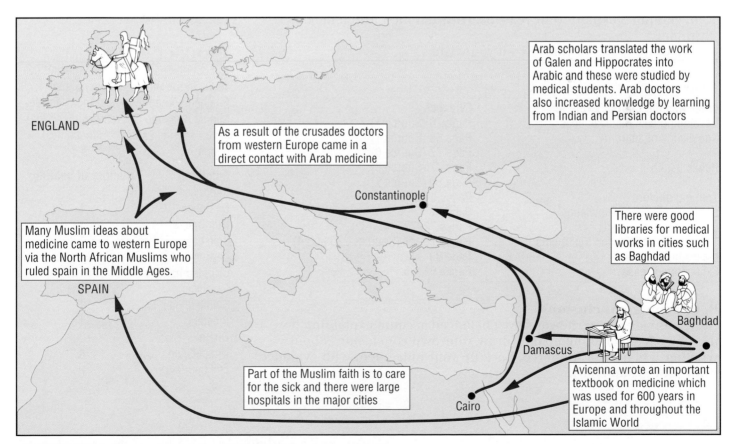

Arab scholars translated the work of Galen and Hippocrates into Arabic and these were studied by medical students. Arab doctors also increased knowledge by learning from Indian and Persian doctors

As a result of the crusades doctors from western Europe came in a direct contact with Arab medicine

ENGLAND

Many Muslim ideas about medicine came to western Europe via the North African Muslims who ruled spain in the Middle Ages.

SPAIN

Constantinople

There were good libraries for medical works in cities such as Baghdad

Damascus

Baghdad

Part of the Muslim faith is to care for the sick and there were large hospitals in the major cities

Avicenna wrote an important textbook on medicine which was used for 600 years in Europe and throughout the Islamic World

Cairo

SOURCE 2 The movement of medical knowledge from and to Europe

Did the Christian Church help or hinder medical progress?

IN THIS DEVELOPMENT study you will be discovering that causal factors vary in importance. In some periods of history religion was an important cause, in others it was not. In the Middle Ages it was very important – you have already seen many examples of the Church affecting medicine. You can now try to draw some overall conclusions as to whether the Christian Church helped or hindered medical progress.

You may think the answer is obvious, but before you tackle the task below take a class vote: based on what you have already studied, do you think the Church helped or hindered medical progress? Keep a record of the vote and take another one at the end of the exercise.

SOURCE 1 Roger Bacon – a thirteenth-century priest. He suggested that a new approach to medicine was needed. He said that doctors should do their own original research instead of learning from the books of ancient writers such as Galen. Church leaders put him in prison for heresy. This nineteenth-century engraving shows him smuggling his work out of prison

■ TASK

A. Research
Work in groups. Draw up a large chart with three colums: Topic; Helped/Hindered?; Explanation.

1. In column 1 of your chart write the topics from the table below, using the list of references. Some references are earlier in the book, others are to these two pages.
2. In column 2 explain whether the Church helped or hindered this aspect of medicine. You may think it did both! That's fine as long as you can explain your reasons.
3. In column 3 explain your reasons. **How** did the Church help or hinder?
4. Add other topics of your own if you wish.

Topics	
What was the Church's role in:	**Evidence**
Developing new medical ideas	Page 76 (Source 1)
Knowledge of anatomy	Page 68 (Source 1)
	Page 77 (Source 6)
Public health	Page 77 (Source 3),
	Page 60 (Source 7)
Training doctors	Pages 57 and 68
Spreading medical knowledge	Page 57
Care of the sick	Pages 72–73
The search for effective treatments	Pages 76–77 (Sources 2, 3 and 4)
Licensing healers	Page 69
Explaining disease	Pages 64–65

B. Reaching conclusions
Now, individually, write your own balanced account explaining how the Church affected medicine – draw your own conclusions about whether it helped or hindered. Back up your judgement with evidence from your group chart.

SOURCE 2 Illnesses and conditions miraculously healed by Jesus in the Bible. Usually he just touched someone to heal them. In the Middle Ages the Church promised that Jesus and the saints could still heal people

Condition	Number of healings
Blindness	5
Deafness	1
Dumbness	1
Epilepsy	1
Leprosy	2
Crippled hand	1
Paralysis	2
Swollen legs	1
Bleeding	1
Death	3
Unspecified	4
Evil spirits	9

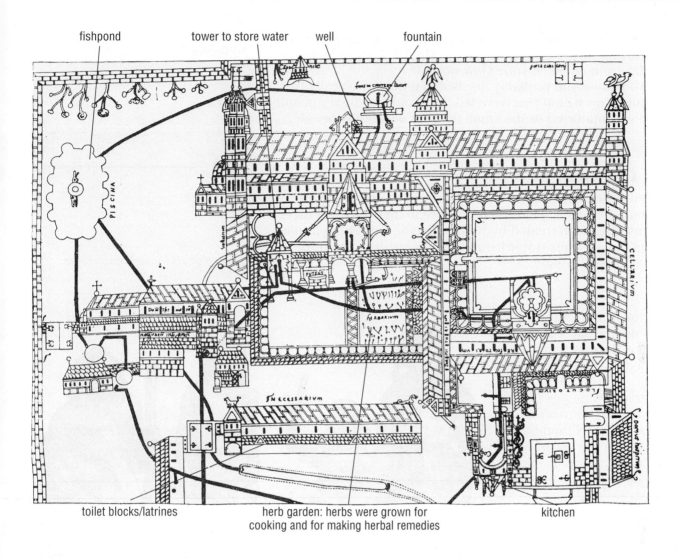

fishpond tower to store water well fountain

toilet blocks/latrines herb garden: herbs were grown for cooking and for making herbal remedies kitchen

SOURCE 3 Diagram of the water supply to Canterbury Cathedral and monastery, 1153, drawn by the engineer who designed and built the system.

All monasteries regarded fresh water supply as a priority. At Canterbury there were five settling tanks to purify the water. Water was piped to the kitchen, the wash rooms, the brewery, the bakery and the fishpond. The waste water was recycled to flush the latrines

SOURCE 4 A cure for toothache, recommended by John of Gaddesden, a leading English doctor in the early 1300s

66 *Write these words on the jaw of the patient. 'In the name of the Father, Son and Holy Ghost, Amen. + Res + Pax + Nax + In Christo Filio.' The pain will cease at once, as I have often seen.* 99

SOURCE 5 From the rules for Benedictine monasteries AD534

66 *Care for the sick stands before all. You must help them as would Christ, whom you really help in helping them. Also you must bear patiently with them as in this way you will gain greater merit [with God]. Let it also be the chief concern of the Abbot that the sick shall not be neglected at any single point.* 99

SOURCE 6 A medieval illustration showing someone caught by a priest illegally dissecting a body. Dissection was banned by the Church until the fourteenth century

Did health and medicine grow worse in the Middle Ages?

ON PAGE 55 you were asked to predict which of three graphs would best describe medicine and health in the Middle Ages. Which did you choose? Have you changed your view now?

Whichever you chose you probably decided that there are really two answers depending on whom you were talking about – ordinary people (who were the vast majority) or the small number of wealthy people.

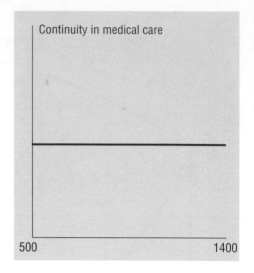

Continuity in medical care

500   1400

Medicine for most people

For ordinary villagers, living in Britain, or elsewhere in Europe, the end of the Roman Empire made little difference to their medical care. They had not usually been treated by Roman doctors or visited Roman baths. They did not get their water from Roman aqueducts, so these things were not greatly missed.

Healers

By the end of the Middle Ages there were some hospitals, and there were a few doctors who treated poor people but these were still rare.

To treat everyday illnesses most Britons depended on the work of local healers and family members who were skilled in the use of herbs and charms.

Treatments

Treatments were usually potions made from plants and vegetables. Many herbal remedies did help people recover. The people who lived in the Middle Ages were not stupid. A lot of care was needed to prepare and use herbal treatments (together with a good memory, since very few of the healers could read or write).

Some of the new herbal remedies introduced by the Romans stayed in use after the empire collapsed.

Life expectancy

There were major epidemics such as the Black Death which killed many poor people. However, during the Middle Ages, as a whole, the health and life expectancy of poor people did not change much either for the better or for the worse.

> **Summary: medicine for most people**
> - The end of the Roman Empire made little difference to most people. They had not benefited much from Roman doctors or public health systems.
> - Throughout the Middle Ages poor people still relied on herbal remedies and charms. Many herbal remedies worked.
> - Throughout the Middle Ages most health problems were treated by family members (usually women) or local healers from the village.

Medicine for the wealthy

The second group of people was wealthier. Perhaps they lived in Roman towns or had large farming estates. During the centuries that followed the Romans' departure their descendants did not have the same standard of medical care. The Roman sewers and clean water supplies disintegrated. There were no doctors, trained to follow Galen's methods of careful observation, diagnosis and advice. They became less wealthy and had a poorer diet and housing. Their life expectancy was probably worse than their ancestors'.

However, this period of regression was followed by a period of recovery. The medical ideas of Greece and Rome did not disappear entirely. They were kept alive in the libraries of monasteries. Gradually, as towns grew once more, a new type of doctor appeared, perhaps owning a copy of *Bald's Leechbook* or something very similar. These contained a sensible mixture of Greek, Roman and native remedies. By the thirteenth century the wealthy were receiving just as good medical care as their ancestors had done under the Romans.

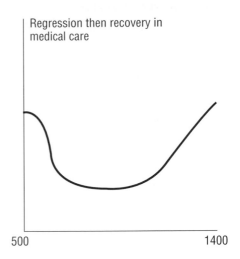

Regression then recovery in medical care

500   1400

Healers

Doctors were trained in universities where they studied Galen, new texts by Arab doctors and occasionally were allowed to observe a dissection which improved their knowledge of anatomy. Some had even studied at the famous medical schools in France and Italy.

Treatments

Treatments (mostly involving the use of herbs) were based on the theory of the four humours. Doctors were proud that they were still following ancient ideas. In the Middle Ages people revered the old ways. It was more important for a medical writer to copy out the words of Galen correctly than to have new ideas of his own. There were some who challenged old ideas but they were often regarded as cranks.

Surgeons too were looked down on. The most respected doctors were the physicians who understood the ancient theories of the four humours and ordered treatments based on them. They did not perform any surgery apart from bleeding a patient. Even surgeons were very limited in what they could do because there were no really effective anaesthetics.

Life expectancy

Because of increasing wealth in the twelfth and thirteenth centuries most people had better houses and a more varied diet. However, despite these improvements people did not live significantly longer lives. This was because the basic problems had not been solved. No one knew exactly what caused disease and so they could not stop deadly infections, which killed over 30 per cent of children before their first birthday. Being wealthy did not stop you getting the Black Death!

Summary: medicine for the wealthy
- The collapse of the Roman Empire affected the wealthy more than the poor.
- By the end of the Middle Ages rich people could visit doctors trained in the ancient ideas of Galen.
- Treatments were based on the theory of the four humours. Herbs were often used. Bleeding was also a common treatment.

---

1. What are the main differences between:
   a) the healers used by the rich and the poor
   b) the treatments used by the rich and the poor?
2. Are there any similarities in healers or treatments used by the rich and the poor?
3. Why did the collapse of the Roman Empire affect rich people's medicine more than poor people's?
4. Who benefited most from the recovery of medical skills in the late Middle Ages?

Did ideas about disease change in the Middle Ages?

In the Middle Ages most doctors followed the ideas of Galen. Like him they believed that illness was caused by an imbalance in the body's humours. Even *Bald's Leechbook* – a book of Anglo-Saxon – remedies contains advice based on Galen's works.

SOURCE 1 From *Bald's Leechbook* AD900. The title itself is a reference to using leeches to bleed patients

66 *Where a great hiccup may come from ...*

It comes from a very chilled stomach or even from an overheated one, or from the stomach being too full or too much emptiness, or from evil humours tearing and scarifying the stomach.

Cough has a varied approach: sometimes it comes from great heat; sometimes from great cold; sometimes from great humidity; sometimes from great dryness. 99

However, doctors in the Middle Ages also had ideas about illness which were different from Galen's.

The most powerful was their belief that **God and the Devil** influenced health. Major epidemics such as the Black Death were seen as God's punishment for people's sins. Even lesser problems, such as the death of a child, might be blamed on the sin of the parents. They therefore believed that God could heal people and that the King (because he was appointed by God) could heal diseases such as SCROFULA, just by touching a sufferer.

Astrology also became very important in the Middle Ages. Trained doctors studied star charts because they believed that the movement of **the planets** affected people's health.

Another very different medieval idea was that **worms** were connected to illness. These are some of the chapter headings from *Bald's Leechbook*:

■ Remedies if a worm eat a tooth
■ Remedies for worms in children's intestines
■ Remedies for worms that eat a man's flesh.

When doctors examined the faeces of sick people they often saw worms. It seemed obvious to link these to whatever illness the person was suffering from.

Common sense also told them that there was a link between **dirt** and disease although they did not know what the link was. So during attacks of plague people in cities cleared rubbish from the streets.

■ TASK 1

Continuity and change in the Middle Ages

A.
Using the completed chart and what you have found out about the Middle Ages write answers to the following questions. For each one find evidence in this chapter to support your answer.

1. Did women's role in medicine change?
2. Were there any important new ideas about the causes of illness?
3. Did treatments stay the same over the period?
4. Did people take intelligent measures to prevent disease?
5. Were there new diseases?

B.
Now use your answers to help you write an essay explaining whether you agree or disagree with this statement: 'There was far more continuity than change in medicine in the Middle Ages.'

1. Get a copy of this summary chart from your teacher. Fill out the second row using the text above. You will also need to refer back to page 52.

	PREHISTORY	EGYPT
Who treated illness?	Women / Medicine men	Priests
What did they think caused illness?	Supernatural explanations / Natural explanations	?
How were illnesses treated?		
How did they try to prevent disease?	Hunter gatherers constantly travelling – reduced the risk of disease	

What factors affected medicine in the Middle Ages?

In the Middle Ages there was little improvement in doctors' basic understanding of disease. Why?

One obvious reason was the disruption caused by war after the Roman Empire collapsed. Medicine had progressed steadily for a number of centuries until Galen's times. It is reasonable to think it might have continued to do so but for the collapse of the Roman Empire.

A second reason is that religion discouraged change. Leaders of the Christian Church often suppressed new ideas in case they challenged the authority of the Church.

Other factors were also important.

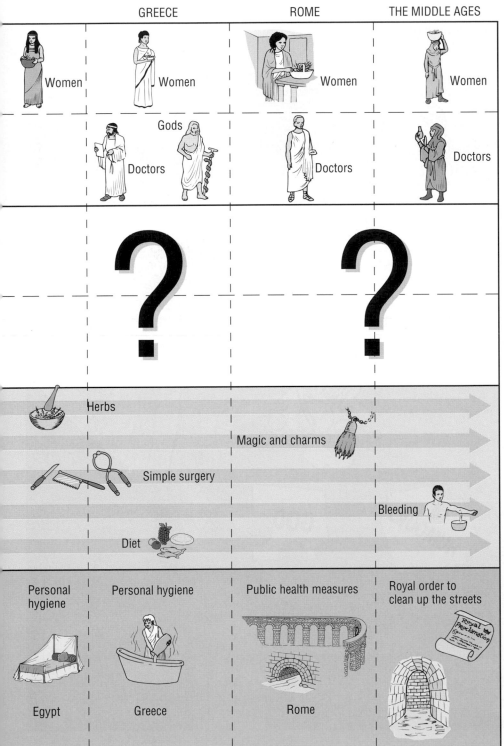

GREECE	ROME	THE MIDDLE AGES
Women / Women	Women	Women
Gods / Doctors	Doctors	Doctors
?	?	
Herbs		
	Magic and charms	
Simple surgery		
		Bleeding
Diet		
Personal hygiene	Personal hygiene	Public health measures	Royal order to clean up the streets
Egypt	Greece	Rome	

■ TASK 2

1. Use the factor charts at the back of your book to record examples of how each of the following affected medicine in the Middle Ages:

   ■ governments
   ■ war
   ■ religion
   ■ communications
   ■ education
   ■ technology.

2. Did any individuals greatly affect medicine in the Middle Ages?
3. Which factor did most to cause change in this period? Which did most to prevent change?

■ TASK 3

Why were medieval doctors still reading Galen?

Write your own answer to this question using these headings:

■ respect for ancient ideas
■ education
■ communications
■ war.

The health jigsaw: AD1400

You have already seen a picture like this (on page 54). This version is attempting to show the ideas and skills that doctors in the Middle Ages had available to them. Some things have changed since the time of Galen, other things have not.

1. Find as many differences as you can between this picture and the one on page 54.
2. For each of the differences explain whether this change improved a patient's health or not.

ACTIVITY

Write a letter from a medieval doctor applying to be the king's physician. Your letter should make clear:

■ what you think causes disease
■ the kinds of treatments you will use
■ the measures you will advise the king to take to help prevent disease spreading in his country.

chapter 3

MEDICINE AND HEALTH AD1400–1750

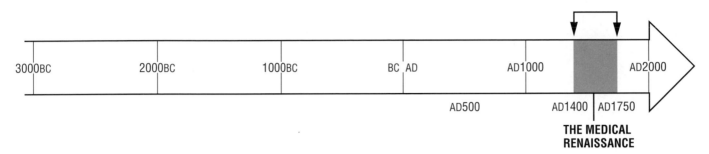

3000BC   2000BC   1000BC   BC AD   AD1000   AD2000

AD500   AD1400   AD1750

THE MEDICAL RENAISSANCE

Did the Medical Renaissance improve people's health?

YOU ARE NOW moving on in your study of medicine and health to investigate a period known as the Medical Renaissance. Between 1500 and 1650 there were major breakthroughs in anatomy, PHYSIOLOGY (understanding how the body works) and surgery. Today you would expect such important discoveries to be headline news and to alter our lives very quickly but in the 1600s it may have been different.

Look at the cartoon opposite. Ridiculous isn't it? Someone made an important scientific discovery and it did not affect the way people lived. Can this be true? Your task in this chapter is to investigate whether these discoveries did change the way doctors and healers treated their patients or whether the news vendor in the cartoon was right.

> Read all about it! Great medical discoveries! Nobody will notice for centuries!

■ TASK

Before you begin try out the same exercise as you started the previous chapter with. Below there are three graphs showing how medical knowledge and health may have changed between 1400 and 1750. Which do you expect to be the right pattern? You may think that none of them are correct and another pattern would be more likely?

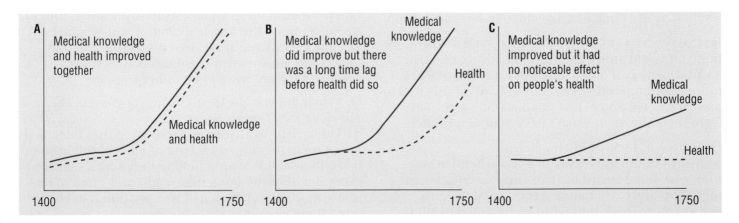

A Medical knowledge and health improved together

Medical knowledge and health

1400   1750

B Medical knowledge did improve but there was a long time lag before health did so

Medical knowledge

Health

1400   1750

C Medical knowledge improved but it had no noticeable effect on people's health

Medical knowledge

Health

1400   1750

How did Vesalius change the way the human body was studied?

Andreas Vesalius

Biography
Born in Brussels in 1514. Studied medicine in Paris and Italy where he met artists who were studying skeletons and dissecting bodies to make their paintings more realistic. Became Professor of Surgery at Padua in Italy. Wrote *The Fabric of the Human Body* (published 1543) with detailed illustrations of the human anatomy. Died in 1564.

SOURCE 1 Vesalius wrote

> *The jaw of most animals is formed of two bones joined together at the apex of the chin where the lower jaw ends in a point. In man, however, the lower jaw is formed of a single bone ... Galen and most of the skilled dissectors after the time of Hippocrates asserted that the jaw is not a single bone. However this may be, so far no human jaw has come to my attention constructed of two bones.*

Specialism
Anatomy

Importance
Before Vesalius: doctors believed that the books of Galen and other ancient doctors were completely accurate and contained all the knowledge they needed. Therefore there was no need to learn more about anatomy by dissecting human bodies.

After Vesalius: Vesalius showed that Galen was wrong in some important details of anatomy. He believed that this was because Galen had to rely on dissecting animals. He said it was vital that doctors dissect human bodies to

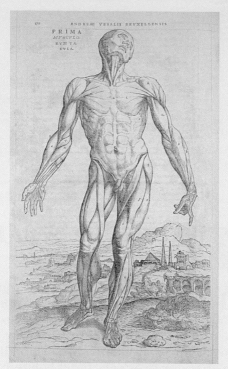

SOURCE 2 An illustration from Vesalius' book

find out about the human structure and exactly how it works. He said doctors needed to test Galen's ideas instead of accepting them uncritically.

An interview with Vesalius
They didn't interview people like this in the 1500s, but if they had done, this is what an interview with Vesalius might have sounded like! The answers are all based on sources from the time.

Question: Why did you want to become a doctor?
Answer: My father was a doctor. What he did always seemed interesting, and I decided to be a doctor too.

Q: I've heard a story that you once stole a corpse so that you could study the human body. Is that true?
A: Yes. I was still only a boy but I wanted to learn more about anatomy. The only way to do this was to dissect a corpse so I stole the body of a criminal from the gallows. It wasn't easy getting it home!

Q: Where did you study medicine?
A: I went to the university at Paris when I was nineteen. I had heard of Jean Guinter who taught medicine there. He had just translated Galen's works from Greek into Latin so I wanted to study

there to learn from him. After three years in Paris I moved to Padua in Italy.

Q: Was working in Padua as exciting as you hoped?
A: Even better. The university was very good. Nobody tried to stop you thinking and having new ideas. I could get plenty of corpses to dissect, and I found artists who could make excellent drawings of parts of the body.

Q: Was it difficult to get artists to draw such things?
A: No. Some of the artists in Padua and Venice had already carried out their own dissections so that they could learn to draw human bodies more accurately. They were keen to help.

Q: When did you decide to write your book *The Fabric of the Human Body*?
A: The artists' drawings were so good that I decided to put them together as a kind of atlas of the human body. I knew this would help my students. I wanted every detail in the book to be right and I had to do many more dissections as I was writing it to check that all the drawings were correct.

Q: How was your book produced?
A: Well, it wouldn't have been possible 100 years ago because printing had not even been invented. The artists engraved their drawings onto blocks for the printers to use. It was important to make sure that all the detail on the drawings was clear so I sent the book to the best printers, in Basle in Switzerland.

Q: Many doctors have criticised your book. How do you feel about their criticisms?
A: I expected them to criticise me because I dared to say that Galen was wrong. In fact, most of my work shows that Galen was very accurate, but doctors have been trained to believe that Galen was right about everything. They find it difficult to accept that there were some things he was wrong about.

Q: Are you sure you are right?
A: Yes. I have checked and double checked. And I've dissected human bodies. Galen of course often had to make do with dissecting animals. It's not surprising he was sometimes wrong because the bodies of monkeys and pigs are different from those of humans.

Q: Can you give me an example of something Galen got wrong?
A: Yes, the human jaw bone. He said the lower jaw is made up of two pieces but it isn't. It's one piece. Animals have lower jaws made from two bones, but my dissections showed that human lower jaws only have one piece.

Q: But that isn't a very important mistake really, is it?
A: No, but if Galen was wrong about that, then he might be wrong about other things too.

Q: Well? Have you found other mistakes?
A: Yes. Take this, for example: Galen said that blood moves from one side of the heart to the other through holes in the septum – that's in the middle of the heart (see Source 3).

Q: And what is wrong with Galen's idea?
A: Well, until recently even I did not dare to think that Galen was wrong about something so important, but if you had ever looked at the septum you would know that he was wrong. I have studied many hearts and the septum is always very thick. There are no holes in it. There is simply no way that the blood can pass through the septum – it must move in another way.

Q: And what is that other way?
A: I don't know yet. I will need to do more research to answer that question.

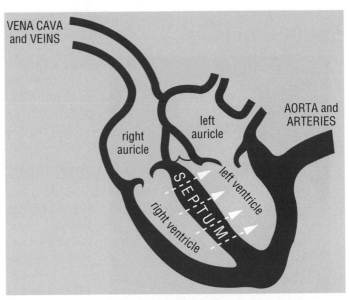

SOURCE 3 Diagram showing Galen's idea about the heart

Q: What are you going to do in the future?
A: I have been offered a new job, as doctor to the emperor Charles V in Spain. It's well paid and it will be restful after writing three huge volumes in three years. I think I'll enjoy working for the emperor – provided I can still get a supply of bodies to dissect.

1. Why did working in Padua make Vesalius's work easier?
2. Which technological developments helped Vesalius make his work well known?
3. Choose either:
   a) the human lower jaw
   b) the heart
   and explain what Galen got wrong.
4. Vesalius probably knew that Galen was wrong about the heart when he first published his book, but he did not say so. Vesalius added his new discoveries about the heart when the book was republished later. Why do you think he did not show that Galen was wrong when the book was first published?

■ **ACTIVITY**

Write a review of Vesalius' book **either**:
a) as a doctor who still thinks that Galen is right about everything. Explain why you find it difficult to believe that Galen could be wrong, **or**:
b) as a doctor who believes that Vesalius has made a big breakthrough. Include an explanation as to why his work is so important.

Why did Paré make new surgical discoveries?

Ambroise Paré

Biography
Born in France in 1510. He was apprenticed to his brother, a barber surgeon and then became a surgeon in Paris at the Hotel Dieu (see page 73). In 1536 he became an army surgeon and spent twenty years on campaign, treating sword and gunshot wounds. He wrote *Works on Surgery*, published in 1575. He died in 1590.

Specialism
Surgery

Importance
Before Paré: wounds were treated by pouring boiling oil onto them. Doctors believed this would help them to heal. They stopped a wound bleeding by sealing it with a red-hot iron. This was called CAUTERISING.

After Paré: Paré discovered that wounds healed more quickly if boiling oil was not used. Instead he put simple bandages onto wounds. He also stopped cauterising wounds. Instead he tied the ends of arteries using silk thread.

Paré's story
Problem 1: helping a wound to heal

It was the young doctor's first battle. Ambroise Paré had been with the French army for only a short time. He had watched the French soldiers begin their attack, but now they were being pushed back by the pikes and guns of the enemy. The wounded began to stagger in for help. Some had to be carried by their comrades.

The old treatment: boiling oil
Paré had never dealt with gunshot wounds before, although he knew how to treat them – in theory. He had read the book by Jean de Vigo called *Of Wounds in General*. Vigo said that gunshot wounds were poisonous and that the only way to stop the poison from infecting the whole leg was to apply boiling oil to the wound, thus killing the poison. This was another method of cauterising a wound.

As the soldiers screamed with pain, Paré checked how the other surgeons were treating the gunshot wounds. 'Go ahead, use the oil,' they said, 'as hot as they can stand. It will save their lives, if they are lucky.'

The crisis: the oil runs out
Paré set to work with boiling oil. He treated one soldier after another until his supply of life-saving oil dwindled and, finally, ran out.

Still the wounded arrived. 'How can I treat them?' thought Paré. 'Something needs to be put on their wounds.'

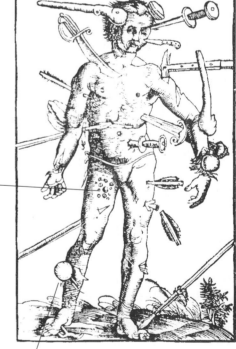

Gunshot wounds

SOURCE 1
This picture of a 'wound man' is from a book on surgery published in 1536. Gunshot wounds were treated with boiling oil

Canonball wounds

The solution: don't cauterise!
Paré was desperate to help the soldiers so he quickly mixed an ointment of his own. It was made out of egg yolks, oil of roses and turpentine, which Paré knew had been used since Roman times to heal wounds. As soon as the mixture was ready Paré began to apply it to wounds.

The surprise: healed wounds

That night Paré tossed and turned, worrying about his patients. He was convinced that in the morning the soldiers whose wounds had been cauterised with oil would be well, but that the others – treated with his own emergency mixture – would be dead or dying.

Finally Paré gave up trying to sleep, and decided to examine his patients. He could hear their groans and curses as he walked towards them.

As Paré bent over the first soldier he realised something strange had happened. This was a man whom he had treated with his own mixture. Instead of suffering in agony he was lying back resting comfortably, and his leg wound looked healthy. It was the same with the other men he had treated after the oil ran out. They were all alive and looked as if they would recover.

It was a different story among the soldiers who'd been treated with boiling oil. Their wounds were swollen and red, and they moaned and threw themselves around in pain. Some were unconscious and others had already died.

Paré decided that he would never again use boiling oil to treat gunshot wounds. It only caused more pain and misery. Instead he would use his own mixture and try to improve it. It would be difficult to go against all the wisdom and beliefs of the great surgeons of the past, but he had to do it.

Problem 2: stopping the bleeding

Paré spent another twenty years as an army doctor. In that time he learned a lot more about how to treat wounds. This included a method of stopping patients' bleeding after an amputation.

The old treatment: red hot irons

The usual treatment to stop bleeding was to press a red-hot iron, called a cautery, against the stump of the limb. This sealed the blood vessels and stopped the patient bleeding to death.

The pain caused by the red-hot iron was excruciating. Paré was sure there must be a better way to stop the flow of blood.

The new treatment: ligatures

Paré's answer was to tie silk thread round each of the blood vessels to close them up. These silk threads were called LIGATURES, and they provided a very effective way of stopping bleeding. This meant that Paré could stop using the cautery, which he called that 'old and too cruel way of healing'.

Paré's idea was not totally new, but it had never become popular because many surgeons still

believed it was too much of a risk. Paré was different. He was prepared to try new ideas even if it meant going against the methods that other surgeons had followed for centuries.

When Paré became an experienced and famous surgeon, people began to take notice of what he said. Paré believed that the idea of ligatures had been sent by God to save people from pain, but many other surgeons did not agree. In one way they were right, although they did not understand why. Paré's ligatures did stop the bleeding, but they were dangerous because the threads themselves could carry infection into the wound. If Paré had had an antiseptic to kill the germs then his ligatures might have worked better. Unfortunately, antiseptics were not invented for another 300 years, and nobody in Paré's time even knew about germs or exactly how infection spread.

Eventually Paré retired from the army. He became a successful surgeon in Paris, treating three French kings. In 1575 he published his book, *Works on Surgery*. This was written in French, not Latin, and was soon translated into many other languages, spreading his ideas throughout Europe.

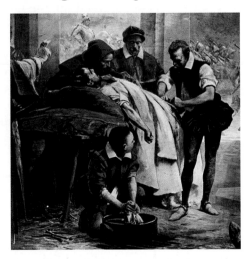

SOURCE 3
A nineteenth-century painting of Paré at the siege of Metz tying ligatures on the wounded

1. A number of factors helped Paré to make his discoveries. Explain how each of these played a part in his discoveries and the spread of his ideas:
   a) war
   b) chance
   c) Paré's own intelligence
   d) printing.
2. Which of the factors above was the most important?
3. Why were many other surgeons unwilling to use Paré's methods?
4. Paré wrote his book in French. How did this help to spread his ideas more quickly?

What was William Harvey's great discovery?

William Harvey

Biography
Born in 1578 in Kent. Studied medicine at Cambridge and Padua. Worked as a doctor in London and then as a lecturer in anatomy. In 1628 he published *An Anatomical Account of the Motion of the Heart and Blood in Animals.* He died in 1657.

Specialism
The circulation of the blood

Importance
Before Harvey: many doctors still believed in Galen's idea that new blood was constantly being manufactured in the liver to replace blood that was burnt up in the body in the same way as wood is burnt by fire. This idea had been challenged by a number of doctors but no one had proved exactly how the blood moved around the body.

After Harvey: Harvey showed that blood flows around the body, is carried away from the heart by the arteries and returns to the heart in veins.

He proved that the heart acts as a pump, recirculating the blood and that blood does not burn up so no other organ is needed to manufacture new blood.

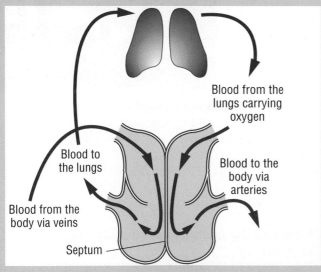

SOURCE 1 Diagram showing the circulation of the blood

88

How did Harvey prove he was right?

The idea that the heart was a pump had been suggested by Erasistratus 1800 years earlier (see page 35) but he had not been able to prove it. Harvey could prove it.

- He dissected live, cold-blooded animals whose hearts beat very slowly. This meant that he could see the movements of each muscle in the heart.
- He dissected human bodies to build up a detailed knowledge of the heart.
- He tried to pump liquids past the valves in the veins but he could not do so. He also pushed thin rods down veins. This proved that the blood flowed in a one-way system around the body.
- He measured the amount of blood moved by each heartbeat, and calculated how much blood was in the body.
- Whenever he disagreed with Galen or his own contemporaries he gave clear, detailed proof of his own conclusions, and explained carefully why other doctors were wrong.

What could Harvey not prove?

Between arteries and veins there are tiny blood vessels called capillaries which carry the blood. They are too small to see with the naked eye but even though Harvey could not see them he said that they must exist.

Later in the 1600s microscopes were developed which allowed doctors to see the capillaries exactly as Harvey had predicted.

1. Do you think Harvey's discovery will improve his patients' health? Explain your answer.

What caused these discoveries?

■ ACTIVITY

Your teacher will give you a chart like the one below.

EXPERIMENT	CHALLENGES	WARS
People were willing to challenge old ideas – by experimenting they could prove whether their theories were correct.	Many old ideas were challenged. Copernicus said the earth travelled round the sun, not the sun round the earth. Protestants challenged the Pope and the Catholic church.	There were many wars in 16th- and 17th-century Europe.

WEALTH
Since the Black Death in the 1300s many people had grown wealthier. They had money to spend on luxuries and education.

EDUCATION
Literacy was increasing and there were many more schools in the 16th and 17th centuries.

MACHINERY
There were improvements in clocks, watches, pumps and other machines.

ART
Skilful artists found work and people to buy their sculptures and paintings.

ANCIENT LEARNING
There was renewed interest in the writings of Roman and Greek thinkers.

PRINTING
From the late 1400s printed books meant that new ideas spread much more rapidly.

1. Write the name of Vesalius, Harvey or Paré in the central box and his specialism.
2. You are now going to try to work out how various developments brought about new discoveries in medicine and health. Look at the developments described in the other boxes. If you think that, for example, printing helped your chosen character to make a new discovery or develop his specialism, then draw a line from 'printing' to the central box. Do this for all the boxes that helped bring about this discovery.

   Sources 1–7 will help you but you will also have to look back through pages 84–89 and think for yourself as well! Some of the connections are less obvious than others.

3. Were there any connections between the developments in the outer ring of boxes? For example, did improvements in education help to improve machinery? If you think so, draw a line between the two boxes. Do this for any other boxes that you think were connected.
4. On a separate sheet of paper, list all the developments that helped to bring about your chosen discovery.
5. Finally, write an essay to explain how at least two of the developments worked together to bring about the discovery. Explain why you have made your choice and explain if you think one of them was more important than another.

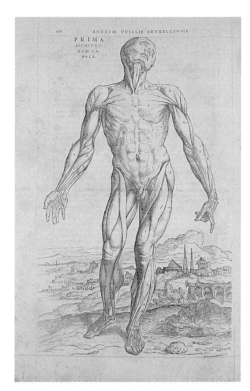

SOURCE 1 An illustration from Vesalius' book, *The Fabric of the Human Body*, published in 1543. In Italy Vesalius found many talented artists who made detailed anatomical drawings

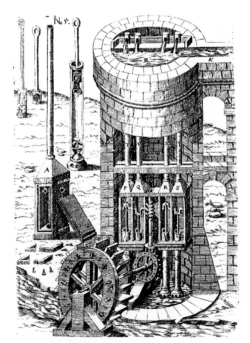

SOURCE 2 A water pump pictured in a book entitled *Various Ingenious Machines*, published in 1588. The valves are shown separately on the left

SOURCE 3 Extracts from Leonardo da Vinci's Notebook, written before 1519. Leonardo da Vinci gave this advice to many ambitious young artists in Italy

66 *The painter who has a knowledge of the sinews, muscles and tendons will know exactly which sinew causes the movement of a limb … he will be able to show the various muscles in the different attitudes of his figures …*

You will need three dissections to have a complete knowledge of the arteries, three more for the membranes, three for the nerves, muscles and LIGAMENTS, three for the bones and cartilages. Three must also be devoted to the female body … 99

SOURCE 4 From William Harvey's *On the Circulation of the Blood*, 1649. Harvey's books were reprinted several times before the 1670s

66 *When water is forced through pipes we can see and distinguish the individual compressions of the pump (perhaps at a considerable distance) in the flow of the escaping water. It is the same from the opening of a cut artery…* 99

SOURCE 5 From the writings of Robert Boyle, a leading English scientist, 1663

66 *A human body itself seems to be but an engine wherein almost all the actions are performed mechanically.* 99

SOURCE 6 Written by Ambroise Paré in *Apology and Treatise*, 1585. He is pleading with other surgeons to adopt his methods of tying up arteries after an amputation. His method was not entirely new, but it was Paré's books which made the method widely known

66 *I confess that I used to staunch the bleeding after amputation in a different way, of which I am now ashamed. But what else could I do? I had watched my masters whose methods I intended to follow. They had various hot irons and burning medicines with which they would treat the dismembered part. This cannot be spoken of without great horror, for this kind of remedy could not help giving the patient great tormenting pain.*

I must earnestly beg all surgeons to give up this old and too cruel way of healing, and take up this new method. I think that it was taught to me by the special favour of God, because I did not learn it from my masters. 99

SOURCE 7 A description of some of the technological advancements during the Medical Renaissance

66 *Guns were used increasingly in wars in the sixteenth century. They set a new problem for the surgeons because bullets might carry infection deep into a wound. Around 1600 craftsmen developed the microscope. There had been improvements in glassmaking in the 1500s and in the science of rays of light. In 1661 an Italian professor used an improved microscope to identify the capillaries, the channels along which blood flows from the arteries to the veins. Harvey knew they must exist but had not been able to see them.* 99

Did the Medical Renaissance improve health and treatments?

SOMETIMES DISCOVERIES ARE important because they immediately change the way people live. At other times discoveries take longer to have an effect. You are now going to look at four case studies to investigate how far developments in medical knowledge actually affected treatments.

■ ACTIVITY

Use the chart below to work out whether the discoveries of Vesalius about anatomy, Harvey about the circulation of the blood and Paré about surgery had an immediate effect on the work of healers and on their patients.

	Grace Mildmay	Richard Wiseman	Treating the plague 1665	James Woodforde
Old ideas				
New ideas from: ■ Vesalius ■ Paré ■ Harvey ■ Others?				

Lady Grace Mildmay (1552–1620)

Lady Grace Mildmay was born in 1552. Like other ladies from wealthy families, she was expected to provide medical care for the people on the family's lands and medicine was therefore part of her education.

How did she learn her skills?

Her governess made her read William Turner's *A New Herbal* (published in 1551) which identified herbs and their medical uses but Lady Grace was no country QUACK. She knew all about the latest medical theories even if she had not been able to attend university. She increased her knowledge by reading widely, including a famous book on surgery by Jean de Vigo which had been translated into English in 1543. Her papers also show that she knew the work of the Arab doctor, Ibn Sinna (Avicenna), and of Galen, whose theories were still the basis of medical treatments. She also had discussions with doctors who clearly respected her work.

Lady Grace clearly believed in Galen's theory that illness was caused by imbalances of the four humours in the body or by sin. She used purges to empty the body of excess humours and bled her patients.

> **SOURCE 1** One of Lady Grace's cures for smallpox began
>
> 66 *Let the patient's blood, from the liver vein of the right arm, and that a reasonable quantity, according as you see the blood, good or corrupt, and according to the patient's age and strength.* 99

However, even though Galen's ideas dominated her thinking, she also followed some of the work of Paracelsus (1493–1541) who attacked Galen's ideas about the four humours and claimed that illnesses were caused by seeds of disease which settled in the infected parts of the body. Paracelsus recommended remedies based on minerals, such as mercury, arsenic and lead, rather than purges, to treat illness.

What treatments did she use?

Lady Grace's medical treatments were detailed and complex. Her favourite medicine, her 'precious balm', took five weeks to make and involved fifteen separate processes. The ingredients of this BALM included 24 types of roots, 68 herbs, 14 different seeds, 12 flowers, 10 spices, 20 kinds of gum, 5 CORDIALS, 6 different purgatives, 2 pints of vinegar, 2 gallons of olive oil and 6 pounds of sugar amongst other things.

Herbs and seeds made up the majority of the ingredients in all her treatments, but she also used metals or minerals such as amber, gold, turpentine, mercury, tin and lead, and items new to Europe such as tobacco. Occasionally her cures also included elk's hooves, crab's claws and powder of human skull! Many of the ingredients came from abroad and a wide range of equipment was needed for boiling, distilling and preserving the medicines.

With her array of medicines Lady Grace tackled a wide range of illnesses – JAUNDICE, smallpox, skin diseases, cramp, ulcers, loss of memory, fevers of all kinds, eye problems and MELANCHOLY. However, she would not perform surgery such as removing cataracts from the eye which is, she wrote, 'a cure is manual, difficult to do and beyond the practice of woman'.

1. Why do you think Mildmay said that surgery was 'beyond the practice of woman'?

Lady Grace wrote down many of her ideas about treatments such as those in Sources 2 and 3.

SOURCE 2 From Lady Grace Mildmay's papers. (Posset was a drink that mixed wine, or ale with hot milk)

A drink for a burning fever

Take diascordium one ounce; mithridate two ounces; syrup of lemons one ounce. Mix these with cardus benedictus water or angelica water quarter of a pint. Take three pints of small ale; three handfuls of sorrel; two handfuls of the tops of marigolds. Steep them in the ale all night and in the morning strain it hard and make some posset drink of it. And every four hours take a spoonful of the cordial water above written, in a draught of this posset ale …

I give this cordial in this manner: once a day for three days at nine of the clock at night. And all the mornings after give every hour to drink, warm broth made with the strength of a good chicken, a crust of bread, a whole mace, endive, borage, violet leaves, cinquefoil, strawberry leaves, of each alike, in all a pretty bundle …

SOURCE 3 From Lady Grace Mildmay's papers

… It is [a] dangerous thing to [upset] the humours in the body by extreme purges or extreme cordials. When humours are stirred and made to fly up to the head, heart and spirits it greatly disturbs all the principal parts of the body … the healing methods which bring the body and parts thereof into union, little by little, work the most safe and effectual operation and the greatest hope to cure any disease in the end, except God determine the same to be incurable.

SOURCE 4 Paracelsus, born around 1483, was a German physician and chemist. He dared to disagree with Galen! Galen had said that diseases were caused by an imbalance of humours and that they would be cured by blood-letting and purging. Paracelsus believed that disease attacks from outside the body and devised mineral remedies with which he thought the body could defend itself. Although his work contained elements of magic, his criticisms of Galen helped medical thinking take a more scientific course. He died in 1541

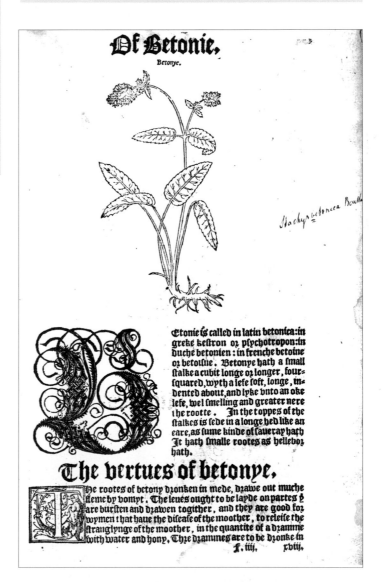

SOURCE 5 A page from William Turner's *New Herbal* published in 1551. This page describes the virtues of betony: 'the roots of betony drunk in mede (a sweet honey wine) draw out much phlegm by vomit'

Richard Wiseman (1622–76): surgeon to Charles II

Biography

1622 – born

1640 – became a surgeon in the Dutch navy

1643 – became a surgeon with the royalist forces in the English Civil War and then went into exile with Charles II

1657 – served in the Spanish navy

1660 – returned to England and became a royal surgeon when Charles II was restored to the throne.

1672 – published *A Treatise on Wounds*

1676 – published *Several Chirurgical Treatises* (CHIRURGY was another word for surgery)

1676 – died

Where did he get his ideas from?

Having spent over 30 years as a surgeon in various countries, Richard Wiseman set about passing on his knowledge to younger surgeons. In the last years of his life he wrote two long books describing the surgical methods he had seen and used.

In his introductions he wrote:

SOURCE 6

66 *Know, reader, that in preparation [of these treatises] I have read all the eminent chirurgical authors, yet in the writing I was more conformed to my own judgement and experience than other men's authority.* 99

SOURCE 7

66 *... such men as have spent their whole time in a perpetual practice are the best instructors ... [I] spent my time in armies, navies and cities, not in universities, nor books ... we do not all spend our time talking in coffee houses and drolling over the accidents that befall one another in our profession.* 99

Wiseman had certainly read the works of Greek and Roman doctors. He frequently referred to Hippocrates and Galen and followed some of their ideas. For example, in choosing a diet for a patient he told his readers to note 'the CONSTITUTION of the patient, whether he be hot or cold, dry or moist, old or young, tough or tender and washy.'

He also used other methods and medicines that had changed little over the centuries, including many herbs.

SOURCE 8

66 *Many [herbs] are mentioned by the [ancient] authors ... the most common are Comfrey, Bugle, Mugwort, Plantain, Wild tansy, St Johnswort, Strawberry leaves... some are to be boiled in water with white wine and honey... their principal use is in wounds of the thorax and abdomen though they be of frequent use in all great wounds ...*

Turpentine for deep wounds which cannot be closed – one of the most powerful medicaments in all wounds. [It] preserves bruises from putrifying ... 99

Less usual was one recipe for oil which required the boiling of 'two puppies until the skin fall off the bones.'

Wiseman also knew and admired the work of more recent writers, including Paré. In *A Treatise on Wounds* he said that 'since Galen's time we have found little augmentation of knowledge, till some bold adventurers in these latter ages have made some fortunate essays at further discoveries.' However, Wiseman gave far more space in his books to describing his own cases – over 600 are mentioned – than he gave to modern or ancient medical writers.

What were his treatments like?

Wiseman's surgical operations were often rushed because they were done in the middle of battle, on land or at sea. He knew the best way to deal with wounds, writing that Paré 'proposes a more easy and sure way, passing the needle with a good strong thread through the skin ... ' but, he continued, 'at sea your cauteries are at such times in readiness. Use them. They will secure your patient from immediate danger.'

During fighting at Weymouth in the Civil War Wiseman treated a soldier shot in the heel. The bleeding was unstoppable. 'I applied my endeavours but after all I was put to the use of the actual cautery which I did successfully.'

Describing the treatment of wounds, Wiseman wrote:

SOURCE 9

66 *[for a stab wound] The weapon thus drawn out, cleanse the wound with rags or ought else and permit the wound to bleed accordingly ... if there be hair growing about the wound shave it off, then wipe away the clotted blood with a sponge dipped in red wine, oxycrate or water.* 99

SOURCE 10

66 *[for a bullet wound] Having taken out the bullet dress it with oil as hot as the part will bear, not giving credit to any that shall persuade you to the contrary. On the second day [after the injury] consider the habit of the body ... in these gunshot wounds it may be convenient for the body to be gently purged, thereby carrying off the bilious humour, which from their heat are most apt to ferment and flow into these wounds and cause pain and inflammation and ill symptoms ...* 99

SOURCE 11

66 *[for a particularly large wound] The way to stop the* FLUX *of blood is by retaining the lips of the wound together by* SUTURE *or bandage and by applying such medicines as have a drying faculty ... some of these mixed with a white of an egg ... spread upon a double cloth and laid over the wound with compress and bandage ... but if the artery bleed you must use the cautery ... by it the vessel shrinks up at both ends, the flux [of blood] is immediately stopped and the part marvellously strengthened.* 99

1. What evidence is there in Sources 9–11 that Wiseman did not agree with Paré's methods?

SOURCE 12 A surgeon cauterising a wound. Paré had warned about the dangers of cauterising wounds and of using boiling oil to help healing

The King's Evil

As the king's surgeon, Wiseman was also present when people came to Charles II seeking a cure for skin disorders, known as the KING'S EVIL. They believed that if the king touched them they would recover. Between 1660 and 1682 Charles II touched over 92,000 people.

Wiseman wrote 'I myself have been a frequent eye-witness of many hundreds of cures performed by His Majesty's touch alone without any assistance of chirurgy'. He rejected the explanation that people were actually cured by the fresh air of the court, away from the city, or that they simply recovered because they believed the king's touch could cure them. However, Wiseman recorded over 50 cases when he himself treated people for the King's Evil. His own cures were based upon diet, medicines and surgery. He did not send anyone to the king.

1. Vesalius said that Galen's ideas should be tested instead of being automatically accepted. Would Wiseman have agreed with Vesalius?
2. Which ideas or methods did Wiseman use that had already been used for centuries?
3. Which new ideas or methods did Wiseman use?
4. Did Wiseman believe that the king could cure the King's Evil?
5. Did Wiseman have more in common with medieval surgeons or modern surgeons? Explain the reasons for your answer.

SOURCE 13 Charles II touching people to cure them of King's Evil

■ ACTIVITY

Work in pairs to make up an interview with Richard Wiseman in the style of the Vesalius interview on pages 84–85. Each of you write out a list of questions, then swap with your partner, and see if you can write some answers from Wiseman, using the evidence on pages 94–96.

The Great Plague: 1665

On pages 62–65 you investigated the Black Death. The plague continued to strike Britain at regular intervals through the 1400s and 1500s. Then in 1665 London was hit by the worst outbreak for three centuries.

In London alone more than 65,000 people died out of a population of less than 400,000.

Fifty years later, Daniel Defoe, the author of *Robinson Crusoe*, wrote an account of life in London during the plague. It was called *Journal of the Plague Year: 1665*. He consulted documents from that year and included some in his book. Although parts of his work are imaginary it provides a dramatic and accurate account of life during the plague. Source 15 contains edited extracts from his book.

SOURCE 14 Defoe's *Journal of the Plague Year* describes how people wore charms such as this abracadabra amulet to ward off the plague

SOURCE 15 From Defoe's *Journal of the Plague Year: 1665*

❝ … *a blazing star or comet appeared for several months before the plague. The old women remarked that those two comets passed directly over the city, and … imparted something peculiar…*

… astrologers added stories of the conjunctions of planets…, one of these conjunctions … did happen in October and the other in November; and they filled the people's heads with predictions on these signs of the heavens, that they foretold drought, famine and pestilence …

… The Government appointed public prayers and days of fasting, to make public confession of sin and implore the mercy of God to avert the dreadful judgement that hung over their heads…

… When anyone bought a joint of meat in the market they would not take it off the butcher's hand, but took it off the hooks themselves. On the other hand the butcher would not touch the money, but have it put into a pot full of vinegar.

… The infection generally came into the houses of the citizens by means of their servants, whom they were obliged to send for food or physic, and who meet with distempered people, who conveyed the fatal breath into them.

… the calamity was spread by infection, by the breath, by the sweat or by the stench of the sores of the sick persons, or some other way, perhaps, beyond even the reach of the physicians themselves. I cannot but with some wonder find some people talk of its being a stroke from Heaven, which I look upon as ignorance; likewise the opinion of others who talk of infection being carried on by the air, carrying with it vast numbers of insects and invisible creatures, who enter into the body with the breath or even at the pores with the air and there generate or emit most acute poisons or poisonous eggs which mingle themselves with the blood and so infect the body … ❞

SOURCE 16 An example of a contemporary treatment for plague

❝ *To draw the poison from the plague sore, take the feathers from the tail of a chicken and apply him to the sore. The chick will gasp and labour for life … When the poison is drawn out by the chicken, the patient will recover.*

Wrap in woollen cloths, make the sick person sweat, which if he do, keep him warm until the sores begin to rise. Then apply to the sores live pigeons cut in half or else a plaster made of yolk of an egg, honey, herb of grace and wheat flour. ❞

■ ACTIVITY

1. Using Sources 14–16 make lists of:
   a) explanations for the plague   b) treatments for the plague.
2. Look back to pages 64–65. For each explanation and treatment, work out whether it was also used at the time of the Black Death or whether it is new.

SOURCE 17 Orders conceived and published by the Lord Mayor and Aldermen of the City of London concerning the infection of the plague, 1665

In every parish there be one, two or more persons by the name of examiners to enquire and learn what persons be sick. And if they find any person sick of the infection, to give order to the constable that the house be shut up.

Every house visited be marked with a red cross of a foot long in the middle of the door, evident to be seen, and with these words 'Lord have mercy upon us'.

To every infected house there be appointed two watchmen, one for every day and the other for the night [so] that no person go in or out of such infected houses.

If any nursekeeper shall remove herself out of any infected house before 28 days after the decease of any person dying of the infection, the house to which the said nursekeeper doth so remove herself shall be shut up until 28 days have expired.

There be a special care to appoint women searchers in every parish to make due search and true report whether the persons whose bodies they search do die of the infection. No searcher be permitted to keep any shop or stall or be employed as a laundress.

1. Study Source 17. Work out what job the following people had to do:

   ■ watchman
   ■ examiner
   ■ searcher
   ■ raker.

2. For each of the measures listed explain why you think it was introduced; whether it would be effective in preventing the spread of the plague; and why.

There be appointed able and discreet chirurgeons to join with the searchers for the view of the body, to the end there may be a true report made of the disease.

The burial of the dead [be] either before sun-rising or after sun-setting and that no neighbours nor friends be suffered to accompany the corpse to church or to enter the house visited. All the graves shall be at least six feet deep.

Bedding and apparel and hangings of chambers must be well aired with fire and such perfumes as are required before they be taken again to use.

Special care be taken that no stinking fish or unwholesome flesh or musty corn or other corrupt fruits be sold about the city. No hogs, dogs, cats, tame pigeons or rabbits be suffered to be kept within any part of the city, or any swine to be or stray in the streets or lanes.

All plays, bear-baitings, games, singing of ballads, buckler play or such-like causes of assemblies of people be utterly prohibited.

Every householder do cause the street to be daily prepared before his door, and so to keep it clean swept all the week long. The sweeping and filth of houses be daily carried away by the rakers.

Nothing is more complained of than the multitude of rogues and wandering beggars that swarm in every place about the city, being a great cause of the spreading of the infection. No wandering beggars be suffered in the streets upon the penalty of the law to be severely executed.

Disorderly tippling, ale-houses, coffee-houses, and cellars be severely looked unto, as the common sin of this time and greatest occasion of dispersing the plague.

■ ACTIVITY

Choose three measures from Source 17 which you think are most important and make a poster to publicise them.

James Woodforde, parson and diarist (1740–1803)

James Woodforde was a parson, born in 1740. He began to keep a diary in 1758 when he was a student at Oxford and continued it nearly every day until his death in 1803.

He spent his life amongst country people in villages in Somerset and Norfolk although he travelled many times to London to meet friends, see plays and visit the sights, such as the Tower of London. Source 18 gives extracts from his diary that deal with illness and medicine.

SOURCE 18

❝ 1776

June 4 … *My tooth pained me all night, got up a little after 5 this morning and sent for one Reeves a man who draws teeth in this parish, and about 7 he came and drew my tooth, but shockingly bad indeed, he broke away a great piece of my gum and broke one of the fangs of the tooth, it gave me exquisite pain all the day after, and my face was swelled prodigiously in the evening and much pain. Very bad and in much pain the whole day long. Paid the old man that drew it however. He is too old, I think, to draw teeth, can't see very well.*

November 3 … *This morning about 11 o'clock Dr Thorne came to my house and* INOCULATED *my servants Ben Legate and little Jack Warton against smallpox … Pray God my people and all others may do well, several houses have got the smallpox at present in Weston. O Lord send thy blessing of health on them all.*

November 22 … *John Bowles's wife … was inoculated by one Drake, formerly a sergeant in the Militia. He makes a deep incision in both arms and puts a plaister over, he gives no camomile but they take salts every morning … My neighbour Downing, father of the children lately inoculated, has got the smallpox in the natural way and likely to have it very bad – therefore I sent Harry Dunnell this evening to Dr Thorne's, to desire him to come tomorrow and see him, which he promised.*

1779

May 15 … *Bled my three horses this morning, two quarts each …*

May 22 … *My boy Jack had another touch of the* AGUE *about noon. I gave him a dram of gin at the beginning of the fit and pushed him headlong into one of my Ponds and ordered him to bed immediately and he was better after it and had nothing of the cold fit after, but was very hot …*

May 27 … *My maid Nanny was taken very ill this evening with a dizziness in the head and a desire to vomit but could not. Her straining to vomit brought on the hiccups which continued very violent till after she got to bed. I gave her a dose of rhubarb going to bed. Ben was also very ill and in the same complaint about noon, but he vomited and was soon better. I gave Ben a good dose of rhubarb also going to bed.*

1781

April 14 … *I got up very ill this morning about 8 o'clock, having had little sleep all the night, owing to the pain in my ear which was much worse in the night and broke, and a good deal of blood only came away. The pain continued still very bad all the morning tho' not quite so bad as before. It made me very uneasy about it. A throbbing pain in my ear continued till I went to bed. I put a roasted onion into my ear going to bed tonight.*

April 15 … *I thank God I had a tolerable night to sleep and was much better this morning for it …*

1784

March 9 … *Nancy [Woodforde's niece] very ill again this morning, kept her bed almost the whole day. I sent for Dr Thorne early, he came about 12 o'clock, says it is the fever which has been so long about these parts. Mr Thorne left a vomit for to be taking tonight and a rhubarb powder to take tomorrow. Nancy however ate some rabbit for dinner.*

March 11 … *Nancy taken very ill this morning about 3 o'clock, worse than ever. Mr Thorne came here about 11 and brought some quinine for her to take to begin at 12 o'clock and then every three hours to bed …*

March 12 … *Nancy a good deal better this morning, she taked* QUININE *today every two hours till bed time. She complained of great lightness in her head and rather giddy …*

March 13 … *Nancy brave today … but the quinine has prevented [the fever's] return …*

1788
March 1 ... *Ben returned about 4 o'clock this afternoon and he brought me a letter [saying that] Juliana was, it was much feared, in a decline, on account of her lately having had the measles and catching cold after, which has affected her lungs, she has been bled seven times ...*

May 17 ... *[Ben] brought me two letters ... which brought the disagreeable news of Juliana's death ...*

1790
May 6 ... *To 18 yards of black ribband, paid. Gave my brother half my black ribband. The ribband is designed to put round our necks to prevent sore throats.*

September 24 ... *Nancy was taken very ill this afternoon with a pain within her, blown up so as if poisoned, attended with a vomiting. I suppose it proceeded in great measure from what she ate at dinner ... some boiled beef rather fat and salt, a good deal of nice roast duck and a plenty of boiled damson pudding. After dinner by way of dessert she ate some greengage plums, some figs and raspberries and cream. I desired her to drink a good half pint glass of warm rum and water which she did and was soon a little better – for supper she had water-gruel with a couple of small tablespoonfuls of rum in it, and going to bed I gave her a good dose of rum and ginger. She was much better before she went to bed ...*

September 25 ... *Nancy thank God much better this morning – the rhubarb made her rise earlier than usual ...*

1791
March 7 ... *the smallpox spreads much in the parish. Abigail Roberts's husband was very bad in it in the natural way, who was supposed to have had it before and which he thought also. His children are inoculated by Johnny Reeve, as are also Richmond's children near me. It is a pity that all the poor in the parish were not inoculated also. I am entirely for it.*

March 11 ... *The* STYE *on my right eyelid still swelled and inflamed very much. As it is commonly said that the eyelid being rubbed by the tail of a black cat would do it much good if not entirely cure it, and having a black cat, a little before dinner I made a trial of it, and very soon after dinner I found my eyelid much abated of the swelling and almost free from pain. I cannot therefore but conclude it to be of the greatest service to a stye on the eyelid. Any other cat's tail may have the above effect in all probability – but I did my eyelid with my own black tom cat's tail.*

March 15 ... *My right eye again, that is, its eyelid much inflamed again and rather painful. I put on a plaistor to it this morning, but in the afternoon took it off again as I perceived no good from it. I buried poor John Roberts this afternoon, aged about 35.*

March 16 ... *My eyelid is I think rather better than it was, I bathed it with warm milk and water last night. I took a little rhubarb going to bed tonight. My eyelid about noon rather worse owing perhaps to the warm milk and water, therefore just before dinner I washed it well with cold water and in the evening appeared much better for it ... Mr Custance gave me a Guinea to pay for the* INOCULATION *of Harry Dunnell's six children.*

March 17 ... *My eyelid much better today, washed it well with cold water this morning. Dr Thorne recommended the same to me when here.* **99**

1. Which remedy did Woodforde use most often? (It appears five times.)
2. What different kinds of remedies did Thorne (Woodforde's doctor) use and recommend?
3. Woodforde records the death of two people in Source 18. What did they die of?
4. Which new method of preventing disease was being used in 1776?
5. Did Woodforde believe it was his cat's tail or his doctor which cured his eye problem?
6. Woodforde died less than 200 years ago. Are his remedies more like the ones we use today or the remedies Galen used almost 2000 years earlier?

■ **ACTIVITY**

Over the coming weeks keep your own medical diary. Record not only what happens to you, but also what happens to your family or friends – just as Woodforde did. Note down illnesses, remedies, treatments and what effect the treatments had.

SOURCE 19
Rhubarb was a popular remedy. It helped purge the bowels and prevent CONSTIPATION

Great medical discoveries! No one healthier!

THE DISCOVERIES MADE by Vesalius and Harvey are a vital part of medical history. They proved to doctors that Galen and other ancient writers could be wrong and that careful dissection and experiment were the way to new understanding. Their work inspired others and became the foundation on which later scientists built their discoveries.

However, the discoveries of Vesalius and Harvey, important though they were, did not make anyone healthier at the time! Life expectancy did not increase much. They had not, after all, discovered new and better ways of treating illnesses. John Aubrey, a seventeenth-century writer and gossip, said of Harvey: 'All his profession agree Dr Harvey to be an excellent anatomist, but I never heard any that admired his treatment of the sick. I knew several practitioners in London that would not have given threepence for one of his prescriptions ...'

Ambroise Paré's work was more immediately useful than that of Vesalius and Harvey. Other surgeons could see with their own eyes that his new methods of bandaging wounds (instead of using boiling oil) were successful and helped patients to survive. However, Paré's idea of using a silk ligature or thread to tie arteries instead of sealing them with a cauterising iron was not widely copied. The cautery had helped to stop infection. The ligature could actually introduce germs into the wound and this meant that soldiers were more likely to die from infection. It was not until 300 years after Paré's death that the development of antiseptics meant that his ligature idea could finally be used successfully.

New treatments

In fact it was probably another development altogether which had the greatest impact on treatments. In 1492 Europeans landed in America for the first time. Over the next two centuries they brought back a wide range of new remedies such as those in Source 3 which were quickly adopted by herbalists such as Lady Grace Mildmay. Once again trade and communication were playing their part in the development of medicine.

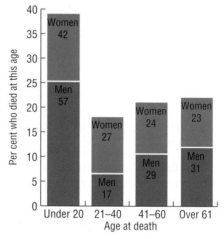

SOURCE 1 This graph shows the age at death of 250 people who were buried at St John's Church, Adel, in Leeds, between 1685 and 1700. Only 20 per cent of people lived beyond the age of 60. Today the vast majority do

■ **TASK**

Study Sources 1 and 2 on this page. Compare with Source 10 on page 61. Then write your own explanation of the significance of these figures.

Infant and childbirth	21
Consumption (TB)	15
Fever (probably flu)	47
Surfeit	4
Smallpox	17
Wearing	15
Palsy	4
King's Evil	1
Flux	2
Measles	1
Drowned	2
Dropsy	1
Bitten	2
Lost among the bogs	1
Hanged	1

SOURCE 2 This table shows the cause of death for 134 out of the 250 people who were buried at Adel between 1685 and 1700. The biggest cause of death – 'fever' – may well have been influenza. Regular epidemics swept Britain. A quarter of a million people died of it between 1727 and 1731

SOURCE 3 Plants from the Americas were brought to Europe from the 1500s onwards. One was the bark of the cinchona tree, used by native South Americans in many effective remedies. In Europe it was known as quinine and was particularly used to treat fevers. It was used by Woodforde (see Source 18 on pages 100–01)

The health jigsaw: 1700

You should be familiar with this idea by now.

The jigsaw pieces represent the knowledge and developments needed by doctors to give people better health and longer life. This doctor in 1700 has some pieces of the jigsaw. The blank pieces are discoveries yet to be made.

1. What do you think should be shown on the blank pieces?
2. Look back to the similar pictures on pages 54 and 82. Does the doctor in 1700 have more in common with:

a) Galen

b) a medieval doctor

c) a doctor today?

Explain your answer in a piece of extended writing. You can get a sheet from your teacher to help you.

103

Who would you go to for treatment?

Licensed healers

Physician

Physicians were fully qualified doctors who had studied for fourteen years at university, seven of those studying medicine. They were all men.

They knew the work of Galen and many other ancient writers as well as of Harvey, Vesalius and other more modern doctors.

For their work they charged large fees, especially in London. Even the fee of a country physician could be a month's wage for a labourer.

Surgeon

Surgeons or surgeonesses trained by watching and copying other surgeons in a long apprenticeship.

They were given licences by the local bishop, allowing them to treat patients and charge fees.

Despite their practical skills they were looked down on by physicians as second-class doctors.

Apothecary

An APOTHECARY sold and mixed medicines that had been prescribed by physicians.

They were not supposed to treat the sick or prescribe medicines but many did so, especially for the poor, for a small fee.

There were many apothecaries in London and several in any town.

Midwife

Midwives were also licensed by the local bishop to supervise the last week of a pregnancy and deliver babies. However, if there were complications, the midwife handed her patient over to a physician.

Unlicensed healers

Family

The first person to treat nearly all sicknesses was the wife or mother of the patient.

Lady of the manor

Girls from wealthy families were expected to learn how to treat illnesses and common injuries.

Books were written especially to give advice on these subjects to ladies of the manor, and some read medical textbooks.

Ladies treated people in their village and local farms as well as their own families and servants.

Wise woman

In every village and town there were wise women who local people trusted because of their deep knowledge of herbs and other treatments which had often been passed down through generations.

However, if a treatment went wrong then the wise woman could suddenly be accused of being a WITCH.

Travelling quack

At every fair and market there were tooth-pullers, herb-sellers and others who made their living as they travelled round the country. Some might do good because they had built up knowledge through experience. Many simply wanted to take the patients' money and run!

■ ACTIVITY

The illustrations above show you some of the healers who might be available in the period. Who do you think each of the following would consult if they were ill:

a) a noble family   b) a rich lawyer
c) a farm labourer   d) a beggar?

Explain the reasons for your choice.

How did the status of women healers change?

IN 1729 A SURGEON in Fulham took on a new apprentice. Nothing surprising about that, you might think, but there was. The surgeon was a woman – her name was Anne Saint and her apprentice was also a woman – Mary Webb.

In fact a number of women surgeons can be found in the records of the sixteenth and seventeenth centuries. They came from families of craftsmen and churchmen, and often had fathers or brothers who were surgeons. A Mrs Cook was appointed as the surgeon-apothecary at Christ's Hospital, London, in the 1570s. As you can see from Sources 1 and 2 such women seem to have been very popular, especially among the poor, who probably made up the majority of their patients.

SOURCE 1 Records of the city of York, 1572. Male doctors had wished to stop Isabel Warwick treating the sick

&& [Isabel Warwick] has the skill in the science of surgery and has done good therein, it is therefore agreed that she, upon her good behaviour, shall use the same without obstruction by any of the surgeons of the city. &&

SOURCE 2 Epitaphs and memorials of several women healers

&& Margaret Colfe of Lewisham. Having been above 40 years a willing nurse, midwife, surgeon, and in part physician to all both rich and poor, without expecting reward. [Lewisham, 1643]

Prudence Potter of Devon – her life was spent in the industrious and successful practice of physic, chirurgery and midwifery. [Devon, 1689]

Dorothy Burton – has excellent skill in chirurgery, sore eyes, aches etc., and has done many famous good cures upon divers poor folks, that were otherwise destitute of help. [1629]

Lady Halkett – she ministered every Wednesday to a multitude of poor infirm persons, besides what she daily sent to persons of all ranks who consulted her in their MALADIES. Next to the study of divinities, she seems to have taken most delight in those of Physic and surgery, in which she was no mean proficient. [1699] &&

By the 1700s, however, women surgeons were disappearing too. One reason for this was education. For centuries anyone who wished to become a physician had to study at university, and women were not allowed to attend the universities. By the 1700s, surgery was going the same way. Many male surgeons were better educated and women, who were rarely allowed to learn Latin and Greek, were unable to match the men's education, however good their practical skills.

In the 1700s it also became fashionable among middle-class families to have a highly educated doctor. Some worried what their friends would think if they continued to consult a woman, no matter how skilful she might be. The fashionable people were only interested in whether doctors had the right kinds of qualifications.

SOURCE 3 John Aubrey, *Brief Lives*, written around 1680. Hobbes is commenting on the fashion of having a learned doctor

&& Hobbes is regarded as one of the greatest philosophers to have lived. Mr Hobbes used to say that he had rather have the advice or take medicine from an experienced old woman, that had been at many sick people's bedsides, than from the learnedest but unexperienced physician. &&

A third reason why women lost their place to men was actually the result of an important invention. In about 1620 Peter Chamberlen invented obstetric forceps, used in the delivery of babies. With forceps a doctor could free a baby from the womb without killing it or its mother. However, anatomical knowledge was needed and it seemed that, as only men had studied anatomy at university, only men could use this life-saving invention. By 1700 men were rapidly taking over the task of delivering babies, something that had probably been the work of women since time began.

■ TASK

Copy these headings and write notes under them to show how each one helped exclude women from the medical professions.

■ Education

■ Fashion

■ Forceps

How would you treat Charles II?

■ ACTIVITY

On 2 February 1685 King Charles II was suddenly taken ill. Twelve doctors clustered around him, trying to save his life.

Your task is to take on the role of one of those doctors and suggest appropriate treatments. The questions below give you a series of choices to make. They are real choices based on actual treatments given to King Charles.

All the details were written up by Sir Charles Scarborough – one of the king's doctors.

SOURCE 1 Charles II

Instructions

1. For each decision choose the option or options that you think will be the most effective, but make sure you have good reasons for choosing them.
2. Record your choices and the reasons for them on a sheet your teacher can give you.

   Remember: if your treatments fail and the king dies, the other doctors may try to blame you for his death! However, if the king lives, you will be richly rewarded. You may win a knighthood, a country house and a large pension!
Good luck!

February 2

At 8 o'clock in the morning the king collapses. For two hours his servants have known he is ill. As he is being shaved he gives a terrible shriek and falls unconscious. Immediately the king's physicians are called.

DECISION 1

Do you recommend to your fellow doctors:
a) opening a vein in the king's arm to bleed sixteen ounces of blood
b) call in Mistress Holder who treated the king's poisoned hand five years ago (see Source 3)
c) do nothing
d) ask for an X-ray to be taken?

SOURCE 2
Sir Charles Scarborough (left). He is demonstrating the anatomy of the arm. Sir Charles Scarborough was one of the doctors who treated Charles II

SOURCE 3 John Aubrey, a scholar and gossip, writing in about 1680

66 *His Majesty King Charles II had hurt his hand which he instructed his surgeons to make well. But they made it much worse, so that it swelled up and poisoned him up to the shoulder. He could not sleep and began to be feverish. Mrs Holder, wife of his Chaplain, among many other gifts has a strange wisdom in the curing of wounds. Mrs Holder was sent for at 11 o'clock at night. She made ready a* POULTICE *and applied it and gave his Majesty sudden ease. He slept well. Next day she dressed it and perfectly cured him, to the great grief of all the surgeons who envy and hate her.* 99

DECISION 2

Within an hour there is no improvement in the king's health. What should you do next:
a) bleed the king again
b) give more time for the first bleeding to work
c) purge the king by giving him pills that will empty his bowels
d) pray?

DECISION 3

Some of the king's servants do not think you are doing enough. They demand that you try another treatment. Do you:
a) give the king more pills to purge him some more
b) tell the servants that you are the experts and you know exactly what you are doing
c) place pigeons against the soles of the king's feet
d) shave the king's head and put burning tongs on his scalp to blister the skin?

February 3

The king can speak again but there is no other improvement. Everyone is growing more worried. Then the king has another attack.

DECISION 4

Should you begin the next stage of treatment by:
a) calling Mrs Holder to give the king a herbal remedy
b) bleeding the king again, this time opening two veins
c) giving the king some more of the Sacred Tincture which will keep his bowels empty
d) leaving the palace as swiftly as possible, saying that you have other patients to attend to?

February 4

The king is much better in the morning. The worst seems to be over but in the afternoon he has another attack.

DECISION 5

Should you:
a) continue bleeding the king
b) continue purging the king
c) prescribe the following medicine recommended by one of your colleagues: spirit of human skull, 40 drops, taken in an ounce and a half of Cordial Julep
d) abandon all treatments?

February 6

The king's health is worsening rapidly. The physicians are undecided about whether to use the remedy below.

> Every other hour – two scruples (two and a half grams) of BEZOAR STONE, a green stone found in the stomach of Persian goats. Bezoar is a much-famed remedy.

DECISION 6

What would you recommend? Should you use this remedy or not?

DECISION 7

The king is dead. Do you:
a) send the palace your bill for payment, knowing that you did your best
b) try to see the new king James II (Charles II's brother) so that you can blame the other doctors for Charles II's death
c) order a carriage and drive towards the coast as fast as you can?

How did you get on?

There is a score sheet on page 110. Use it to calculate your total score.

30 or more
If you scored 30 or more you would have been a very successful doctor in the 1680s.

20–29
If you scored 20–29 you have done well but need to be a little more ruthless in trying your remedies. Perhaps you are too kind to your patients?

10–19
If you scored 10–19 you clearly need a lot more training!

Less than 10
If you scored less than 10 you would have been a failure as a doctor in the 1680s. However, with your treatments the king might have lived!

Medicine from prehistory to 1750: a summary

■ TASK 1

Get a copy of this chart from your teacher. Using all that you have found out about medicine from 1400–1750 fill in the final column.

■ TASK 2

Continuity and change in the Medical Renaissance

A.

Using the completed chart, and what you have found out about medicine during the period 1400–1750, write answers to the following questions. For each one find evidence in the chapter to support your answer.

1. Did women's role in medicine change?
2. Was any important new medical knowledge discovered in this period?
3. Were there any important new ideas about the causes of illness?
4. Were Galen's ideas still important in this period?
5. Did treatments stay the same over the period?
6. Did people live much longer in 1750 than they had done in 1400?

B.

Now use your answers to these questions to help you write an essay explaining whether you agree or disagree with this statement: 'There was far more change than continuity in medicine during the Medical Renaissance.'

	PREHISTORY	EGYPT	GREECE
Who treated illness?	Women / Medicine men	Women / Priests	Women / Gods / Doctors
What did they think caused illness? (Supernatural explanations)		Spirits and gods	
What did they think caused illness? (Natural explanations)		The channels of your body are blocked	The four humours are out of balance
How were illnesses treated?		Herbs / Simple surgery	Diet
How did they try to prevent disease?	Hunter gatherers constantly travelling – reduced the risk of disease	Personal hygiene / Egypt	Personal hygiene / Greece

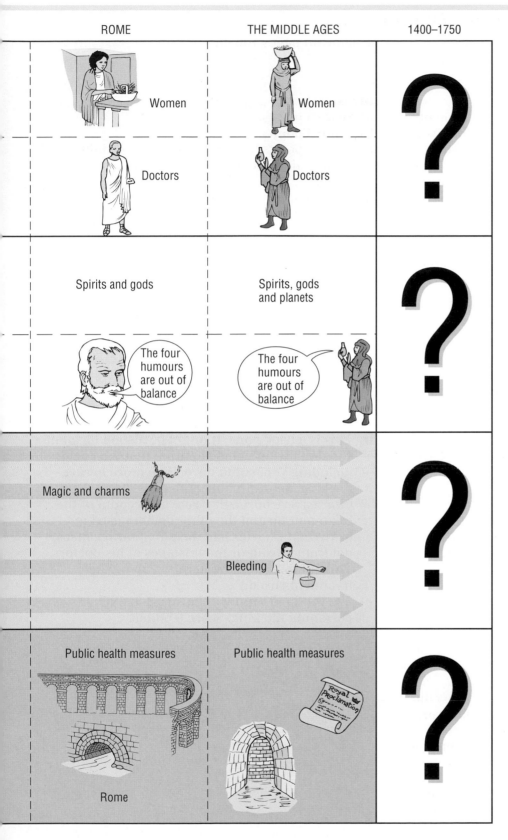

ROME	THE MIDDLE AGES	1400–1750
Women	Women	?
Doctors	Doctors	?
Spirits and gods	Spirits, gods and planets	?
The four humours are out of balance	The four humours are out of balance	?
Magic and charms	Bleeding	?
Public health measures	Public health measures	?
Rome		

■ TASK 3

1. Choose at least one example from this period of medical history to support each of these statements:

a) War has led to medical improvements.

b) Better education helps to improve medical understanding.

c) Better communication helps to improve medical understanding.

d) Great medical discoveries do not always improve treatments immediately.

2. Now write your own statements to sum up how the following factors affected medicine during this period:

■ Individual genius
■ Religion
■ Chance.

■ TASK 4

Write an essay explaining whether you think this was an important period in medical history. You can get an outline from your teacher to help you.

How would you treat Charles II: score sheet

Use this table to add up the points you have scored in the game on pages 106–07.
Mark them on your sheet.

DECISION 1

a) Exactly what the doctors did. Score 3 points.

b) Never! She has not been trained at a university. She's a woman. What can she know about medicine? Score 0 points.

c) This might have done Charles some good, but people may think that you don't know what to do and if the king dies they'll blame you for doing nothing! Score 0 points.

d) Score 0 points, but this is the least of your problems. You are about to be burned as a witch.

DECISION 2

a) Exactly what the doctors did! Score 2 points.

b) Do you believe in the theory of the humours or don't you? The more bleeding the better! Score 0 points.

c) Excellent idea, it will help balance the humours – score 3 points.

d) Very good idea. Pray for the king and yourself but don't let it interrupt the bleeding. Score 1 point.

DECISION 3

a) Good idea – score 2 points.

b) Yes, shout and scream at the servants by all means. You are the expert. However, this won't help the king. Have 1 point for showing that you're in charge.

c) This would be a good idea if the king had the plague but he has a different illness. Score 0 points.

d) Excellent, just what the doctors did in 1685. Score 3 points.

DECISION 4

a) No! You don't want that woman stealing the credit just when your treatments may work. Score 0 points.

b) Excellent again. Hippocrates and Galen would have been proud of you. Score 3 points.

c) Another good idea! Score 3 points.

d) This is the fastest way to execution. People will think you have secretly poisoned the king. Score 0 points.

DECISION 5

a) Score 3 points.

b) Score 3 points.

c) Score 3 points. (If you thought you should have chosen all three of A, B and C have a bonus point!)

d) Score 0 points. How will the king get better if you don't treat him?

DECISION 6

Yes – if you decided to use the bezoar stone score 3 points. It might work and at this stage anything is worth trying. Records show that the king's doctors used 58 different drugs in five days.
No – score 0 points if you decided not to use bezoar.

DECISION 7

a) Score 3 points. You have spent five days trying to save the king with the best methods and medicines. Of course you deserve payment.

b) This is a tricky one. It might be a good idea but you don't want people to think that the doctors, including you, could have done more to save the king. Score 1 point. (After the king's death Charles Scarborough wrote an account of the treatment he and the other doctors used to prove that Charles had died of natural causes, not from poison or the mistakes of his doctors. This is how we know so much about the treatments used.)

c) Are you mad? You will be suspected of poisoning the king. Score 0 points.

chapter 4

MEDICINE AND HEALTH 1750–1900

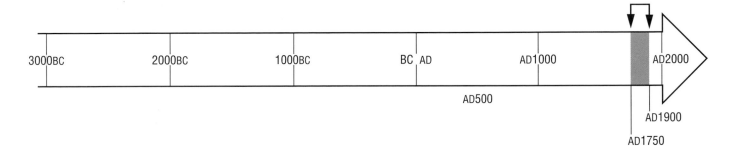

3000BC   2000BC   1000BC   BC AD   AD1000   AD2000

AD500

AD1900

AD1750

Why was there so much progress in this period?

OH NO, NOT AGAIN! You've seen this kind of 'progress' claim before on page 83. However, in Chapter 3 you saw that 350 years of medical progress did very little to improve the health of ordinary people.

In this story of medicine and health you are now coming to a period which is often talked about as a time of great progress. Between 1750 and 1900:

■ scientists and doctors made giant steps forward in understanding the true causes of disease

■ they discovered ways of preventing some of the killer diseases

■ there were enormous improvements in public health. Many towns improved sewers and fresh water supply.

In Chapter 4 you will investigate why historians regard this period as a time of such great progress in medicine and health, and you will discover some of the factors which helped bring about this progress.

You will also look at whether, in this period, unlike the previous one, medical progress at last began to affect the health of ordinary people. Is the news vendor right or is it just wishful thinking?

Read all about it! A century of medical progress. You've never been healthier

Why had they stopped reading Galen in the nineteenth century?

Galen's ideas are questioned

FOR MORE THAN 1500 years Galen's ideas had dominated medicine. In the sixteenth and seventeenth centuries, however, the advances in anatomy and science which you studied in Chapter 3 had begun to challenge Galen's authority.

In the 1700s what we now think of as modern science began to grow up. Instead of looking at ancient books for ideas, scientists now used their own detailed observation, experiment and measurement to build up an accurate picture of the natural world. During this scientific revolution old explanations were questioned – Galen's included – and if they were found to be inaccurate they were abandoned. Gradually the works of Galen and other ancient writers became less and less important.

... but some of Galen's treatments live on!

In the history of medicine you will find that treatments and ideas about disease do not always change at the same pace. People sometimes continue to use treatments long after the ideas on which they are based have been abandoned. This is either because the treatments work, or because there are no alternatives. In the nineteenth century some of Galen's treatments continued to be used as you can see from Source 2.

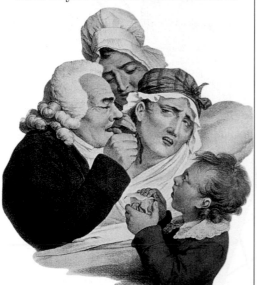

SOURCE 2 Doctor applying leeches to bleed a patient in the late 1700s

SOURCE 1 Why had they stopped reading Galen in the nineteenth century?

New understanding of the body
In the 1500s Vesalius (page 84) had begun a revolution in the understanding of the human body. He showed that Galen's descriptions were incomplete and, sometimes, even wrong. He encouraged all doctors to do their own dissections on human corpses rather than relying on Galen's work.

Knowledge of the world
Scientists gradually discovered that many ancient ideas about the natural world – particularly the Greek theory of the four elements which had formed the basis for the theory of the four humours – were wrong. For example, they discovered that air itself is made up of different gasses.

The microscope
The invention of the microscope helped further to undermine Galen's work. For example, it proved that Harvey's ideas were right (page 89).

From the 1600s doctors and scientists increasingly used microscopes to investigate medical details which Galen could not possibly have discovered. Galen was simply irrelevant to such work.

New explanations for disease
It was difficult to disprove the theory of the four humours by experiment, but by the nineteenth century scientists did not accept it as an explanation of disease – it simply did not fit in with their new understanding of the natural world. They developed their own explanations of disease based on careful observation and research.

The most popular theory in the early 1800s was that 'bad air' caused disease, but by 1860 scientists had found a much more accurate explanation.

PASTEUR GERM THEORY

Training of doctors
These new ideas and techniques were being spread through better training for doctors. It became part of their training to carry out dissections, to use microscopes and to think scientifically. Galen's books were no longer important. The Catholic Church, which had been such a strong supporter of Galen in the Middle Ages, was no longer in control of medical training.

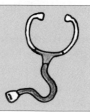

How did changes in the nineteenth century affect medicine and health?

YOU WILL ALREADY know about some of the changes which took place in Britain in the nineteenth century. New industries appeared; workers flocked to the factory towns and the population grew very quickly.

Britain led the way, but similar changes were also taking place in other countries at the same time. Many of these changes had a major impact on medicine and health as you can see from Source 3.

■ TASK

Look at Sources 1 and 3. Choose three changes which you think are particularly important in influencing medicine and health in the period 1750–1900. Explain your choice.

Urbanisation
The growth of towns created many health problems. Poor housing and infected water supplies made killer diseases spread more rapidly than ever before.

Political change
In 1800 Parliament believed it should not interfere in people's lives. If people were unhealthy that was their business! By 1900 Parliament was making laws to improve people's health in a way that would have been unthinkable in earlier centuries: for example, forcing towns to install sewers.

Scientific medicine
Science helped medicine. Scientists discovered the links between micro-organisms and disease. Chemists researching the properties of different substances found, for example, a gas which could be used as an anaesthetic and a dye which killed bacteria.

Technology
New technology helped medicine. For example, developments in steel-making helped to produce a thin syringe needle that did not break; improvements in glass-making led to better microscope lenses and the first thermometer.

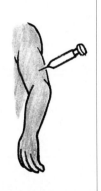

Improved communications
Communications were revolutionised in this period.

Faster trains allowed scientists and doctors to gather at conferences and learn from each others' ideas. By 1900 you could get from London to Edinburgh in nine hours and from London to Paris in less than a day.

There were more newspapers and improved education meant more people could read. News could be reported more quickly because of the invention of the telegraph. For example, details of important scientific experiments carried out in France were reported in British newspapers the next day.

Entrepreneurs
Medicine became big business. Some entrepreneurs made millions of pounds from almost useless remedies. However, others put money into scientific research to find drugs which would help to cure disease.

War
Major wars during the period affected developments in health. For example, the Crimean War in the nineteenth century, led to improvements in the standards of nursing and hospitals.

SOURCE 3   How did life in the nineteenth century affect medicine and health?

What did people die of in the nineteenth century?

DURING THE EIGHTEENTH century no official figures were collected for births, marriages and deaths. It was not until 1801 that the whole population was counted. In 1837 it became law that every birth, marriage and death had to be registered.

1. Source 1 shows how life expectancy and infant mortality changed through the nineteenth century. Do the graphs suggest that health was improving in the nineteenth century or not?

As well as these national statistics, from the middle of the nineteenth century, different groups and individuals around the country also started to keep information about the population of their own area. MEDICAL OFFICERS OF HEALTH were employed by the local authorities and they sent statistical information to the government every year. Source 2 is part of a report from Algernon Adams, Medical Officer of Health for Maidstone in Kent, 1889.

SOURCE 1 Graphs showing life expectancy and infant mortality, 1841–1901

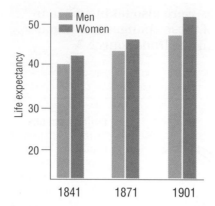

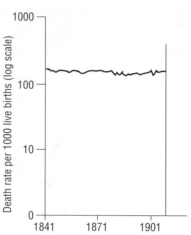

■ TASK

1. Look at Source 2. Which age group suffered the most deaths?
2. List the four most common causes of death among the under fives.
3. The page opposite lists the main infectious diseases of the nineteenth century. Which of these was the most serious problem in Maidstone in 1889?
4. Which were not problems in 1889?
5. Write a paragraph comparing the causes of death in Source 2 with those in Source 2 on page 102.
6. Write a further paragraph comparing the causes of death in Source 2 with causes of death today. You may need to refer to pages 170–71 or ask your teacher for an information sheet.

SOURCE 2 (below) Transcript of a table from the report of the Maidstone Medical Officer of Health, 1889. You can see from the first column that Maidstone was not a big town. Even so it suffered some of the same problems as the large industrial towns

TABLE OF DEATHS during the Year 1889, in the Urban Sanitary District of Maidstone

	Population Estimated to middle 1889	Registered Births	DEATHS FROM ALL CAUSES								DEATHS FROM SPECIFIED CAUSES														
			At all ages	Under 1 year	1 and under 5	5 and under 15	15 and under 25	25 and under 60	60 and up-wards		Smallpox	Measles	Scarlatina	Diphtheria	Croup	Whooping Cough	Typhus	Typhoid	Diarrhoea and Dysentery	Cholera	Phthisis	Bronchitis, Pneumonia, and Pleurisy	Heart Disease	Injuries	All other Diseases*
EAST MAIDSTONE Males........	15,422	280	113	38	9	9	3	26	28	Under 5		6		2	1				4		1	5		4	24
										5 upwrds				1							11	13	6	4	31
Females....		246	120	35	17	8	4	15	41	Under 5		9	1	1	2				3			7	2	2	25
										5 upwrds		1		2							2	9	9	2	43
Total.......		526	233																						
WEST MAIDSTONE Males........	14,201	207	107	30	20	5	10	19	23	Under 5		4	1	5					3		1	7		1	28
										5 upwrds				5							4	6	4	10	28
Females....		196	110	23	18	13	4	21	31	Under 5		1		6					1			6	1		26
										5 upwrds				7				1	1		8	15	8		29
Total.......		403	217																						
Totals....	29,623	929	450	126	64	35	21	81	123	Under 5		20	2	14	3				11		2	25	3	7	103
										5 upwrds		1		15				1	1		25	43	27	16	131

TB (Tuberculosis)
(also called consumption and phthisis)
Method of infection: the bacteria spread in the tiny droplets of moisture produced when coughing. Sometimes spread through UNPASTEURISED cows' milk.
Symptoms: coughing with blood-stained spit, weight loss, chest pains. Charles Dickens wrote this description of TB:
'… the forehead covered with drops of sweat, the cheeks painted a livid crimson, the eyes sunk, the palms of the hands hot and painfully hot to the touch; the breath offensive, quick, and laborious; and the cough so incessant as scarce to allow the wretched sufferer the time to tell his complaints'.
Who: all ages. TB affected about 15 per cent of the population during the nineteenth century.

Measles
Method of infection: the VIRUS spreads through droplets of moisture produced when coughing and sneezing; highly infectious.
Symptoms: at first the child suffers from catarrh and then a speckled rash appears which spreads across the body.
Who: mainly children.

Smallpox
Method of infection: the virus is spread like flu from person to person by coughing and sneezing and by touching an infected person.
Symptoms: starts with a rash that develops into pus-filled blisters which are very unpleasant. The blisters become crusted and fall off leaving deep scars.
Who: had been a major killer of all ages, but by 1850 smallpox was gradually being eliminated by vaccination.

Cholera
Method of infection: acquired from CONTAMINATED water.
Symptoms: watery diarrhoea and sickness followed by rapid dehydration and death, sometimes within 24 hours.
Who: all ages. There were major cholera outbreaks in 1832, 1848 and 1866.

1. Use your own research to write an entry for scarlatina (scarlet fever).

Diphtheria
Method of infection: the bacteria spread through droplets of moisture produced when coughing and sneezing and through contact with articles of clothing soiled by the infected person.
Symptoms: there are three different types of diphtheria. They are characterised by paralysis, bleeding and the blocking of the throat resulting in suffocation.
Who: particularly children.

Whooping cough
Method of infection: the bacteria spread through droplets of moisture produced when coughing and sneezing; very infectious.
Symptoms: catarrh followed by sickness and fits of coughing that sometimes last for six weeks. Gradually the coughing gets better and after three months the disease can have cleared up.
Who: children suffer badly often becoming so weak that they die of other infections like pneumonia.

Typhoid
Method of infection: an infectious disease where bacteria are passed on through food and water contaminated by excreta (urine, faeces, sweat) of a human carrier. It can also be carried by flies which infect food.
Symptoms: after two weeks the bacteria cause headaches, prolonged fever, constipation and then diarrhoea. The disease usually lasts for four weeks but can be fatal.
Who: attacks all ages. Another disease called **Typhus** has similar symptoms and was sometimes confused with typhoid but it is passed on by bites from body lice.

Lung infections such as **bronchitis** and **pneumonia** were also common. They are secondary infections which often kill people who are already weakened by another infection or by bad diet.
The people who were most vulnerable to these killer diseases were the poor, very young children, and those living in bad housing. If you were all three – an infant, born into a poor family, and living in bad housing – then your chances of suffering one of these diseases were much higher.

Influenza
Method of infection: the virus spreads through droplets of moisture from the nose produced by coughing and sneezing.
Symptoms: coughing, pain, shivering, sickness and headaches.
Who: all ages particularly those who are weak. There were regular flu epidemics throughout the nineteenth century.

■ ACTIVITY

One of the most important features of the nineteenth century was 'urbanisation'. Cities and towns in Britain were growing fast. In these towns many people lived in overcrowded housing with little ventilation; they had no clean water supply, and their diet was poor.

Make a table listing the diseases on this page in one column. Alongside each disease explain whether you think urbanisation would increase the risk of the disease spreading. Give reasons for your answers.

Smallpox: how did Jenner make his breakthrough?

THE GREATEST MEDICAL triumph before 1850 was the discovery of a way to prevent smallpox, which had previously been one of the biggest killer diseases.

The first method of prevention – inoculation

Epidemics of smallpox broke out in Britain every few years. Many died from it. The horror of smallpox was not just the danger of death but the physical scars it caused. For many, especially the poor, smallpox also left a family isolated. Tradesmen and friends were frightened away. When someone had the disease their house, belongings and goods were disinfected, and the damage that this caused would not be paid for. Sufferers feared they would lose their jobs. To avoid financial ruin families often hid smallpox cases, using treatments similar to those used by Grace Mildmay in the seventeenth century (see page 92).

In the eighteenth century a method of avoiding smallpox was introduced to Britain from China where it had been used for centuries. Chinese doctors had noticed that people who had suffered a mild form of smallpox often survived during later epidemics. They developed a method of inoculation which involved spreading matter from a smallpox scab onto an open cut in the skin. This gave people a mild dose of the disease and protected them from the full force of a severe attack.

This method of inoculation gradually spread through Asia helped by the growing trade between China and the rest of Asia. It was observed in Turkey by Lady Mary Wortley Montague. She had only just survived an attack of smallpox and was keen that her children should not suffer the same disfiguring disease. In 1721 she had her children inoculated and they survived the next smallpox epidemic. Lady Montague was an influential woman; she had many friends who were doctors. They saw the potential of preventing smallpox and of making money from inoculation. Soon it became big business whenever smallpox epidemics raged during the eighteenth century. As you saw from Source 18 on pages 100–01 inoculations were common, and some doctors made a fortune from mass inoculation (see Source 2).

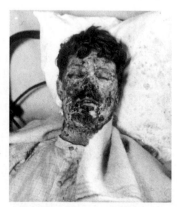

SOURCE 1 A patient with severe smallpox scabs

SOURCE 2 Dorothy Fisk, *Doctor Jenner of Berkely*, 1959. You can find other examples of inoculations on page 100, recorded by James Woodforde

❝ *The Suttons in eleven years inoculated 2514 people, for substantial fees. They also sold, for anything between fifty and a hundred pounds, to doctors living at a safe distance from them, the secrets of their methods. They had their own inoculation house in Ingatestone in Essex where patients were prepared for the operation and rested after it.* ❞

In Maidstone mass inoculations were carried out by Daniel Sutton during an epidemic in 1766. Source 3 shows their impact. This information was recorded by Reverend John Howlett who was a supporter of mass inoculation.

1. Draw a graph to show the figures in Source 3.
2. Mark on the graph the date when mass inoculations were carried out in Maidstone.
3. How effective was inoculation in your opinion?

Date	Total deaths	Deaths from smallpox	
		Total	As % of all deaths
1740–51	1594	260	16.3
1752–63	1616	202	12.5
1764–75	1798	76	4.2
1776–87	1992	122	6.1
1788–99	2308	31	1.3

SOURCE 3 Deaths from smallpox in Maidstone, 1740–99

There seems little doubt that inoculation reduced the likelihood of dying from smallpox but even inoculation involved some risk. Some people died of the mild dose that they were given. Others became carriers of the disease and it is probable that they spread smallpox to people with whom they came into contact. Therefore some people refused the treatment.

As you can see from Source 2, doctors also charged a substantial fee for their work, so the very poor could not afford inoculation.

1. What factors led to inoculation being introduced to Britain in 1721?
2. Why did inoculation not totally solve the problem of smallpox?
3. If you had lived in Maidstone in the 1700s would you have paid to be inoculated?

The second method of prevention – Edward Jenner and vaccination

Edward Jenner was a doctor in Gloucestershire. When Jenner offered inoculation against smallpox he was puzzled to find that many people refused. He discovered from the local farmers that people believed that they would not catch smallpox if they had already had a mild disease called cowpox. They did not think they needed Jenner's inoculations. Jenner examined this idea and discovered that dairy maids, who often caught cowpox, did seem less likely than other people to catch smallpox. He wondered whether he could use cowpox as a method of preventing smallpox.

> **SOURCE 4** Extracts from Dr Jenner's Casebook, published in *An enquiry into the causes and effects of Variola Vaccinae, known by the name of cowpox*, 1798
>
> 66 **Case 16**
> *Sarah Nelmes, a dairy maid near this place, was infected with cowpox from her master's cows in May 1796. A large sore and the usual symptoms were produced.*
> **Case 17** *James Phipps*
> *I selected a healthy boy, about eight years old. The matter was taken from the [cowpox] sore on the hand of Sarah Nelmes and it was inserted on 14 May 1796 into the boy by two cuts each about half an inch long. On the seventh day he complained of uneasiness, on the ninth he became a little chilly, lost his appetite and had a slight headache and spent the night with some degree of restlessness, but on the following day he was perfectly well.*
>
> *In order to ascertain that the boy was secure from the CONTAGION of the smallpox, he was inoculated with smallpox matter, but no disease followed. Several months later he was again inoculated with smallpox matter but again no disease followed.* 99

Jenner tried the same experiment and recorded his observations with 23 different cases. Only then did he conclude 'that the cowpox protects the human constitution from the infection of the smallpox'.

Jenner wrote up his findings and submitted them to the Royal Society for publication in 1798. However, as you will see from page 118, there was much opposition to Jenner's ideas and the Society rejected his work.

Jenner therefore published his findings himself (see Source 4). He called the technique vaccination because the Latin word for cow is *vacca*. His book was widely read and distributed. Parliament thought Jenner's work was very significant and he was given a grant of £30,000 to open a vaccination clinic in London.

By 1803 doctors were using the technique in America. Thomas Jefferson, President of the United States, championed it. He believed Jenner had made the complete eradication of smallpox a possibility. In 1805 Napoleon had all his soldiers vaccinated, and by 1812 Arabic and Turkish translations of Jenner's work were being sold in central Asia. In 1852, more than 50 years after Jenner's discovery, the British government made vaccination compulsory. You can see the results in Source 6.

1. Look back at Source 2 on page 114. What effect has vaccination had on Maidstone?
2. How were:
a) chance
b) scientific investigation
c) government action
   important in the discovery and development of vaccination?

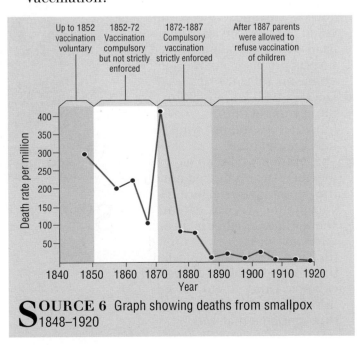

SOURCE 5 Cowpox scabs on Sarah Nelmes's arm

Up to 1852 vaccination voluntary | 1852-72 Vaccination compulsory but not strictly enforced | 1872-1887 Compulsory vaccination strictly enforced | After 1887 parents were allowed to refuse vaccination of children

SOURCE 6 Graph showing deaths from smallpox 1848–1920

Why was there opposition to vaccination?

You might think that vaccination sounds like a good idea. Many people agreed, and Jenner's methods were widely copied. However, you will also be aware from your study of the history of medicine that new ideas have often been opposed. The Royal Society refused to publish Jenner's research because of opposition to his ideas. After Jenner had published his findings, more than 100 leading London doctors signed a declaration of confidence in his research and announced their support for vaccination. Despite this, opposition still continued.

There were many reasons why people were against vaccination.

- Some people simply did not like anything new. What's more, this particular idea sounded very odd.
- Others did not accept the evidence that Jenner had recorded. Sceptics thought it was unbelievable that a disease that comes from cows could protect people against a human disease such as smallpox. Jenner still could not offer any explanation as to why vaccination worked so he was unable to answer the criticisms satisfactorily.
- Doctors who were making money out of doing inoculations did not want to lose that income.
- Vaccination was seen as dangerous, and indeed not all the doctors who performed vaccination were as careful as Jenner. Some patients died when careless doctors mixed up the vaccines and infected them with smallpox instead of cowpox. Other doctors used infected needles and killed their patients that way.

SOURCE 7 'The cowpock – or – the Wonderful Effects of the New Inoculation' by James Gillray

SOURCE 8 'The curse of humankind' by George Cruikshank, 1808

Added to all these problems was the fact that vaccination was not free. Some people, particularly the poor, were not vaccinated, and had to run the serious risk of catching smallpox – 40,000 people died in a dreadful epidemic in the late 1830s.

The greatest opposition to vaccination came after the government made it compulsory in the 1850s. Never before had any government forced a medical treatment on the entire population. There was outrage against this attack on personal liberty. Compulsory vaccination was seen by some as an attempt by doctors and the medical profession to take over all health care. Opposition to it was particularly strong among herbalists. In 1887 the opposition succeeded and parents could refuse to have their children vaccinated.

1. Look at Sources 7 and 8. Which of the cartoons was inspired by the Anti-vaccine Society in 1802 when Jenner, with the aid of a government grant, opened his vaccination clinic in St Pancras, London?
2. Which cartoon was in favour of the use of Jenner's new vaccine?
3. Why was there so much opposition to vaccination in the nineteenth century?

■ ACTIVITY

Divide into pairs. One person in each pair list the arguments for vaccination. The other list arguments against vaccination. Now present your case to your partner as persuasively as you can.

How important was Jenner's work?

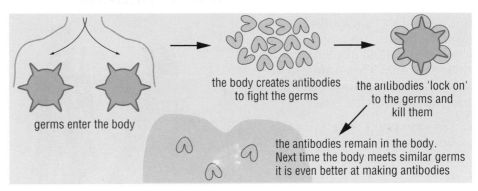

SOURCE 9   How immunity works

We now know why Jenner's vaccination worked: cowpox is almost the same virus as smallpox so that when the body reacts to cowpox it also becomes IMMUNE to the very similar disease of smallpox. Jenner did not realise this; he did not even know that smallpox was caused by a virus. There were no powerful microscopes which would have enabled him to examine smallpox matter and see what it contained. He could not explain how or why his method worked. It was simply the result of careful observation and experiment.

Jenner's vaccination undoubtedly saved many lives, and he is now considered significant for other reasons as well. Jenner was the first immuniser. He made deliberate use of the knowledge that recovering from a mild form of a disease gives human beings protection (or IMMUNITY) against a more severe form. This was the basis of the science of immunology which was to be pursued with such success by Pasteur and others half a century later – a story which you will follow up on page 128.

4. Why couldn't Jenner explain why vaccination worked?
5. If doctors could prevent smallpox, why could they not prevent other diseases?
6. How do you think the ideas of Jenner might prove useful to other doctors searching for the causes of disease?

■ ACTIVITY

Source 10 is to be used to illustrate an encyclopaedia entry about Jenner. Write the text for the encyclopaedia entry to go with it. Describe what the statue shows, then explain:

■ who Jenner was
■ how he developed vaccination
■ why his work was important.

SOURCE 10   A nineteenth-century statue of Jenner injecting the arm of James Phipps

Would your child survive in nineteenth-century Britain?

■ ACTIVITY

You have seen this kind of exercise before, on pages 50–51 when you looked at medicine in ancient Rome. This time you are in nineteenth-century Britain, and it is your child who is ill.

1. Get into pairs. You will each need a counter to move around the game board.
2. Choose one of the **families** from Box A.
3. Your child has a terrible cough and a high temperature. Choose one of the **healers** from Box B.
4. On the board opposite start by putting your counter on the number your healer instruction tells you to.
5. Take turns following the instructions in your square. At each turn note down what happened, using the sheet you can get from your teacher.
6. If your child dies or recovers before your partner's, try the game again using a different healer.
7. When you have finished the game discuss with your partner whether the different healers, treatments and remedies were helpful. You will find out more about them on pages 122–23.

Box B: Healers

Visit a doctor – go to square 1.

Using a patent remedy – go to square 21.

Treat the child yourself **at home** – go to square 7.

A chemist – go to square 8.

A herbalist – go to square 4.

Box A: Families

Mr and Mrs Grace are very well off. They inherited land and money from their parents.

Mr Gilbert is a clerk in a shipping office, working ten hours a day. He does not want his wife to work as that would not be 'respectable'. They have just enough money to live on, provided there are no unexpected bills.

Mrs Williams earns a few pennies doing laundry. Her husband works at the docks, provided an 'ill wind' does not keep the ships out of port. If there are no ships he earns nothing.

WILL YOUR CHILD SURVIVE?

1

Your choice of doctor depends on how much money you have. Graces go to 11. Gilberts go to 20. Williamses go to 27.

2

Your sister says you must keep the child wrapped up warm at home with the window closed. If you agree, go to 14. If not, go to 7.

3

Buy Morrison's Vegetable Universal Compound, pills that cure everything by purging the patient. Go to 14.

4

At the herbalist the Williamses cannot afford the prices. Choose another healer. The Graces and Gilberts decide to try a herbal cure. The herbalist recommends treacle, tincture of lobelia and aniseed water. If you agree, go to 29.

5

The dispensary gives free medicine to working people who don't have much money. You try the medicine. Go to 25.

6

The Williamses discover they cannot afford any more pills. Go to 22. The Graces and Gilberts buy some more. Go to 25.

7

You are given lots of advice. If you listen to your friend, go to 26. If you listen to your sister, go to 2. If you listen to your brother, go to 18.

8

The chemist mixes you a remedy made from sodium tartrate, Ipecacuhana wine and laudanum. The Williamses cannot afford this mixture. Choose another healer. If the Graces and Gilberts choose this remedy, go to 15. If they do not, choose another healer.

9

On your way home you meet a man selling Dr Drummond's Herbal Tonic which he says cures any disease or disability. If you buy some, go to 16. If not, choose another healer.

10

There is still no improvement. The doctor suggests you take the child to the seaside to drink seawater. It can be very effective. If you agree, go to 19. If you disagree, go to 22.

11

Your physician is very confident. He has seen plenty of these cases. He recommends bleeding the child, followed by purging. If you agree, go to 24. If not, choose another healer.

12

The bleeding and purging bring no improvement. The doctor recommends another medicine to help your child vomit to clear out her system. You can't afford the medicine so he sends you to 5.

13

You take the child home, but you have no work so it is hard to feed her. Go to 17.

14

The treatment has no immediate effect. You could try some more and go to 6 or, if not, go to 22.

15

The remedy is not working. The chemist suggests doubling the dose. The Gilberts cannot afford more. Choose another healer. The Graces can afford another dose. If you choose this, go to 23. If not, choose another healer.

16

Dr Drummond's Herbal Tonic cures almost everything but not your child's fever. Choose another healer.

17

The doctor says the child is no better. He says he will try bleeding her, but he is not hopeful. Go to 30.

18

Your brother says the best remedy is to skin and roast a mouse and then get the child to eat it whole. If you agree, go to 28. If not, go back to 7.

19

The journey is too much for the weak child. She dies. When the physician's bill arrives you pay it. He did everything he could.

20

Your doctor recommends bleeding the child and then regular doses of purging. If you agree, go to 12. If you disagree, go to 22.

21

At the shop there are many patent medicines to choose from. Choose 3 or 31.

22

It is time to choose another healer or go to 9.

23

Your child recovers. Perhaps there was something in the remedy or perhaps it was because your child had clean bedding, plenty of food and fresh water.

24

The bleeding and purging have not helped. Your doctor bleeds the child again and also makes her vomit. Go to 10.

25

There is still no improvement. Choose another healer or go to 30.

26

Your friend says that the best remedy is for the child to ride a donkey seven times in a circle or be passed under it seven times. If you agree, go to 14. If not, go back to 7 or choose another healer.

27

The doctor for the poor thinks it is best to bleed the child but says she is too weak through lack of food. He recommends you take her home to rest and to feed her and then bring her back. If you agree, go to 13. If not, choose another healer.

28

Your child dies. Your brother says there was nothing wrong with his suggestion. You should have listened to him sooner.

29

The fever falls briefly then returns. If you decide to go back to the herbalist, go to 32. If not, choose another healer.

30

Your child grows weaker and dies. You do not blame the doctor or the medicines. They were the best you could get.

31

Buy Holloway's pills and ointment which cure everything by purging the patient. Go to 14.

32

The herbalist recommends a mixture of dropwort and comfrey. The Gilberts cannot afford another treatment and choose another healer. The Graces buy the mixture and go to 23.

Were doctors and medicines helpful?

IF YOU HAD an infectious disease such as whooping cough (the disease in the activity on pages 120–21) doctors and other healers could have done little to help you for most of the nineteenth century. Many of their methods such as bleeding and purging were similar to remedies which had been used a thousand years earlier. Nevertheless, some important changes were under way.

Doctors

From the 1750s ordinary people were able to call on the services of a local doctor or general practitioner. Doctors usually trained through an apprenticeship. They attended medical lectures and walked the wards of a hospital as the pupil of a respected surgeon or physician. They learned to use new devices such as the stethoscope which was invented in 1816. The modern-style stethoscope was developed in 1860. They were aware of the most effective drugs and herbal remedies for common ailments. In addition to this, doctors acted as 'male midwives'. The majority of local doctors were well respected because they worked hard. They usually had standard charges but these were often waived if a patient was too poor to pay. At the beginning of the 1800s doctors had good incomes, mainly from their wealthy patients but also from contracts with the local parish for the care, midwifery and vaccination of the poor.

Medicines

Even so, the cost of medicines was a problem when doctors treated the poor. Dispensaries began to appear. These were created to provide the poor with cheap medicines and doctors were then paid by the trustees of the dispensary who gave their money out of charity. In many towns the work of the dispensaries increased so much that they became hospitals, offering a large range of services. Other dispensaries were opened by doctors to provide a shop for their services. By the 1840s half the population of England were enrolled at dispensaries by paying weekly contributions.

Domestic medicine

Many illnesses were still treated at home, as they had been throughout the centuries. Home care had changed little – providing comfort, food and warmth so long as the family could afford them. This approach was dominated by common sense and useful information passed from generation to generation.

Domestic medicine of this sort rarely provided a cure but it gave the patient a sense of security and control over their own treatment. However, one useful development was the introduction of thermometers which helped home carers to make simple diagnoses.

Home carers used treatments such as herbal remedies which they had learnt from their ancestors or which had been published in early medical books.

Patent medicines

By 1800 people were supplementing these cures with visits to 'quack' doctors or remedies bought from shops, 'patent' medicines or 'cure alls'. These made little or no contribution to the improvement of health but were cheaper than prescriptions from doctors.

Another reason why people bought patent medicines or visited 'quacks' was that qualified doctors could not cure many illnesses. In the 1850s James Ward set up in Leeds as a 'cancer curer' using herbal remedies. He was criticised by local doctors but challenged them to a contest, each to treat twenty patients. The winner was to be the one who had most surviving patients. No doctor took up his challenge. Even though they thought Ward's remedies were useless they knew that their own more scientific methods were no better.

Patent medicines in the nineteenth century were big business. They did not come under any government control until the 1880s. That meant that false claims could be made without any fear of prosecution. There was also no control over the manufacturing standards or the ingredients in the medicines – some of which were positively dangerous. Deaths and illnesses resulting from overdoses and addiction were common if the pills were taken regularly.

James Morrison started manufacturing his Vegetable Universal Medicines in 1825. They were made of lard, wax, turpentine, soap and ginger. They had no active ingredient yet the pills were supposed to cure everything from fever, scarlatina, TB, smallpox and measles to the effects of old age. By 1834 Morrison was selling over one million boxes of pills a year throughout Europe and the British Empire.

SOURCE 1 From F.B. Smith, *The People's Health*, 1971

66 *The man who came to see Dr Strachan of Clackmannan, Scotland in 1861 was one of many poor patients who were suffering from leg ulcers. We now know that this, with typhus, is a classic indication of poor diet and hygiene. The doctor recorded that his patient 'had been at many doctors, and had tried all the Holloway's ointments and other infallible remedies. [Holloway's ointments were 'cure all' medicines advertised and sold widely.]*

The doctor examined him and 'with great difficulty ... got him a larger allowance from the poor's funds, and some of his friends assisted him ... As soon as the man's system got into good condition the ulcers began to heal and ... the poor man was restored and fitted for his work'.

When the man next met Dr Strachan he informed the doctor that he was getting on very well. 'Well doctor, I tell you what it was that cured my legs, and it will be useful to other folk. It was just moose wels [spider's webs]. Jenny Donald advised me to try them, and they cured my legs at once.' 99

A DRESSMAKER'S DILEMMA

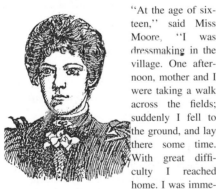

"At the age of sixteen," said Miss Moore, "I was dressmaking in the village. One afternoon, mother and I were taking a walk across the fields; suddenly I fell to the ground, and lay there some time. With great difficulty I reached home. I was immediately put to bed, and two doctors were summoned, both of whom were of opinion that my fainting was due to anaemia and neuralgia. I was like a mad thing at times: the pain drove me almost frantic."

"You look robust and healthy enough now."

"Yes, and I feel well and strong too. But for nearly four years, I was racked with pain in my head, neck, and shoulders. People thought I should die, and death to me would have been a happy release. My heart was also disordered for I had palpitation, and dreaded going upstairs. But now" (she concluded), "I can run up with anyone, and can do a day's sewing with perfect ease."

"To what do you attribute so great a change?"

"To nothing else than Dr. Williams' Pink Pills for Pale People."

MOTHERS
OUGHT
TO
KNOW
THIS.

If your Daughters have Pale Faces, Weakness, Palpitation, Bloodlessness, NICHOLL'S MAYHATINE BLOOD PILLS quickly bring the rosy colour to the pallid cheeks, and change a delicate, undeveloped irregular girl into a strong, well-developed woman. They are tasteless, make rich, red blood; invaluable to Ladies as a Strengthening Regulator. All Chemists, or post free 3 doz., 1s. 1½d.; 9 doz., 2s. 9d.; 18 doz., 4s 6d.

I. W. NICHOLL, Phar. Chemist, **25 High St., BELFAST.** Thousands of Testimonials.

SOURCE 2 Advertisements for patent medicines

---

1. What cured the patient in Source 1?
2. What sort of treatment did the patient think had cured him?
3. Was the doctor able to cure the patient's illness?
4. Look at Source 2. What did these patent medicines claim to cure?
5. Why do you think people bought 'cure all' products in the nineteenth century?

Improved medicines

In the late 1800s there was some progress in the production of medicines. In the 1880s the government introduced laws to control the making of patent medicines. By 1900 many of the harmful ingredients were removed from the 'cure all' pills.

The rapidly-developing chemical industry also discovered the first really effective chemical drugs in the 1880s – the painkillers aspirin and antipyrin. As scientific research into drugs developed so did the interest of manufacturers. By 1900 companies like Boots, Wellcome and Beecham had formed the basis of the pharmaceutical industry which we know today.

■ ACTIVITY

1. Draw two spider diagrams to summarise who treated illnesses in 1700 and in 1900. You can look at page 104 to help you.
2. On the 1900 diagram circle the changes in one colour and the continuities in another.
3. How much change was there in who treated illnesses between 1700 and 1900?

Could you see a woman doctor in the 1850s?

THE SIMPLE ANSWER to that question is 'No'! Six hundred years of change had steadily reduced the status of women in medicine.

In the Middle Ages the Church allowed only men to train as physicians.

In the 1600s the Church also took over the licensing of all healers. It did not give licences to wise women or village healers because they were often suspected of being witches.

As you saw on page 105, by the 1700s, surgeons also had to have a university degree. As women could not go to university they were barred from becoming surgeons.

In the 1700s male doctors became fashionable, and began to take over the traditional role of midwives among wealthy families because they were the only ones trained to use the new forceps.

Finally, in 1852, the government introduced the Medical Registration Act which required all doctors to belong to one of the Colleges of Physicians, Surgeons or Apothecaries. All of these were closed to women!

Of course, women still played the major role as healers in the home, and as nurses, but the days when they could become doctors were long over.

In the 1850s women began to fight back. However, the problems for ambitious women began long before they reached the age when they might want to study medicine. Schools for girls were a rarity before the 1860s – certainly ones that taught anything other than reading, writing, cooking and dressmaking. Science? That was a subject for boys! Even those girls lucky enough to be educated at a good school found that their days of learning were over when they reached their mid-teens because women were not allowed to attend universities. Most men could not see any sense in educating women when their most important roles were as obedient wives, dutiful mothers and efficient housekeepers.

Despite these obstacles a handful of women fought for the right to become doctors. Elizabeth Blackwell was the first woman to qualify as a doctor in the United States in 1849. She visited England ten years later, inspiring Elizabeth Garrett to follow in her footsteps. Elizabeth Garrett was the first woman to qualify in Britain as a doctor but she had to overcome immense difficulties first to get training, then to be allowed to practise as a doctor.

■ ACTIVITY

Boxes A–D tell the story of four stages in the fight by women to become doctors. Boxes E–H explain the different ways in which men tried to block women's progress. Can you match up the boxes in pairs, showing how men tried to push back each advance by women?

Box A
During the 1860s Elizabeth Garrett worked as a nurse and then attended lectures at the Middlesex Hospital.

Box C
In 1874 six women, led by Sophia Jex-Blake, completed the medical course at Edinburgh University.

Box B
Elizabeth Garrett passed all the exams to qualify as a doctor. The final step before she could work as a doctor was to become a member of one of the Colleges of Surgeons, Physicians or Apothecaries.

Box D
In 1876 a law was passed opening all medical qualifications to women.

Box E
The Colleges of Surgeons and Physicians refused to allow women members which therefore stopped Elizabeth from working as a doctor. She had to take the College of Apothecaries to court before it accepted her as a member. After that it too changed its rules so that women could not become members.

Box F
Male students at the hospital protested that Elizabeth Garrett should not be allowed to attend lectures.

Box G
For five years after 1876 the Royal College of Surgeons refused to allow anyone to take exams in midwifery as a way of preventing women learning alongside men.

Box H
Edinburgh University said that it could only give medical degrees to men. The women had to complete their degrees at Dublin or Zurich in Switzerland.

SOURCE 1 Letter from Elizabeth Garrett to a friend, 1859. Her father did help her later

❝ I have just concluded a satisfactory talk with father on the medical subject. He does not like it, I think. He said the whole idea was disgusting and he could not entertain it for a moment. I asked what there was to make doctoring more disgusting than nursing, which women were also doing and which ladies had done publicly in the Crimea. He could not tell me … I think he will probably come round in time. I mean to renew the subject pretty often. ❞

SOURCE 2 Thomas Huxley, a leading scientist, 1851

❝ In every excellent characteristic, whether mental or physical, the average woman is inferior to the average man. ❞

SOURCE 3 The views of the novelist W.M. Thackeray in the 1850s on what an ideal woman should be like

❝ An exquisite slave: a humble, flattering, tea-making, pianoforte-playing being, who laughs at our jokes, however old they may be; coaxes us and fondly lies to us throughout life. ❞

SOURCE 4 A statement made by students at Middlesex Hospital, London, in 1861 in protest at Elizabeth Garrett attending lectures

❝ We consider that the mixture of sexes in the same class is likely to lead to results of an unpleasant character.

Lecturers are likely to feel some restraint through the presence of females in giving that explicit enunciation of some facts which is necessary.

The presence of young females as spectators in the operating theatre is an outrage on our natural instincts and feelings and calculated to destroy those sentiments of respect and admiration with which the sex is regarded by all right-thinking men. Such feelings are a mark of civilisation and refinement. ❞

■ ACTIVITY

Write a reply from Elizabeth Garrett to the medical students who wrote the letter in Source 4. Try not to be too rude! It might make them worse.

SOURCE 5 Elizabeth Garrett, the first woman to qualify as a doctor in Britain

1. Were men or women doing more to care for the sick around 1860?
2. Read Source 1. Why did many men accept women as nurses but not doctors?
3. What does Source 3 suggest are the qualities of an ideal woman?
4. Why was it nearly impossible for women to become doctors?
5. Explain how each of these factors helped limit or increase the role of women in medicine:

   ■ religion
   ■ governments
   ■ technology
   ■ education
   ■ individuals.

Nursing

Despite the obstacles to women becoming doctors, they continued to exercise a powerful influence over other areas of medicine – particularly nursing which, as you can see from Source 1, was one of the 'acceptable' medical jobs for a woman.

In the 1850s female nurses went to work in the Crimea. These nurses included two women who later became celebrated figures: Mary Seacole, a Black nurse who fought racial prejudice to establish her career, and who paid her own way out to the Crimea; and Florence Nightingale who was sent by the British government to run the army hospitals with a team of nurses. This was the first time women had been used as army nurses. The story of how Florence Nightingale changed hospital care is told on the next two pages.

■ TASK

Use your own research to find out about Mary Seacole. Your teacher can give you a research sheet to help you.

How did Florence Nightingale improve hospitals?

FLORENCE NIGHTINGALE IS one of the most celebrated individuals of the nineteenth century. Most people have heard of her work as a nurse in the Crimea, but more important was what she did after she returned to Britain from the Crimea.

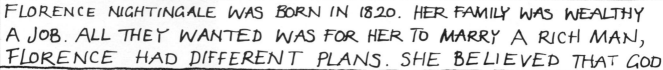

FLORENCE NIGHTINGALE WAS BORN IN 1820. HER FAMILY WAS WEALTHY A JOB. ALL THEY WANTED WAS FOR HER TO MARRY A RICH MAN, FLORENCE HAD DIFFERENT PLANS. SHE BELIEVED THAT GOD

1. Over the previous 100 years a lot of hospitals had been opened. Secretly, Florence Nightingale visited hospitals and read about them. Conditions in many were awful.

No one knows how to look after her. That nurse is drunk. Bringing her here is as good as giving her poison.

2. Florence Nightingale told her family she was going to be a nurse.

A nurse!

You might as well be a servant!

You don't expect me to hang about this drawing room all my life. I will go out and work. You must look at me as if I were your son.

5 SOME MEN DIDN'T LIKE HAVING A WOMAN TELLING THEM HOW TO RUN THINGS. BUT IN SIX MONTHS, FLORENCE NIGHTINGALE DID CHANGE THINGS.

You must have privacy for an amputation.

Boil those sheets and towels — we need everything completely clean.

Patients need good food.

I don't care if the army say no — we need those things now.! I'll pay for them.

She hired 200 builders to rebuild a ward block although the army said it could not be done.

8. But she travelled under a false name on a different ship. She avoided all the publicity. She had other plans.

If I can improve the hospitals in the Crimea, then I can do it here.

9. Florence went to see the Queen. She gave an 800 page report to the government, telling them what had to be changed.

fresh air... clean floors and sheets... better food... trained nurses... plenty of light...

10. In three years the death rate in army hospitals was cut by half.

With hospitals like this you might as well be taking soldiers out onto Salisbury Plain and shooting them.

11. In 1860, Florence Nightingale published her 'Notes for Nursing'. It was a bestseller.

It's very practical. This one has an extra section on looking after babies.

■ **ACTIVITY**

It is 1907. Florence Nightingale is being cited for the Order of Merit (see frame 14). Write out the citation using the information on these two pages and your own research. The citation should explain what Florence Nightingale achieved and why her achievements are important.

AND HER PARENTS DID NOT EXPECT THEIR DAUGHTER TO GET HAVE CHILDREN AND LIVE HAPPILY EVER AFTER. HOWEVER WANTED HER TO BE A NURSE.

3. In 1851, Florence secretly went to Germany to work in a hospital for three months. Then back in London, she got her first job running a hospital for sick 'gentlewomen'. It was not what she really wanted. The patients in the hospital were rich; Florence wanted to help the poor. It was a start.

In 1854, war broke out between Russia and Britain. The army set up hospitals to care for the wounded, but conditions were so bad that almost half of the wounded soldiers brought into the military hospitals died there. Something had to be done. A member of the cabinet appealed to Florence Nightingale for help and she agreed to lead a group of trained nurses to the Crimea.

4. The conditions were even worse than Florence Nightingale had expected.

You can't care for people in these conditions. There isn't even a scrubbing brush or a towel. We must reorganise the whole place.

6. In six months, Florence Nightingale had cut the death rate of wounded soldiers to only two out of every hundred. The newspapers back in Britain called her The Lady with the Lamp. Supporters raised thousands of pounds.

FLORENCE NIGHTINGALE – THE LADY WITH THE LAMP.

7. After two years in the Crimea, Florence returned to Britain. She was a heroine. The newspapers wanted her story...

WELCOME THE HEROINE OF THE CRIMEA

12. In 1860, Britain's first Training School for nurses was set up by Florence Nightingale with money raised for her while she was in the Crimea.

You are all going to work in ordinary hospitals. You can make them better, healthier places.

13. Whenever a new hospital was built its designers would ask advice from Florence. She showed them how to lay out a hospital so nurses could do their job better. She even improved conditions in workhouse hospitals.

14. In Victorian times, women were expected to stay in the background and let men make all the decisions. Florence Nightingale refused to do this and, as a result, hospitals in Britain became much healthier places.

Madam, may I present you with the Order of Merit.

How did scientists discover the causes of disease?

IN THE 1860s understanding of disease reached a turning point. Scientists proved that germs cause disease. Over the next six pages you are going to investigate why this breakthrough occurred in the 1860s, and why it was important for the future development of medicine.

How did people explain disease in the 1800s?

For centuries common sense had told people that there was a connection between dirt and disease, but they had not been able to explain what the link was. In the early 1800s the popular explanation was miasma or bad air. Poisonous fumes (called miasma) were given off from rubbish and decaying matter. The fumes were swept from one place to another by the wind.

This was not a new theory. During the Great Plague of 1665 people had carried strong-smelling herbs with them to overcome the fumes which they thought spread the plague. In the nineteenth century, bad air seemed a better theory than ever. The growing towns were full of refuse which gave off terrible smells – no wonder the towns were so full of disease! Florence Nightingale believed in this theory. That is why she wanted hospitals to be well-ventilated, clean and airy (see page 126).

This idea may have been wrong, but it was closer to the truth than the theory of the four humours, and measures based on it often worked. Clearing away rubbish did help to prevent disease.

1. The miasma theory of disease was mistaken. Why do you think people believed it?

To see how scientists finally explained the link between germs and disease you need to look back 150 years to the 1600s.

Step 1: the discovery of micro-organisms

In the late 1600s a Dutch clockmaker called Anthony van Leeuwenhoek made some of the earliest microscopes. His first microscopes had only one lens, and the image was distorted and fuzzy, but Leeuwenhoek patiently used them to study everything from water drops to peppercorns. To his amazement, almost everything he looked at contained tiny organisms which he called animalcules. He found them in food, drops of water, human excreta, animal intestines. He even found them in the waste material he scraped from between his own teeth. He described his findings in a series of 200 papers to the Royal Society in London.

Step 2: Improved microscopes

Leeuwenhoek's discovery interested other scientists but at that time microscopes were not good enough for his idea to be pursued further. However, by the early 1800s purer glass was being produced and the science of optics was better understood. In 1830 Joseph Lister, a British scientist, developed a microscope that magnified 1,000 times without distortion. With these improved microscopes scientists could observe in detail the behaviour of micro-organisms.

Step 3: Louis Pasteur's germ theory

In the 1850s Louis Pasteur, a French scientist, became interested in micro-organisms when he was asked to help a brewing company find out why their vats of alcohol were going bad. Pasteur discovered that a particular micro-organism was growing vigorously in the liquid. He developed a theory that these germs (called germs because the micro-organism is germinating or growing) were the cause of the problem.

Pasteur solved the brewer's problem, showing him how to kill these harmful germs by boiling the liquid. As a result, Pasteur became well known in France and he was called in by other industries who had similar problems. He found that micro-organisms seemed to be responsible not only for milk turning sour, but also for beer, wine and vinegar fermentation going bad.

Pasteur was an ambitious man who was keen to spread his theories further. In 1860 he got that opportunity when the French Academy of Science organised a competition for scientists to prove or disprove 'SPONTANEOUS GENERATION', an old theory about what causes decay (see Source 1).

The old theory: spontaneous generation

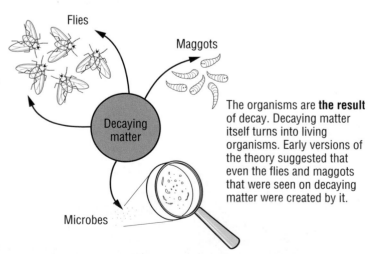

The organisms are **the result** of decay. Decaying matter itself turns into living organisms. Early versions of the theory suggested that even the flies and maggots that were seen on decaying matter were created by it.

SOURCE 1 Explanations of decay in the nineteenth century

Step 4: The battle between germ theory and spontaneous generation

The miasma theory of disease made scientists very interested in decaying matter. They had long been aware that decaying matter was full of flies and maggots. Now through their microscopes they also saw micro-organisms. The question was where did these things come from? There were two theories (see Source 1).

The competition found Pasteur up against another leading French scientist – Pouchet. Pasteur devised a series of ingenious experiments to prove that his theories were correct (see Source 2). They succeeded triumphantly, and in 1861 Pasteur published his 'GERM THEORY'.

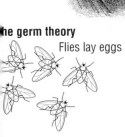

THEORY	EXPERIMENT	
The air contains living micro–organisms	He took sterile flasks out into the streets of Paris, opened them briefly, then sealed them again. Bacteria grew in them.	
Microbes are not evenly distributed in the air	He repeated the experiment in various places around France including high mountains. The number of bacteria varied.	
Microbes in the air cause decay	He filled two flasks; one with sterile air and the other with ordinary air. In the first there was no decay; in the second decay proceeded as normal.	
Microbes can be killed by heating	He heated a material in a flask to make it sterile. He drove the air out, then sealed the flask. It remained sterile even 100 years later.	

SOURCE 2 Pasteur's theories and experiments

Step 5: Linking micro-organisms to disease

Pasteur had proved the power of micro-organisms to make beer go bad. In his germ theory he also said:

'If wine and beer are changed by germs, then the same can and must happen sometimes in men and animals.'

He speculated: could disease be caused by the same process as wine going sour or material decaying? Harmful germs get into a body, grow rapidly and cause the disease.

He soon had an opportunity to put this to the test. The French silk industry was being ruined because of a disease which was affecting their silkworms. Pasteur was called in to investigate. Here again he found that a particular micro-organism seemed to be causing the silkworms' disease.

Step 6: Proving the link between bacteria and human disease

Pasteur was a scientist, not a doctor. He carried out his early experiments with beer, wine and silkworms. It was a German doctor, Robert Koch, who took up the challenge of applying Pasteur's ideas to human diseases. As you can see from page 130, Koch conducted a series of painstaking experiments which proved once and for all that specific micro-organisms cause specific human diseases.

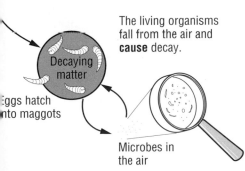

he germ theory
Flies lay eggs
The living organisms fall from the air and **cause** decay.
Decaying matter
Eggs hatch nto maggots
Microbes in the air

■ TASK

1. Draw a flow chart with boxes to show steps 1–6 above.
2. Explain how each step was important.
3. For each step indicate what factors helped scientists make that step.

How important was Robert Koch?

Robert Koch was born in Germany in 1843. As a doctor he became interested in Pasteur's germ theory. He bought a microscope and from 1875–78 he methodically studied anthrax, a disease which affects both animals and humans.

Koch's meticulous research so impressed people that the German government gave him a full-time job and a talented team of bacteriologists to continue his research. His methods were followed by other scientists in their search for the causes of disease.

This imaginary interview is how he might explain the importance of his work.

Question: Which experiment first started your research?
Answer: Some scientists thought they had found the bacteria that cause anthrax. I wasn't happy. I wanted to prove it, beyond a shadow of a doubt.

Q: So describe this famous experiment?
A: I took some organs from sheep that had died of anthrax. In the organs I found the BACTERIUM which everyone said caused anthrax. I extracted it, grew it, studied it, and then injected a mouse with it. After a time the mouse developed anthrax.

Q: So you proved it?
A: Not so fast! There is a lot more yet. I took some blood from the infected mouse. Again I isolated out the anthrax bacterium. Again I grew it on a medium, to check it was still the same. I injected it into a new mouse and it developed anthrax too. I repeated this process over and over again through twenty generations of mice. They all caught anthrax, and at the end I still had the same bacterium as at the beginning. Then, and only then, did I pronounce that this was the bacterium which causes anthrax.

Q: So why was that a useful experiment?
A: Because it provided a method which everyone could follow. Using my methods they have already identified the causes of typhoid, tuberculosis, the dreaded cholera, tetanus and so on. [You can see the list in Source 4.] I am confident more will follow.

Q: Is your anthrax experiment the only thing which makes you famous?
A: No. That was only the beginning. My next step was to make a better medium for growing and observing bacteria. If you want to find out about bacteria you have to be able to see them! Some of my rivals such as Pasteur were still using liquids.

I perfected a solid medium, then a better way of growing bacteria, and finally a way of staining them so they could be observed more easily.

Q: Staining – what's that?
A: I was looking for the bacteria that cause blood poisoning. I couldn't see them although I knew they must be there. My solution was to stain them purple so I could see them.

Q: What advice would you give to someone wanting to find out more about medicine?
A: Be scientific. Be systematic. Record everything. Repeat everything. You will only avoid false conclusions if you try everything out again and again. Check your results: don't believe them the first time.

SOURCE 3 A contemporary cartoon. Koch is shown slaying the tuberculosis bacillus

1. What answer do you think Koch would have given to these questions:
a) What is your greatest achievement?
b) How will your research help people find cures for disease?
c) What was the most important factor in your success?

Did germ theory help scientists cure diseases?

There was no doubting the importance of Koch's achievements. They inspired other scientists to search for the causes of many diseases.

> **SOURCE 4** Using Koch's methods, the causes of these diseases were identified very quickly. The starred ones were discovered by Koch and his team
>
> | | |
> |---|---|
> | 1880 Typhus | 1886 Pneumonia |
> | 1882 Tuberculosis* | 1887 MENINGITIS |
> | 1883 Cholera* | 1894 Plague |
> | 1884 Tetanus | 1898 Dysentery |

Koch's success spurred Louis Pasteur into action again. Pasteur was nationalistic and ambitious. France and Germany were deadly rivals at this time. France had lost a bitter war to Germany in 1870–71. Pasteur was already a world-famous scientist but it greatly troubled him that Koch and Germany seemed to be getting ahead of France in the battle to explain disease. For the rest of his life, despite a severe stroke which paralysed the left side of his body, Pasteur applied himself to what he considered the greatest challenge of all – finding cures for disease.

Pasteur knew he could not compete with Koch's work on his own. By this time he was powerful enough to be able to raise money from the French government and he gathered around him a team of doctors and vets to help with the research.

A new vaccination: chicken cholera

Pasteur had thought a lot about Jenner's work on smallpox. He was sure that smallpox was not the only disease that could be prevented by vaccination, but as he did not know how vaccination worked he had to continue his search by trial and error.

In 1879 Pasteur was researching chicken cholera because that was a disease which was troubling French farmers at the time. He extracted the germ which caused the disease and then started the process of trying to make a weak form of it. His team injected chickens with different strengths of culture to see if they worked.

During the summer of 1879, when the research was temporarily abandoned during the holidays, some chicken cholera solution was accidentally left unused in the laboratory. On returning to work, Charles Chamberland, a member of the team, happened by chance to inject chickens with these old germs that had been left exposed to the air throughout the summer. As you can see from Source 5 below, this led to an amazing discovery. The old solution had IMMUNISED the chickens against the disease. Clearly, exposure to the air had weakened the germs.

Pasteur called this method vaccination to show his debt to Jenner.

1. Pasteur always denied that the chicken cholera discovery was pure chance. He said 'chance only favours the mind which is prepared'. What do you think he meant by that?

SOURCE 5 How an effective vaccine against chicken cholera was discovered

Vaccination number three: anthrax

Anthrax was a dangerous disease in animals and it could also kill humans. In one area of France anthrax killed 9 per cent of the sheep and 7 per cent of the cows every year. After patient experiment Pasteur's team announced that they had produced an attenuated (weak) culture which they believed could immunise animals against anthrax.

The Agricultural Society of Melun invited Pasteur to a public display to prove his ideas about anthrax were correct. This would have scared many scientists, but not Pasteur. In May 1881 he took up the challenge.

SOURCE 6 This is how Pasteur's experiment was reported in the London *Times* on 2 June 1881 by telegraph from it's Paris correspondent

66 On 5th May, M. Rossignol's farm and 60 sheep were placed at M. Pasteur's disposal. Ten of the sheep were left untouched in order that they might later serve for a comparison. Of the remaining 50, 25 were marked with a hole in their ear and were inoculated on 5th May with weak virus and on 17th May with stronger virus. On 31st May none of them had lost fat or gaiety or appetite.

On 31 May the 50 sheep were taken and all inoculated with the strongest virus. M. Pasteur predicted that today, 2nd June, the 25 sheep not inoculated would be dead and that the inoculated animals would show no symptoms of sickness. Today at half past one a number of spectators came together to witness the results. At 2 o'clock, 23 of the sheep which had not been inoculated were dead. The 24th died at 3 o'clock and the 25th an hour later.

The 25 inoculated animals were sound and frolicked and gave signs of perfect health.

The agricultural public now knows that an infallible preventative exists against anthrax. 99

SOURCE 7 Pasteur vaccinating sheep against anthrax

Pasteur's critics found plenty to attack in his methods. Koch accused Pasteur of sloppy science, saying he did not accurately measure his anthrax vaccine. However, they could not argue with the results – the sheep were protected. He had risked public humiliation if the anthrax experiment had failed. Instead he succeeded triumphantly and his fame quickly spread.

Vaccination number four: rabies

Pasteur was now more confident of his method and in 1882 he turned his attention to rabies. This disease is passed to humans from a bite by an infected dog. It was not a common disease in humans, but it caused certain death and the patient suffered terribly in the process. After two years of careful research Pasteur developed a rabies vaccine which worked. Soon people from all over Europe were flocking to Paris to be treated by Pasteur.

■ TASK

1. Work in pairs to study the achievements of Pasteur and Koch. Copy and complete the chart below to show the reasons for their success.

   These are some of the extra factors you might consider to go in place of the question marks:

   ■ individual genius
   ■ role of chance
   ■ the support of governments
   ■ warfare
   ■ links with industry
   ■ improved communications
   ■ improved technology.

2. Use your chart to write your own essay 'Why were the causes of disease finally discovered in the 1860s and 1870s?'

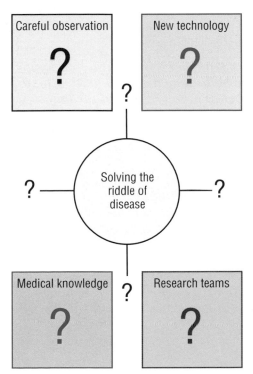

The first cures

Pasteur's vaccinations could only prevent disease, but as you can see from Source 8 the first cures were soon to follow.

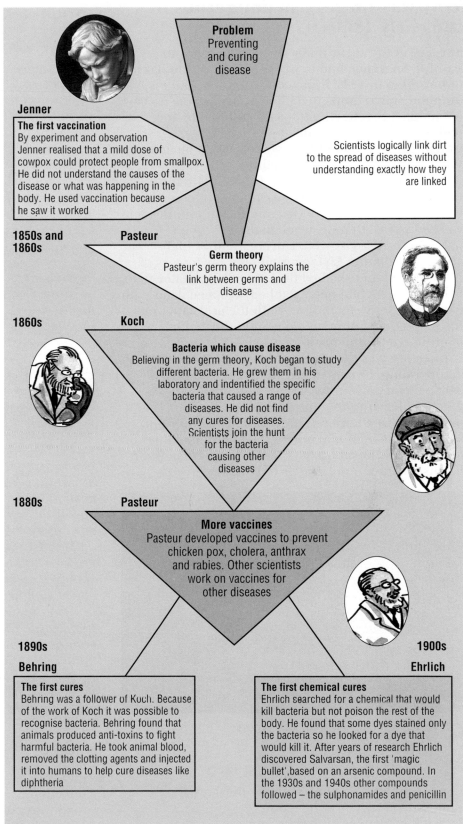

Problem
Preventing and curing disease

Jenner
The first vaccination
By experiment and observation Jenner realised that a mild dose of cowpox could protect people from smallpox. He did not understand the causes of the disease or what was happening in the body. He used vaccination because he saw it worked

Scientists logically link dirt to the spread of diseases without understanding exactly how they are linked

1850s and 1860s   **Pasteur**
Germ theory
Pasteur's germ theory explains the link between germs and disease

1860s   **Koch**
Bacteria which cause disease
Believing in the germ theory, Koch began to study different bacteria. He grew them in his laboratory and indentified the specific bacteria that caused a range of diseases. He did not find any cures for diseases. Scientists join the hunt for the bacteria causing other diseases

1880s   **Pasteur**
More vaccines
Pasteur developed vaccines to prevent chicken pox, cholera, anthrax and rabies. Other scientists work on vaccines for other diseases

1890s   **1900s**
Behring   **Ehrlich**

The first cures
Behring was a follower of Koch. Because of the work of Koch it was possible to recognise bacteria. Behring found that animals produced anti-toxins to fight harmful bacteria. He took animal blood, removed the clotting agents and injected it into humans to help cure diseases like diphtheria

The first chemical cures
Ehrlich searched for a chemical that would kill bacteria but not poison the rest of the body. He found that some dyes stained only the bacteria so he looked for a dye that would kill it. After years of research Ehrlich discovered Salvarsan, the first 'magic bullet',based on an arsenic compound. In the 1930s and 1940s other compounds followed – the sulphonamides and penicillin

SOURCE 8 How scientists discovered cures for disease

How did surgery improve in the nineteenth century?

Why was surgery so dangerous in the early 1800s?

Surgery in the early 1800s was dangerous and painful. Surgeons had to work quickly. At the Battle of Borodino in 1812 Napoleon's surgeon, Dubois, amputated 200 limbs in 24 hours. There was no way of completely relieving the pain suffered by the patient, nor was it possible to replace blood by transfusion although blood vessels could be tied with ligatures to stop the bleeding.

Sometimes operations went dreadfully wrong. Robert Liston was a famous London surgeon who once amputated a leg in two-and-a-half minutes but worked so fast that he accidentally cut off his patient's testicles as well. During another high-speed amputation Liston amputated the fingers of his assistant and slashed the coat of a spectator who, fearing that he had been stabbed, dropped dead with fright. Worse was to follow. Both the assistant and the patient died of infection caught during the operation or in the hospital ward.

Infection was the greatest danger to patients after an operation. Germs might enter the wound and cause blood poisoning. Almost half of all patients who had leg amputations died from blood poisoning. One famous surgeon, James Simpson, said that 'the man laid out on the operating tables of our hospitals has more chances of death than the English soldier on the fields of Waterloo'.

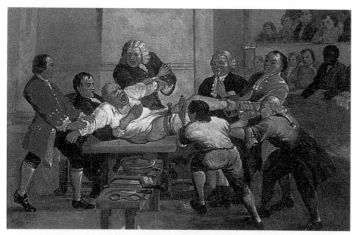

SOURCE 1 An operation around 1800

SOURCE 2 The novelist Fanny Burney's account of her mastectomy operation in 1811. She survived and lived for many years afterwards

66 ... *when the dreadful steel was plunged into the breast – cutting through veins – arteries – flesh – nerves – I needed no injunctions not to restrain my cries. I began a scream that lasted unintermittingly during the whole time of the incision – I almost marvel that it does not ring in my ears still! so excruciating was the agony. When the wound was made, & the instrument was withdrawn, the pain seemed undiminished, for the air that suddenly rushed into those delicate parts felt like a mass of minute but sharp & forked poignards [daggers], that were tearing at the edges of the wound, but when I felt again the instrument ... I thought I must have expired, I attempted no more to open my eyes – they felt so firmly closed, that the eyelids seemed indented to the cheeks ...* 99

SOURCE 3 An account by Professor James Syme of his amputation of a leg at the hip joint. Syme was Clinical Surgeon at Edinburgh Royal Infirmary 1833–69

66 *I introduced a narrow knife about a foot long ... I cut along the bone, which started, with a loud report, from its socket. Finally I passed the knife around the head of the bone, cutting the remaining portion of the LIGAMENT, and this completed the operation, which certainly did not occupy at the most more than one minute.*

[My assistant] relaxed [the torniquet so] that we might estimate the size and number of the bleeding vessels. It seemed at first sight as if the vessels which supplied so many jets of arterial blood could never all be closed ... a single instant was sufficient to convince us that the patient's safety required all our [speed], and in the course of a few minutes HAEMORRHAGE was effectually restrained by the application of ten or twelve ligatures. 99

1. On your own copy of Source 1 mark all the possible sources of infection.
2. What evidence is there in Sources 1–3 that surgeons had copied the ideas of Ambroise Paré (page 86)?

3. Use Sources 1–3 to explain in your own words why:
a) pain
b) bleeding
c) infection
made surgery so dangerous.
4. From what you already know about nineteenth-century medicine which of these problems do you expect to be solved first?

Problem 1: Pain

Look up the following references which show how surgeons dealt with the problem of pain in earlier periods: Source 3, page 38; Source 9, page 70. Such herbal remedies had some effect but in the early 1880s there were still only three operations which surgeons could carry out with some success: the amputation of limbs, trephining, and the removal of superficial TUMOURS. All were carried out as swiftly as possible to reduce the pain suffered by the patient. Surgeons were used to ignoring the pain of their patients. However, medical knowledge was advancing rapidly and some surgeons felt that if the patient could be 'knocked out', then there would be no resistance and this would give them more time to operate and could improve their techniques. During the same period chemistry was developing and scientists were finding that certain chemicals could have an effect on the human body. In 1799 Sir Humphry Davy discovered that laughing gas reduced the sensation of pain: 'It seems capable of destroying pain and might probably be used in surgical operations'. Forty years later dentists used it to ease the pain of tooth extractions and other surgeons were experimenting with different substances. Source 4 describes the first successful operation using ether.

> **SOURCE 4** An account of an operation to remove a neck tumour using ether as an anaesthetic by John Collins Warren, senior surgeon at Massachusetts General Hospital in 1846
>
> 66 *The patient was arranged for the operation in a sitting posture, and everything was made ready … The patient was then made to inhale a fluid from a tube with a glass globe. After four or five minutes he appeared to be asleep, and was thought by Dr Morton to be in a condition for the operation. I made an incision between two or three inches long in the direction of the tumour, and to my great surprise without any starting, crying, or other indication of pain.* 99

A year later, ether was used by J.R. Liston in London to anaesthetise a patient during a leg amputation. However, ether had severe drawbacks as an anaesthetic. It irritated the lungs, causing the patient to cough during the operation. It was also unstable and produced inflammable vapour. Soon other surgeons were searching for a better alternative.

Why was there opposition to anaesthetics?

James Simpson was Professor of Midwifery at Edinburgh University. One evening in 1847 he invited several colleagues to his home. They sat around the table experimenting with different chemicals. Simpson wrote later 'I poured some of the [CHLOROFORM] fluid into tumblers in front of my assistants, Dr Keith and Dr Duncan and myself. Before sitting down to supper we all inhaled the fluid, and were all "under the table" in a minute or two, to my wife's consternation and alarm.'

SOURCE 5 Simpson and friends recovering from effects of chloroform. A drawing made in 1857

Simpson realised that in chloroform he had discovered a very effective anaesthetic. He soon started using it to help relieve women's labour pains during childbirth. He wrote articles about his discovery and other surgeons started to use it in their operations.

However, with painless operations now a real possibility, it may surprise you that the first reaction of many surgeons was intense opposition to the use of anaesthetics.

Some had medical arguments. Chloroform was a new and untested gas. No one knew for sure if there would be long-term side effects on the bodies or minds of patients. They did not know what dose to give to different patients. The first death from the use of chloroform (see Source 8) scared surgeons and gave opponents of anaesthetics powerful evidence of their danger.

There were also moral and religious arguments as you can see from Source 6. Some people were particularly opposed to the idea of easing the pain of childbirth – believing that this would be unnatural.

What's more, anaesthetics did not necessarily make surgery safer. With a patient asleep the doctor could attempt more complex operations, thus carrying infections deeper into the body and causing more loss of blood. The number of people dying from surgery may even have increased after the discovery of anaesthetics!

SOURCE 6 Letters to the medical journal *The Lancet* in 1849 and 1853

66 *The infliction [of pain] has been invented by the Almighty God. Pain may even be considered a blessing of the Gospel, and being blessed admits to being made either well or ill.* 99

66 *It is a most unnatural practice. The pain and sorrow of labour exert a most powerful and useful influence upon the religious and moral character of women and upon all their future relations in life.* 99

SOURCE 7 Army Chief of Medical Staff, 1854

66 *... the smart use of the knife is a powerful stimulant and it is much better to hear a man bawl lustily than to see him sink silently into the grave.* 99

SOURCE 8 In 1848 Hannah Greener died whilst being given chloroform during an operation to remove her toenail

Why were anaesthetics accepted?

James Simpson presented a powerful case for anaesthetics. He brought the example of Ambroise Paré to his defence.

SOURCE 9 James Simpson speaking to a meeting of doctors in Edinburgh in 1847

66 *Before the sixteenth century surgeons had no way of stemming the flow of blood after amputation of a limb other than by scorching with a red hot iron or boiling pitch. The great suggestion of Ambroise Paré, to shut up the bleeding vessels by tying them, was a vast improvement. It saved the sufferings of the patient while adding to their safety. But the practice was new, and like all innovations in medical practice, it was at first and for long, bitterly decried ... attacked ... suppressed.*

We look back with sorrow on the opponents of Paré. Our successors in years to come will look back with similar feelings. They will marvel at the idea of humane men confessing that they prefer operating on their patients in a waking instead of an anaesthetic state, and that the fearful agonies that they inflict should be endured quietly. All pain is destructive and even fatal in its effects. 99

The struggle continued for ten years with anaesthetics gradually winning wider acceptance. The final breakthrough came when Queen Victoria accepted the use of chloroform during the delivery of her eighth child in 1857. She publicly praised 'that blessed chloroform'. With the support of the queen opposition to anaesthetics was doomed. From now on they became a standard part of surgical practice.

■ TASK

Explain how the following factors played a role in either encouraging or opposing the development of anaesthetics:

- ■ religion
- ■ war
- ■ individual genius
- ■ Queen Victoria
- ■ chance
- ■ government.

SOURCE 10 Written by Margaret Matthewson of Shetland. She was from a poor family. She worked as a servant. In 1877 she went to Edinburgh for a shoulder operation by Professor Cheyne. The operation would not have been possible before the days of anaesthetics. She survived the operation although she died one year later from a recurrence of the problem. She wrote this account while convalescing

  66 *The big theatre door was open and we went in. Professor Cheyne bowed and smiled. There were a lot of people sitting in the gallery and four people sitting around the table.*

Doctor Cheyne came and laid a towel saturated with chloroform over my face and said 'Now breathe away.' I then felt the Professor's hand laid gently on my arm as if to let me know that he was near … I felt myself go weaker and weaker and every nerve and joint relaxing and breaking up as it were, a very solemn moment thus staring death in the face, and I believed I never should awaken to look on the things of time any more but was indeed entering eternity.

[Finding he needed more time to complete the operation, the surgeon gave her an extra large dose of chloroform. After the operation she took seventy minutes to regain consciousness.]

I was conscious of no more until I awoke in a bed in a strange ward. My first thought was 'My arm! Is it off or not?' I at once sat up to feel for it. I found it bandaged to my waist and breathed a sigh of thankfulness.

I felt very sick and kept on vomiting … at intervals for several hours … I doubt it will be sometime ere I get over this horrid chloroform taste and its effects. **99**

■ ACTIVITY

Source 2 on page 134 and Source 10 above describe surgery before and after the development of anaesthetics. Imagine James Simpson wants to use these two sources to show how valuable the development of anaesthetics has been to patients and surgeons. Use Sources 2 and 10 to write an extra paragraph for his speech in Source 9.

Problem 2: Infection

With anaesthetics surgery was certainly less painful. But it was not safer. Until the acceptance of germ theory in the 1860s, surgeons did not take any precautions to protect open wounds from infection. They reused bandages, thus spreading gangrene and skin infections from patient to patient. Doctors did not wash their hands before an operation, nor did they STERILISE their equipment, and some of them operated wearing old pus-stained clothes.

Ignaz Semmelweiss

Semmelweiss was a Hungarian doctor working in Austria. He was very concerned by the deaths of apparently healthy women after childbirth. Some doctors regarded this as inevitable, but Semmelweiss observed that women whose babies were delivered by midwives were much less likely to die from infection than women who were delivered by medical students. He believed the reason for this was that the medical students came straight to the delivery rooms after they had been dissecting dead bodies. If they simply washed their hands, he thought, they would reduce the risk of infection to women.

SOURCE 11 A notice placed by Dr Ignaz Semmelweiss at the entrance of the maternity ward in the General Hospital in Vienna, 15 May 1847

From today, 15 May 1847, any doctor or student coming from the postmortem room must, before entering the maternity wards, wash his hands thoroughly in the basin of chlorinated water placed at the entrance. This order applies to everyone, without exception.

Semmelweiss pursued his crusade with great passion. He even called doctors who did not wash their hands murderers. However, at the time, he was regarded as a crank and a fanatic, and was said to be mentally unstable. It would be many years before the sensible measures he was suggesting would be adopted by others.

1. Could Semmelweiss have known about Pasteur's germ theory in 1847?
2. Why do you think Semmelweiss faced opposition to such a simple measure?
3. Who did more to help women in childbirth: James Simpson or Ignaz Semmelweiss?

Joseph Lister

Joseph Lister was one of the outstanding surgeons of the nineteenth century. He had researched gangrene and infection, and had a keen interest in the application of science to medicine. His father had been the pioneer of the improved microscope. He read the work of Pasteur on germ theory, published in 1861.

SOURCE 12 From an article in *The Lancet*, 1869, by Joseph Lister, Professor of Surgery, Glasgow University

❝ *When it had been shown by the researches of Pasteur that the septic property of the atmosphere depended on minute organisms suspended in it, it occurred to me that decomposition in the injured part [following an operation] might be avoided by applying as a dressing some material capable of destroying the life of the floating particles.* ❞

Lister had seen carbolic spray used to treat sewage. After experiments he found that a thin mist of carbolic acid sprayed over the wound during surgery limited infection. By following this with careful bandaging the wound would heal and not develop gangrene.

SOURCE 13 Operation with carbolic spray. One assistant is using chloroform to anaesthetise the patient, another is mopping up blood with a sponge

SOURCE 14 *On the New Method of Treating Compound Fractures*, Joseph Lister (1867)

❝ *James, aged 11 years, was admitted to the Glasgow INFIRMARY on August 2, 1865, with compound fracture of the left leg caused by the wheel of an empty cart passing over the limb a little below the middle. The wound, an inch and a half long and three quarters of an inch broad, was over the line of the fracture.*

A piece of lint dipped in carbolic acid was laid on the wound, and splints padded with cotton wool were applied. It was left undisturbed for four days and, when examined, it showed no sign of suppuration. For the next four days the wound was dressed with lint soaked with a solution of water and carbolic acid and olive oil which further prevented irritation to the skin. No pus was present, there seemed no danger of SUPPURATION, and at the end of six weeks I found the bones united, and I discarded the splints. The sore was entirely healed … ❞

SOURCE 15 From Lister's own record of amputations

	Total amputations	Died	% who died
1864–66 (without antiseptics)	35	16	45.7
1867–70 (with antiseptics)	40	6	15.0

■ ACTIVITY

You are a journalist who has been asked to report on Lister's antiseptic surgery. Describe in detail the measures he has taken to reduce the risk of infection. You could include a comparison of Source 1 on page 134 and Source 13. Explain why he has taken each of these measures.

Why was there opposition to antiseptics?

You already know that new medical techniques often meet with great opposition. Antiseptics were no exception.

To start with, many surgeons opposed Lister's methods, and he was seen as a fanatic. His carbolic spray, which soaked the operating theatre, seemed very extreme. It cracked the surgeon's skin and made everything smell. The new precautions caused extra work, and made operations more expensive and less pleasant for the surgeons.

Surgeons were still convinced that speed was essential in an operation and, with the problem of bleeding it often was. It seemed that Lister's antiseptic methods just slowed operations down.

When some surgeons did try copying Lister's methods they got different results. This was usually because they were less systematic, but that didn't stop them criticising Lister. Others argued that antiseptics actually prevented the body's own defence mechanisms from operating effectively.

Pasteur's ideas of germ theory had spread very slowly. Even trained surgeons found it difficult to accept that there were tiny micro-organisms all around which could cause disease. One surgeon regularly joked with his assistants that they should shut the door of the operating theatre in case one of 'Mr Lister's MICROBES' might fly in.

For many centuries surgeons had lived with the idea that a lot of their patients would die. When Lister said he had achieved such good results, their first reaction was one of disbelief. For many the next reaction was to feel defensive.

Lister was not a showman like Pasteur. He did not give impressive public displays. Indeed, he appeared to be cold, arrogant and aloof and was sometimes critical of other surgeons.

Lister was always changing his techniques. He did this because he wanted to find a substance that would work equally as well, but without the corrosion that carbolic spray caused. His critics simply said he was changing his methods because they did not work.

SOURCE 16   Opposition to the use of antiseptics

■ ACTIVITY

Work in pairs. Role play an argument between Lister and one of his critics. You should get plenty of ideas from the text and sources above. You can also get a sheet from your teacher to help you.

How did Lister change surgery?

Despite opposition, Lister's methods marked a turning point in surgery. In 1877 he moved to London to train young surgeons under his own supervision. In 1878 Koch found the bacterium which caused SEPTICAEMIA. This gave a great boost to Lister's ideas. By the late 1890s his antiseptic methods (which killed germs on the wound) became aseptic surgery which meant removing all possible germs from the operating theatre. To ensure absolute cleanliness various measures were introduced.

- Operating theatres and hospitals were rigorously cleaned.
- From 1887 all instruments were steam-sterilised.
- In 1894, sterilised rubber gloves were used for the first time. However well surgeons' hands were scrubbed they could still hold bacteria in the folds of skin and under the nails.

In 1892 Lister and Pasteur were together given an award at the Sorbonne University in Paris for their contribution to the fight against disease.

With some of the basic problems of surgery now solved, surgeons attempted more ambitious operations. The first successful operation to remove an infected appendix came in the 1880s. The first heart operation was carried out in 1896 when surgeons repaired a heart damaged by a stab wound.

■ TASK

Draw a timeline from 1850–1900. Above the line mark important dates in the work of Pasteur and Koch (see pages 128–33). Below it mark important dates in the development of safer surgery. Then use it to write answers to these questions.

1. How was Lister's work linked to Pasteur's germ theory?
2. What other factors helped lead to improvements in surgery?

Problem 3: What about the bleeding?

The third great problem of surgery was bleeding. Lister also made a contribution here. He improved on Paré's ligatures by using sterilised catgut which did not pose such a great risk of infection.

Other surgeons experimented with blood transfusion, but despite their many attempts it often failed. The blood clotted, and even when it was successful many patients mysteriously died. The explanation for that would not be found for another twenty years – a development which we return to on page 152.

Why were sewers and water supply improved in the nineteenth century?

FOR HUNDREDS OF years people had known that there was a link between dirt and disease although no one was sure exactly what the connection was. During the late eighteenth century and the first half of the nineteenth century conditions in many British towns became worse than ever. The population was growing so rapidly that towns could not cope with the need to house people and provide them with water and facilities to remove their sewage. In these conditions the killer diseases spread with terrifying ease and speed. The conditions were so bad that many people's health may even have grown worse than it had been in earlier centuries.

A COURT FOR KING CHOLERA

SOURCE 1 A drawing of London made in the 1840s. Similar conditions could be found in other growing towns around Britain and Europe

1. Look at Source 1. List as many threats to health as possible.
2. Why do you think people let the towns get like this?

The battle over public health

Some people thought that the government should force local councils to clean up their towns. However, there were also many who believed that the government should keep out of people's lives – this attitude is called LAISSEZ-FAIRE. They believed the government should allow each local area to control its own affairs. This usually meant letting the local ratepayers make all the decisions. They certainly did not want the government to force them to pay for improvements to their towns. Such people were nicknamed 'the Dirty Party'.

This battle between local authorities and the government played a central part in the story of public health in nineteenth-century Britain.

The debate rumbled on inconclusively until ...

Cholera!

Whole families exterminated

NO RANK ESCAPES ITS ATTACK!

CIVILIZED NATIONS REDUCED TO SAVAGE HORDES!

These newspaper headlines are talking about cholera. They reflect the fear that struck the country when cholera reached Britain for the first time in the early 1830s. There were other diseases which killed far more people but cholera was the most frightening because it was a 'shock disease' that struck quickly. Sufferers were suddenly gripped by diarrhoea and vomiting. More than 500 millilitres of fluid could be lost each hour in the diarrhoea and, if not replaced, caused death in only a few hours. It was a swift, painful and unpleasant death, hence the fear it inspired.

SOURCE 2 *Methodist* magazine, 1832

To see the number of our fellow creatures, in a good state of health, in the full possession of their wonted strength, and in the midst of their years, suddenly seized with the most violent spasms, and in a few hours cast into the tomb, is calculated to shake the firmest nerves, and to inspire dread in the strongest heart.

SOURCE 3 A cigar advertisement, 1831

When cholera struck for the first time in 1831 many ideas were put forward to explain its causes. Sources 4–8 are some of them.

1. Copy and complete this table using Sources 4–8 to help you.

What people believed caused the Black Death in the 1300s	Was it used as an explanation of cholera?	Evidence
A punishment from God		
Movements of the planets		
Earthquakes		
Children's misbehaviour		
Dirt in the streets		
Poisons in the air		

2. Add other explanations for cholera given by Sources 4–8.
3. Why were some medieval explanations for disease still being used?

SOURCE 4 Edinburgh Board of Health, 1833

66 *Experience proves that notorious drunkards were amongst the victims … the intemperate, the old and the infirm, and poor … half starved children … worn out prostitutes.* 99

SOURCE 5 Bishop Blomfield, 1832

66 *Cholera is a sign to increase the comforts and improve the moral character of the masses.* 99

SOURCE 6 Dr Southwood Smith, 1841

66 *Cholera was due not to want of food and great misery … but to EFFLUVIAL poisons [bad air that carried disease].* 99

SOURCE 7 William Farr, a doctor and Superintendent of the Statistical Department of the Registrar General

66 *Although elevation of habitation … does not shut out the cause of cholera, it reduces its effect to insignificance.* 99

SOURCE 8 Thomas Wakely, a doctor writing in the medical journal *The Lancet*, 1831

66 *We can only suppose the existence of a poison which progresses independently of the wind, of the soil, of all conditions of the air, and of the barrier of the sea; in short, one that makes mankind the chief agent of its dissemination.* 99

Discovering the causes of cholera – the work of John Snow

Cholera is actually spread by infected water. The faeces of a sufferer contain the cholera germ and if they get into the water supply the disease spreads rapidly. Many people studied the 1832 epidemic and, after careful observation of the disease, deduced that there was a link between cholera and water supply. Of course, as Source 9 shows, people at the time (30 years before Pasteur) did not understand that germs caused cholera.

SOURCE 9 Part of a letter from a Mr Perkins to the government's Board of Health in 1848

66 … *my impression is that [the miasma] chemically infects exposed water, and the poorer classes using such water are consequently the greatest sufferers.* 99

Cholera returned regularly throughout the century. The next major epidemics were in 1848 and 1854.

In 1854 Dr John Snow made a breakthrough in proving that there was a link between cholera and water supply. Snow, a London doctor, used meticulous research, observation, and house-to-house interviews to build up a detailed picture of a limited cholera epidemic which hit one particular area of central London. Sources 10 and 11 come from his published reports on the outbreak.

1. Read Source 10. What methods of investigation did Snow use to investigate the epidemic?
2. How does Snow explain the many deaths in Broad Street?
3. How does Snow explain that there were no deaths in the brewery?
4. Which parts of Snow's evidence do you think would be the most important in convincing doubters about the link between water supply and cholera?

■ **ACTIVITY**

Write a letter from John Snow to the public health officials for London advising them what to do to help prevent further outbreaks of cholera.

SOURCE 10 Extract from Snow's account *On the Mode of Communication of Cholera*, 1854

66 *The most terrible outbreak of cholera which ever occurred in this kingdom is probably that which took place in Broad Street, and the adjoining streets, a few weeks ago. Within two hundred and fifty yards of the spot where Cambridge Street joins Broad Street, there were upwards of five hundred fatal attacks of cholera in ten days. The mortality in this limited area probably equals any that was ever caused in this country, even by the plague; and it was much more sudden, as the greater number of cases terminated within a few hours. The mortality would undoubtedly have been much greater had it not been for the flight of the population …*

… On proceeding to the spot, I found that nearly all the deaths had taken place within a short distance of the [water] pump. There were only ten deaths in houses situated decidedly nearer to another street pump. In five of these cases the families of the deceased persons informed me that they always sent to the pump in Broad Street, as they preferred the water to that of the pump that was nearer. In three other cases, the deceased were children who went to the school near the pump in Broad Street …

… There is a Brewery in Broad Street, near to the pump, and on perceiving that no brewer's men were registered as having died of cholera, I called on Mr Huggins, the proprietor. He informed me that there were above seventy workmen employed in the brewery, and that none of them had suffered from the cholera – at least in a severe form – only two having been indisposed, and that not seriously, at the time the disease prevailed. The men were allowed to drink a certain quantity of malt liquor, and Mr Huggins believes they do not drink water at all; he is quite certain that the workmen never obtained water from the pump in the street. There is a deep well in the brewery, in addition to the New River water …

… As there had been deaths from cholera just before the great outbreak not far from this pump-well, and in a situation elevated a few feet above it, the evacuations [excreta] from the patients might of course be amongst the impurities finding their way into the water … 99

SOURCE 11 Map of the Broad Street area

A widow living in the suburbs, in an area otherwise clear of cholera, died of the disease. It was later discovered that she had a bottle of water from Broad Street sent to her every day because she liked it.

535 people lived in this workhouse. They got their water from another source. Only five died.

70 people worked at this brewery. It had its own water supply and gave its workers free beer to drink. No one died.

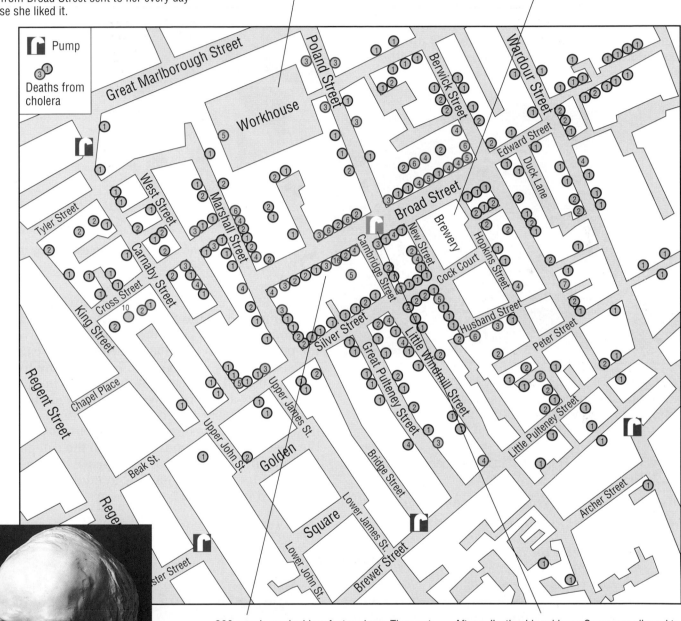

200 people worked in a factory here. They got their water from the Broad Street pump. Eighteen died.

After collecting his evidence Snow was allowed to remove the handle of the water pump in Broad Street. There were no more deaths. It later came to light that a cesspool, one metre away from the pump, had a cracked lining allowing the contents to seep into the drinking water.

SOURCE 12 Plaster-cast bust of John Snow. Snow died in 1858, aged only 45, three years before the publication of Pasteur's germ theory which helped explain the results Snow had recorded

Why were public health reforms begun?

Cholera was the most frightening disease but it was far from being the only danger to health. Conditions in the countryside were often as bad as in the towns.

Bad water supplies, inadequate drains, damp houses, and indifference to rubbish all helped spread disease. Diarrhoea, typhus and the dreaded typhoid and cholera sometimes ravaged cottages as severely as they did the slums of the city.

SOURCE 13 *Punch* cartoon, 1861. Mr Punch (to landlord): 'Your stable arrangements are excellent. Suppose you try something of the sort here?'

SOURCE 14 From *The Times*, 1850, describing the village of Wark

66 *The very picture of slovenliness and neglect. Wretched houses piled here and there without order – filth of every kind scattered about or heaped up against the walls – horses, cows, and pigs lodged under the same roof as their owners and entering the same door – in many cases a pigsty beneath the only window of the dwellings – 300 people, 60 horses and 50 cows, besides hosts of pigs and poultry – such is the village of Wark.* 99

Edwin Chadwick

SOURCE 15 Edwin Chadwick as represented by the *Pictorial Times* in 1846

In the 1830s a civil servant called Edwin Chadwick was employed by the POOR LAW COMMISSION. The Commission supervised the help that was given to the poor out of the local taxes which were called rates. Chadwick was asked to report on the living conditions and the health of the poor in both town and country areas. Chadwick's report concluded that much poverty was due to ill health caused by the foul conditions in which people lived, and that the best way of reducing the cost to the ratepayer of looking after the poor was to improve their health. His recommendations on how to do this are described in Source 17.

SOURCE 16 Average age of death in Liverpool (urban) and Rutland (rural area) in 1840. These statistics were gathered by Chadwick for his report. He used them to show the contrasts in life expectancy in different places and for different social classes

Why was there opposition to public health reforms?

Chadwick's recommendations posed a problem for the government. It knew it should action the recommendations of the report, but such matters were usually handled by the local ratepayers. They were the ones who were responsible for the care of the poor in their area. Local ratepayers were trying to reduce the cost of looking after the poor, not increase it.

The government knew that any attempt to force local councils to follow the recommendations would be unacceptable. Local businessmen and politicians would certainly not accept being told by the government to pay for public health reforms.

For the next 30 years a struggle went on between towns and central government as to how to solve these problems.

Following Chadwick's report the government first did nothing. Then, in 1848, faced by the second major epidemic of cholera, Parliament reluctantly approved the Public Health Act of 1848. This set up a system, run by the government's Board of Health, to encourage (but not force) local authorities to improve conditions in their area. The Act allowed local authorities to make improvements if they wanted to and if they had the support of their ratepayers. It enabled them to borrow money to pay for the improvements. Sources 18 and 19 comment on the effectiveness of these voluntary measures.

SOURCE 17 From Edwin Chadwick's *Report on the Sanitary Conditions of the Labouring Population* which he wrote in 1842

66 *First – That the various forms of epidemic disease amongst the labouring classes are caused by atmospheric impurities produced by decaying animal and vegetable substances, by damp and filth, and close and overcrowded dwellings. The annual loss of life from filth and bad ventilation are greater than the loss from death or wounds in any war in which the country has been engaged in modern times.*

Second – That the most important measures and most practical are drainage, the removal of all refuse from the streets and the roads and the improvement of the supplies of water. The expense of public drainage and supplies of water would save money by cutting the existing charge resulting from sickness and mortality.

Third – For the prevention of disease it would be a good economy to appoint a district medical officer with special qualifications. 99

SOURCE 18 Report on discussions in Leeds in the 1840s by James Smith

66 *A proposal was made for the complete sewerage of the streets. I was present for nearly six hours of this debate. The chief theme of the speakers in opposition related to the means of saving the pockets of the ratepayers with very little regard to the sanitary results.* 99

The cost of improving public health was indeed very high. Eleven million pounds was borrowed by local councils between 1848 and 1872 but, not surprisingly, only a few local authorities took any new measures. By 1872 only 50 councils had appointed Medical Officers of Health, although this had been one of Chadwick's main proposals. Six years later the government's Board of Health was disbanded to the great delight of its critics.

SOURCE 19 Published in *The Times*, 1 August 1854

66 *The Board of Health has fallen. We prefer to take our chance with cholera than be bullied into health. Everywhere the board's inspectors were bullying, insulting and expensive. They entered houses and factories insisting on changes revolting to the habits or pride of the masters and occupants. There is nothing a man hates so much as being cleaned against his will, or having his floors swept, his walls whitewashed, his pet dung heaps cleared away, all at the command of a sort of sanitary bumbailiff. Mr Chadwick set to work everywhere, washing and splashing, and Master John Bull was scrubbed and rubbed till the tears came to his eyes and his fists clenched themselves with worry and pain.* 99

1. Why did Chadwick want improvements in public health?
2. Why was there little progress in public health in the 1850s?

■ ACTIVITY

You are a local councillor who has decided to oppose new public health schemes in your town. Write a speech that you will deliver to your fellow councillors explaining your views and trying to win their support.

Why was public health finally improved?

Through the 1850s progress continued very slowly. Councils could ignore public health if they wished, and many did. The decisive change came with the 1875 Public Health Act which finally forced local authorities to provide clean water, proper drainage and sewers, and to appoint Medical Officers of Health. Why did the government pass this Act?

SOURCE 20 Numbers of Medical Officers of Health and average amount borrowed by councils for public health improvements

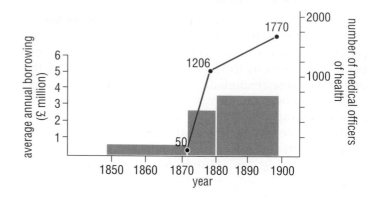

■ TASK

1. On your own copy of Source 21 draw arrows to show how these different causes are connected to each other.
2. Add other causes if you think there are things we have missed out. Show how they are connected to the other causes.
3. Now use your completed diagram to help you write an essay explaining why you agree or disagree with this statement: 'It was impossible to make any real improvements in public health in Britain before 1861.' You can get an outline from your teacher to help you.

Scientific developments
Pasteur's germ theory had finally proved the link between dirt and disease.

New voters
In 1867 working-class men had been given the vote. This meant that MPs were more likely to take notice of the needs of the people in their towns who were the main victims of poor public health.

The weakening of *laissez-faire*
As a result of all these changes the government saw it could no longer leave important public health measures to individuals or councils. The government realised that it was in everyone's interest to force towns to clean up.

Statistics
From 1837 the government collected statistics on births, marriages and deaths. William Farr used these to compile an accurate picture of where the death rate was highest and what people died of. He was able to prove, beyond any shadow of a doubt, a link between unhealthy living conditions and high death rates. He also published details of which were the most unhealthy towns which shamed some of them into action.

HM REGISTRY OF BIRTHS DEATHS & MARRIAGES

The 1875 Public Health Act
This laid down in detail all the duties that were expected of a local council. All towns were forced to perform these tasks. They included the provision of clean water, proper drainage and sewage, and the appointment of a Medical Officer of Health.

Education
Education was improving. In 1870 the government made every local authority set up schools.

Cholera
In 1865 cholera came back again. With the link between the disease and dirty water proved once and for all by John Snow, and then explained by Pasteur's germ theory, ratepayers were finally prepared to take action to clean up their towns.

Some cities led the way
Look at Leeds – a major industrial town – for example. Until 1866 very little action had been taken (see Source 18). Then in 1866 the town appointed its first Medical Officer of Health. In the same year a pressure group was formed to force the council to act. It was backed by the local newspaper who publicly blamed the council for 2,000 unnecessary deaths in Leeds each year. In 1870 a local firm got a court order to prevent sewage being pumped into the river from which it drew its own water. In 1874 Leeds had its first sewage purification works. In other towns, throughout the country, similar changes were taking place, and towns began to compete with each other to be the cleanest.

SOURCE 21 Factors leading to the 1875 Public Health Act being passed

Public health is more than sewers and water!

The improved water supply and better sewers were only one part of a range of measures taken by the government and local councils which had an effect on people's health. Source 22 summarises some of the other measures.

■ TASK

Research

Working in groups, research one or more of the items shown in Source 22. You might also want to research other topics which we have not included.

Then on your own copy of Source 22 add notes to explain when, how and why each of these measures was introduced, and why they had an impact on health, in the same way that we have done for education.

A never-ending story?

The last few pages might have given you the impression that all public health problems were solved in the 1870s. This was far from the case. Improvements in medicine and health always take a lot of time. When Charles Booth investigated the East End of London in 1889 he found many people living in appalling conditions of poverty and ill health. From 1881 infant mortality actually started to go up again after a decade of progress. The struggle to improve the living conditions and therefore the health of ordinary people continued into the twentieth century and to the present day. You will pick up the story again on page 160.

> **SOURCE 23** Written by the Reverend Samuel Barnet, 1889
>
> *66 The mother among the poor, in her joy that a son is born into the world, cannot look forward to his life. What is it to her that science has proved stronger than disease? The rich man's family may grow up unbroken around the hearth … The children of the poor must die, and the family circle is broken by death which carries off the weakly … What is it to the poor that it has been proved how cleanliness is the secret of health? They cannot have the latest sanitary appliances. They cannot take baths … or have constant change of clothing; they cannot secure that the streets shall be swept, or, as the inhabitants of Belgrave Square, protect themselves from the neighbourhood of the tallow-factory. 99*

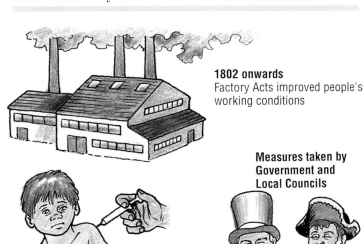

1802 onwards
Factory Acts improved people's working conditions

1852
Compulsory vaccination

Measures taken by Government and Local Councils

1858
Regulation of doctors qualifications

1876
Building regulations

Improved education: 1870 onwards
From 1870 every local authority had to set up schools. Health education was taught at many schools. Improved literacy made it possible for people to read pamphlets from Medical Officers giving advice about drainage, ventilation, diet, personal cleanliness, care of children and care of the sick.

1889
Isolation hospitals for infectious diseases

1876
Laws against pollution of rivers

1876
Food regulations improve the quality of food sold in shops

SOURCE 22 Public health measures

A century of medical progress?

■ TASK

This chart shows three areas of progress in nineteenth-century medicine. On your own copy of the chart:

1. Explain what you consider to be the most important progress in each area. Support your explanation with evidence from pages 111–47.
2. For each area explain whether changes in this area worked through to affect the health of ordinary people. Again support your explanation with evidence from pages 111–47.
3. Use your annotated chart to write an essay explaining which of the areas you think saw the most important changes, and giving reasons for your choice with evidence to support it.

■ ACTIVITY

There is no jigsaw picture on this page as there was at the end of the previous three chapters. Instead you are going to produce one. Look back at the previous three on pages 54, 82 and 103. Then either:

a) draw your own '1900 version' showing all the new ideas and information which were available to doctors in 1900; or
b) describe in words what you would put in the picture for 1900.

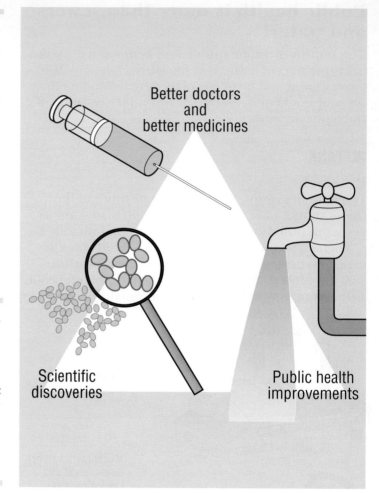

Better doctors and better medicines

Scientific discoveries

Public health improvements

5 MEDICINE AND HEALTH IN THE TWENTIETH CENTURY

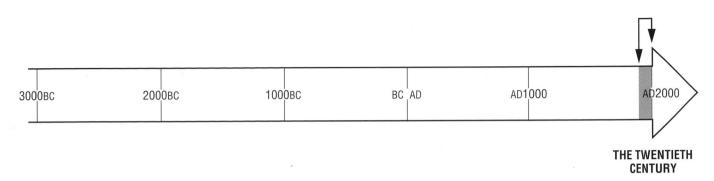

Why has medicine and health improved so rapidly since 1900?

AT THE END of the nineteenth century one writer summed up the achievements of the century as follows: 'The authorities in the great provincial cities have been pushing their activities into the dark places of the earth; slum areas are broken up, sanitary regulations have been enforced, the policeman and the inspector are at every corner. A series of factory acts, building acts, public health acts have continually attacked the worst of the evils ... the forces of progress are against these older social diseases, which must eventually disappear ...

However, despite all the important changes that took place in the 1800s, at the end of the century there was still a great deal of ill-health and misery.

- Life expectancy in 1900 remained below 50 years of age.
- In 1899, 163 out of every 1,000 babies born died before their first birthday.
- Doctors and surgeons were often unable to cure their patients. There were no antibiotics to fight internal infection.
- In surgery, although anaesthetics and antiseptics had taken much of the fear, pain and danger out of operations, the problems of bleeding and infection remained.
- The majority of families could not afford to go to a doctor.
- Many people were still living in unhealthy housing.

There was still much to discover and to improve.

In the twentieth century some of these outstanding problems have been tackled effectively for the first time. Since 1900 there have been greater improvements and more rapid changes in medicine and health than ever before.

Read all about it. Infection conquered at last! Health improved.

What medical progress did the First World War bring about?

THE FIRST WORLD WAR was a massive conflict. More people were killed and wounded than in any war before it. New and deadly weapons were used for the first time. Bullets and shrapnel from high explosive shells produced severe injuries, particularly to the head.

You will have seen from your study so far that war sometimes brings about changes for the better in medicine and health. The First World War was no exception as you can see from Source 1.

Millions were wounded giving surgeons the opportunity to experiment with new techniques.

The powerful guns used in the First World War caused more severe wounds.

Broken bones were commonplace. Surgeons developed new techniques to repair broken bones, and to perform skin grafts – which formed the basis for plastic surgery.

Head wounds were particularly common. Surgery of the eye, ear, nose and throat all improved rapidly. Brain surgery also advanced.

Many of the surgeons who learned their skills quickly in battlefield hospitals set up as specialist surgeons after the war.

Bullet wounds carried infection deep into the body. Surgeons had to search for better ways to prevent the infections. They never fully succeeded, but the suffering of the First World War inspired some doctors to search harder for an effective way to fight infection.

X-rays were invented before the war. During the war their use became routine to find bullets and shrapnel lodged in the body.

Blood transfusion was used effectively for the first time. Methods of storing blood and transporting it to where it was needed were improved.

The low standard of health among recruits to the army made the government very worried about the health of the population generally. It made them more eager to improve health care at home.

The soldiers who fought in the war were promised good housing when they returned – 'homes for heroes'. This speeded up the process of getting rid of unhealthy slum housing in Britain.

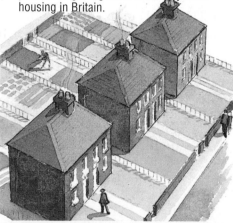

SOURCE 1 How the First World War improved medicine and health

150

Case study: how did the First World War improve surgery?

In 1900 surgeons could operate using anaesthetics and they had developed aseptic surgery (see page 139) to reduce the risk of infection in wounds during and after an operation. Some surgeons were sufficiently confident to operate inside the chest and skull. However, they still faced the problem of bleeding and internal infection.

In some ways the First World War hindered the development of surgical techniques. It stopped a great deal of medical research. In Britain 14,000 doctors were taken away from their normal work to cope with the casualties of the war. However, the war helped more than it hindered. During the conflict surgeons did their best for the wounded but their methods, which worked well in a clean hospital operating theatre, were not so effective on a dirty battlefield. They had to develop new techniques to deal with the problems. Some of these techniques had an impact on surgery in civilian hospitals after the war.

Source 3 illustrates the scale of the problem during a major battle. For five months, during the Battle of the Somme, waves of soldiers charged enemy trenches, and artillery pounded them with shells. There were over a million casualties. Blake Sullivan was just one of the tens of thousands of soldiers who needed surgery every week. The medical services were stretched to their limit.

Look at Source 1.
1. What different kinds of medical care did Blake Sullivan receive?

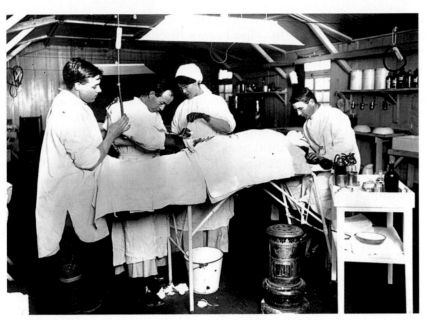

SOURCE 2 A makeshift operating theatre during the First World War

SOURCE 3 Second Lieutenant Blake Sullivan of the Connaught Rangers was wounded in the shoulder during the Battle of the Somme in September 1916. The account was written whilst he was in Chelsea Hospital shortly after his return to 'Blighty'

66 *Near the edge of the village a groaning and agonised German, with half his thigh blown off, feebly beckoned to me; and before going on I made some futile efforts to staunch his bleeding...*

Once well into Guillemont the masses of dead simply staggered me... I needed rest and, after spotting two stretcher bearers coming towards me, I sat down in the midst of the sprawling corpses. The first aid men...dressed the wound and put a sling on my left arm, before going quickly ahead again...

I was soaked in sweat and ready to drop long before reaching the first Dressing Station, where the presiding orderly gave me a drink of water so petrol tainted that I promptly vomited it out again. Pushing on, and feeling as if a hundred pound load were perched on my shoulder I gradually made my way up the hill to Montauban. There was no transport in sight, filthy and dead horses littered the ground; but a rest had become absolutely necessary – and choosing the least [decayed] of the horses I flopped down nearby.

Sergeant Casey passing on an old horse ambulance woke me and helped me on board for a ride to the casualty Clearing Station...

I lined up with the others and got a massive tetanus shot – which promptly developed a plum-sized blob on my chest. Motor ambulances then took us to the hospital in Dernancourt. At midnight they shipped me to Heilly and thence by train to Rouen hospital.

At Rouen the X-ray located the bullet. It had stabbed in under the left arm, chipped the spinal vertebra and then lodged in my right shoulder. Two days after its excision I was sent by train to Le Havre and on, by Australian Red Cross ship, to arrive 4am 9 September at Southampton. 99

Improvement 1: X-rays

X-rays had been discovered 20 years before the war.

In 1895 Wilhelm Röntgen, a German scientist, was experimenting with cathode rays which cause splashes of light in a glass tube. He had covered the tube with black paper but was amazed to find the rays were still lighting up the other side of the room. They were passing through the paper! He investigated further and found that they could also pass through wood, rubber and even human flesh, but not through bone or metal.

He called these mysterious rays X-rays since he did not know what they were. However, their importance was immediately obvious to Röntgen. He published his findings on 28 December 1895. The discovery caused great public excitement, and it had an immediate impact on medicine.

Within six months hospitals had installed X-ray machines. However, it was the First World War which really confirmed the importance of the X-ray in surgery. More machines were quickly manufactured to meet the new demands and they were soon installed in major hospitals all along the Western Front. X-rays immediately improved the success rate of surgeons in removing deeply lodged bullets and shrapnel which would otherwise have caused fatal infections.

Improvement 2: Blood transfusion

Blood transfusion had been regularly tried in the 1800s but, mysteriously, it sometimes worked and sometimes failed. Then in 1901 scientists discovered that there were different blood groups. They realised that transfusion only worked if the donor's blood group matched the receiver's.

This discovery finally made transfusion practical. However, in the years before the war it was still performed with on-the-spot donors because doctors had no way of storing blood properly – it just coagulated (changed into clots or semisolid mass).

During the First World War vast amounts of blood were needed. This made the use of on-the-spot donors very difficult. Many soldiers bled to death in the trenches before blood could be got to them. The search began for a better method of storage and transfusion.

This led doctors to the discovery that the liquid part of the blood (the plasma) could be separated from the tiny particles in the blood (corpuscles). The cells could be bottled, packed in ice and stored where they were needed. The cells only had to be diluted with a warm saline solution and usable blood was ready. This discovery helped save many lives both in the trenches and on the operating table.

SOURCE 4 A portable X-ray machine – X-rays were a vital means of finding bullets and shell fragments in wounded soldiers

2. Did the First World War have a greater role in the development of X-rays or of blood transfusion? Explain your answer.

Improvement 3: Fighting infection

In Britain aseptic surgery was practised in all hospitals and success rates in operations were much higher than they had been 30 years earlier. However, on the battlefield and under the pressure of enormous numbers of operations it was often difficult to prevent the infection of wounds. This was made worse by the presence of bacteria which lodged in clothing. When soldiers were wounded, fragments of clothing would enter the wound and the bacteria would cause GAS GANGRENE.

SOURCE 5 In the insanitary conditions of the trenches even minor wounds could quickly become infected

SOURCE 6 A medical description of gas gangrene

After forty-eight hours the edges of the wound begin to swell up and turn ... making a gape. The cut surface takes on a curious half-jellied, half-mummified look; then the whole wound limb begins to swell up and distend in the most extraordinary fashion, turning as it does so, first an ashy white and then a greenish colour. This is because the tissues are being literally blown out with gas, and on pressing the fingers down on this balloon-like swelling, a distinct crackling or tiny bubbling sensation can be felt.

By trial and error on the massive number of casualties, surgeons arrived at the answer to this problem. They cut away infected tissue and soaked the wound with a saline solution. This was a practical advance made possible by experiment during wartime.

However, this was only a limited improvement and surgeons were all too well aware of their helplessness against serious infection.

Other improvements

Faced by hundreds of thousands of casualties surgeons learned fast. They:

- developed new techniques to repair broken bones
- improved methods of grafting skin which later formed the basis for plastic surgery
- improved surgery of the eye, ear, nose and throat
- successfully attempted brain surgery.

Many surgeons who learned these skills in battlefield hospitals set up as specialists back at home after the war. There were also similar developments in the other countries involved in the war.

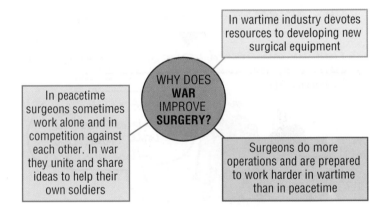

In wartime industry devotes resources to developing new surgical equipment

WHY DOES **WAR** IMPROVE **SURGERY?**

In peacetime surgeons sometimes work alone and in competition against each other. In war they unite and share ideas to help their own soldiers

Surgeons do more operations and are prepared to work harder in wartime than in peacetime

SOURCE 7 Chart summarising the views of Heneage Ogilvey, a British surgeon, about the relationship between war and surgery

3. What evidence is there on pages 150–53 to support the views in Source 7?

■ TASK

'The First World War helped more than it hindered developments in medicine.'

Explain whether you agree with this statement. You can get a sheet from your teacher to help you.

The fight against infection: from magic bullets to guided missiles

DURING THE NINETEENTH century doctors and scientists discovered the causes of many illnesses and infectious diseases. They identified the bacteria and started two lines of research in the hope that they would eventually be able to prevent and cure those diseases.

Line 1 : Prevention

Pasteur began the first line of research with his germ theory

Koch then identified the bacteria which caused specific diseases.

So these are the bacteria which causes anthrax

Using Koch's methods the bacteria causing other diseases were quickly discovered.

Pasteur discovered ways of using weakened forms of bacteria to give the body immunity

If it works for rabies then it will work for other diseases.

Following Pasteur other vaccines were developed although very slowly.

In 1906 Calmette and Guerin discovered a vaccine against tuberculosis

In 1913 Behring perfected a diphtheria vaccine.

Line 2: Cure

Koch set off the line of research by discovering that he could stain certain bacteria

I've stained them purple so that I can see them

Paul Ehrlich searched for a stain that would also kill the bacteria.

If the stain could also kill the bacteria it would be like a magic bullet to shoot the microbe

At first this line of research met with little success. It seemed to be hoping for the impossible. But after many patient experiments...

It works! 606 works!

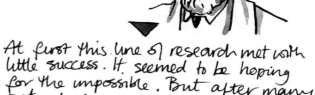

Following Ehrlich, others continued the search for magic bullets.

SOURCE 1 The two lines of research

The first magic bullet: Salvarsan 606

Paul Ehrlich was part of Robert Koch's research team. Koch had shown that certain dyes sought out certain bacteria – that is how he had been able to stain septicaemia bacteria (see page 130).

Ehrlich spent hours staining bacteria and observing the effects of the dye. He worked with Behring on diphtheria, and was fascinated by the way that the body created anti-bodies which killed bacteria but did not harm anything else. Ehrlich compared these antibodies to 'magic bullets'; he was convinced that a chemical could be found which might do the same and he set out to find one.

Despite years of research Ehrlich had little success. In 1905 he was looking for a magic bullet to treat SYPHILIS. Instead of dyes he experimented with a variety of chemical compounds based on arsenic. Ehrlich's team tried 605 variations before they found one that worked. They nearly missed the discovery that 606 worked and it was only when it was being retested that another assistant, Sahashiro Hata, realised that it killed the syphilis bacteria.

The drug was named Salvarsan but it was difficult to use. It could kill not only the microbes causing the disease but the patient as well. The importance of Ehrlich's discovery was that a chemical compound had been used for the first time to destroy bacteria.

1. Explain what Ehrlich meant by the phrase 'magic bullet'.
2. How was Ehrlich's work different from that of Pasteur?

The second magic bullet: Prontosil

Research into the use of chemical compounds was interrupted by the First World War, but in the 1920s it was picked up again.

In 1932, Gerhardt Domagk tried out Prontosil, a red dye. Domagk started a series of tests using mice. The results were good. It definitely had an effect on the bacteria which caused blood poisoning.

> **S**OURCE 2 The entry in the laboratory notebook of Domagk on Christmas Day 1932
>
> 66 *Prepared D4145 K1 730.*
> *Gave orally at the dose of 0.5 grams. So far [the mouse] is very lively, eats heartily, the swellings on the digits … have disappeared …* 99

Domagk got an opportunity to test Prontosil on a human much sooner than he had expected. His daughter Hildegarde was playing with her pet guinea pig near to some medical equipment when she pricked her finger on an infected needle. She soon developed severe blood poisoning. With his daughter near to death, Domagk decided to risk using Prontosil even though he had not tried it on any human before. He gave her a large dose. She recovered. The second magic bullet had been found.

The sulphonamides

The obvious next step was to find what the active ingredient was in Prontosil. It only took two years for French researchers to find it. It was a sulphonamide derived from coal tar. The speed of this discovery was because of the invention in 1931 of new powerful ELECTRON MICROSCOPES.

Soon all the major drug companies joined a race to discover cures based on sulphonamides (which meant any drug derived from coal tar). This was a period of great excitement. Within a few years drugs had been developed to cure and control scarlet fever, meningitis, GONORRHOEA and pneumonia.

The new drugs soon improved health. Maternal mortality, for example, was reduced because infections following childbirth could now be controlled (see Source 3).

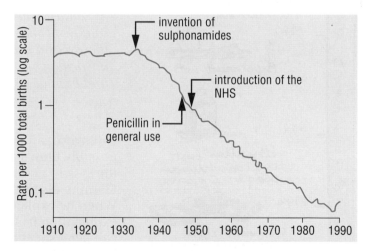

SOURCE 3 Maternal mortality in Britain 1910–90

■ TASK

Draw your own diagram to show the factors which led to the development of sulphonamide drugs, and the results that flowed from their development.

Case study: the development of penicillin

The story of penicillin begins well before the Second World War as you can see from Source 4.

1928 Fleming discovered mould has killed germs

1929 Fleming writes articles about Penicillin

1937 Chain and Florey begin research in Oxford on Penicillin after reading an article by Fleming

1940 Experiment with mice

THE SECOND WORLD WAR

1941 Penicillin first tested on a human being in Oxford

1942 U.S. and British governments co-operate to fund production of penicillin

1944 Enough penicillin to treat all the allied forces wounded in the D-Day invasion of Europe

SOURCE 4 The discovery and development of penicillin

156

When was penicillin discovered?

Penicillin itself is made from a mould called penicillium. It was first discovered in the early nineteenth century by John Sanderson who found that very little grew near it. In the 1880s Joseph Lister noted these observations and wrote to his brother saying that he intended to try penicillin on infected wounds. Lister successfully used penicillin to treat a young nurse who had an infected wound. However, he did not leave any notes on this case and apparently stopped using the mould. Several other scientists investigated the mould but were unable to produce sufficient quantities or discover a way of applying it to a patient.

It was in the laboratory of St Mary's Hospital, London, in 1928, that Alexander Fleming rediscovered the properties of penicillin. This is how Fleming's biographer describes the discovery. Fleming's friend Pryce had gone to visit him in his laboratory.

> **S**OURCE 5 A. Maurois, *The Life of Sir Alexander Fleming*, 1963
>
> 66 *Fleming was in his little laboratory as usual, surrounded by innumerable dishes. The cautious Scot disliked being separated from his* CULTURES *before he was quite certain that there was no longer anything to be learned from them … Fleming took up several old cultures and removed the lids. Several of the cultures had been contaminated with mould … 'As soon as you uncover a culture dish,' he said to Pryce, 'something tiresome is sure to happen. Things fall out of the air.'*
> *Suddenly he stopped talking, then, after a moment's observation, said … 'That's funny …' On the cultures at which he was looking there was a growth of mould, as on several of the others, but on this particular one, all around the mould, the colonies of* STAPHYLOCOCCI *had been dissolved …* 99

On investigation he found that penicillin bacteria had got onto the dish, possibly blown in through an open window. The penicillin was killing the STAPHYLOCOCCI. There are other versions of the story of how Fleming discovered penicillin. Indeed, Fleming's own versions varied. When he explained in 1945 how he grew the mould it was a different explanation from his original report for a research paper in 1929. You can get a sheet from your teacher about that if you want. However, the important point is that Fleming observed the results and recognised their significance – that penicillin could be applied to or injected into areas infected with penicillin-sensitive microbes. However, Fleming did not have the facilities or the support to develop and test his idea that penicillin could fight infection.

1. Why was it Fleming is usually thought of as the discoverer of penicillin?
2. Why do you think that so many people observed the power of penicillin yet did not develop it as a cure?

How was penicillin developed?

It was the Second World War which finally brought about the successful development of penicillin.

In the 1930s two Oxford scientists, Howard Florey and Ernst Chain, became interested in Fleming's 1929 paper about penicillin. In 1939 they gathered together a skilled research team, including pathologists, chemists and BIOCHEMISTS, and three days after the outbreak of the Second World War Florey asked the British government for money to fund the team's research into penicillin.

SOURCE 6 Part of the proposal made by Florey to the Medical Research Council, 6 September 1939

66 I enclose some proposals that have a very practical bearing at the moment.

The properties of penicillin hold out the promise of its finding practical application in the treatment of infections. In view of the great practical importance of penicillin it is proposed to prepare these substances in purified form suitable for injection and to study their antiseptic action on living creatures. 99

SOURCE 7 Sir Ernst Chain describing the team's research in the *Journal of the Royal College of Surgeons,* 1972

66 The only reason that motivated me was scientific interest. That penicillin could have a practical use in medicine did not enter our minds when we started work on it. 99

Stage 1: growing the penicillin

The process devised by Chain to make penicillin was a combination of the latest freeze-drying technology and some much more traditional equipment: thousands of milk bottles (in which to grow the bacteria), milk churns, a dog bath and a hand pump! Slowly the team gathered a few grams of pure penicillin.

Stage 2: testing the penicillin on animals

There was just enough penicillin to try an experiment on eight mice. They were all injected with dangerous microbes. Four mice were then given penicillin. Four were not. Twenty-four hours later the mice who had not been injected with penicillin were dead. Those who had been given penicillin were fine.

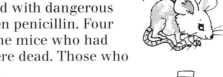

Stage 3: the first human trial of penicillin

The team needed more penicillin for a human trial than they had for the mice. It was not until early 1941 that they had enough to test it on a human patient.

SOURCE 8 Professor Fletcher (one of Florey's team) remembering events in Oxford, 19 February 1941

66 The patient had a sore on his mouth a month previously, and the infection had spread to his scalp. He'd had an abscess there. It had spread to both his eyes and one had to be removed. He had abscesses open on his arm. He had abscesses on his lung – he was well on his way towards death from a terrible infection. We'd nothing to lose and everything to gain. So we thought we'd try [penicillin].

The shortage of penicillin was such that after the first day I collected his urine and I took it over to where Florey was working so that the penicillin could be extracted from the urine and used again.

On the fourth day the patient was really dramatically improved, he was sitting up in bed and his temperature had gone down. On the fifth day the penicillin began to run out and we couldn't go on. Of course when they extracted it from the urine they couldn't get it all back and it gradually ran out... He gradually relapsed and eventually died. 99

Although this patient still died, the trial confirmed that penicillin was a powerful drug. Florey was sure that if enough had been available the man would have lived. Production of penicillin remained painfully slow, but as new batches were produced two more patients were successfully treated. A year later, in August 1942, Fleming himself used penicillin successfully to treat a friend who had meningitis.

■ ACTIVITY

Work in pairs. Either write or role play a discussion between members of Florey's team discussing the progress the team has made so far.

How was penicillin mass produced?

It was clear that penicillin could be a very powerful treatment if only it could be mass produced. The growing casualties of the Second World War added urgency to this need. Florey knew that a massive amount of research and investment would be necessary to produce the thousands of doses of penicillin needed.

A setback

Production in Britain was always going to be a problem because of the threat of German bombing, so, in June 1941, Florey travelled to America to try to interest drug companies there in developing penicillin. At that stage, America was still not involved in the war, there had been only three successful trials of penicillin and there was no proven method for speeding up production.

However, in December 1941 the USA entered the war and this completely changed the situation.

Timetable of success

In 1942 the American government gave $80 million to four drug companies to find a way to mass produce penicillin.

In 1943 production began. The first use in war was by the British army in North Africa (see Source 10).

By June 1944 there was enough penicillin to treat all the casualties suffered on D-Day.

By 1945 the American army was using two million doses a month. It is estimated that another 12–15 per cent of wounded Allied soldiers would have died without penicillin to fight their infection. Penicillin also roughly halved the average time the Allied wounded spent in hospital.

Soon after the war penicillin became available for civilian use – it was called an antibiotic.

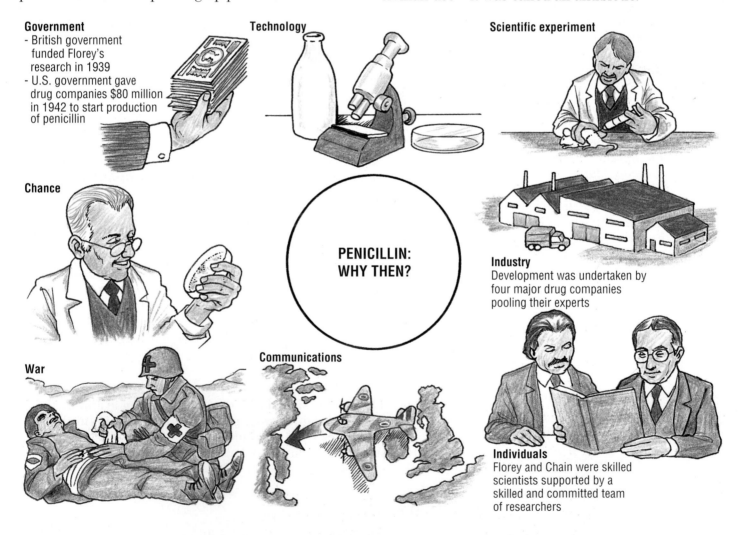

Government
- British government funded Florey's research in 1939
- U.S. government gave drug companies $80 million in 1942 to start production of penicillin

Technology

Scientific experiment

Chance

Industry
Development was undertaken by four major drug companies pooling their experts

PENICILLIN: WHY THEN?

War

Communications

Individuals
Florey and Chain were skilled scientists supported by a skilled and committed team of researchers

SOURCE 9 Factors influencing the development of penicillin

S**OURCE 10** Lt Colonel Pulvertaft describes the first use of penicillin by the British army in 1943

66 We had enormous numbers of infected wounded, terrible burn cases among the crews of the armoured cars. Sulphonamides had absolutely no effect on these cases. The last thing I tried was penicillin … The first man I tried it on was a young New Zealand officer called Newton. He had been in bed for six months with compound fractures of both legs. His sheets were soaked with pus and the heat of Cairo made it smell intolerable. Normally he would have died in a short time. I gave three injections a day of penicillin and studied the effects under the microscope … the thing seemed like a miracle. In ten days' time the leg was cured and in a month's time the young fellow was back on his feet. I had enough penicillin for ten cases. Nine out of ten of them were complete cures. 99

Penicillin – why then?

By now you will have identified a number of causes of change in medicine – war, the role of governments and scientific discoveries by research teams. These causes have often been interconnected as you can see in this case study of penicillin.

■ **TASK**

1. Describe the main events in the development of penicillin.
2. Explain the part played by Fleming in the development of penicillin.
3. Why was penicillin mass produced in 1942–45, and not before?

How have drugs and treatments developed since 1945?

There are enormous profits to be made for companies who develop successful drugs. Drug companies now spend billions of pounds on research.

The range of new drugs being produced each year is impossible to summarise. There are now many new antibiotics with thousands of variations of 'magic bullets'. They all work in roughly the same way as penicillin – by killing bacteria. However, there are also many diseases they cannot help with. They do not attack viruses, for example, so the search for other ways to prevent and control disease has continued. Since 1945, polio, whooping cough, German measles and measles vaccines have been developed. Other developments have included drugs which use the body's hormones, for example the contraceptive pill.

Problems

There have also been some tragic failures and mistakes in drug development. Between 1959 and 1962 a drug called THALIDOMIDE was sold to women to help alleviate morning sickness during pregnancy. It had not been adequately tested before it was put on the market. Thalidomide was found to cause severe abnormalities to FOETUSES. Children were born with severely deformed limbs. It is now known that these problems can be passed on to their own children. The drug was withdrawn and testing procedures were tightened up. All drugs now undergo rigorous trials before becoming available to the public.

Over the last 40 years researchers have also found that some bacteria have begun to become resistant to antibiotics which could cause great problems in the future.

Genetic engineering

More powerful microscopes have made it possible for doctors to see not just the body's CELLS, but the genes and CHROMOSOMES within them.

This has made possible a whole new type of treatment: GENETIC ENGINEERING. Genes can be manipulated to correct problems in a patient's body. For example, DNA can be made to produce the important PROTEIN INSULIN, which occurs naturally in most people, but in people with diabetes is absent. Genetic engineering can also artificially produce antibodies which seek out and destroy specific cells within the body – a kind of guided missile!

■ **TASK**

List any treatments which members of your class or your family have used recently. Divide the treatments into groups:
a) those which were available in the nineteenth century
b) those which were developed between 1900 and 1945
c) those developed since 1945.
Use these lists to help you prepare for a class debate on the topic:
'There has been more change than continuity in treatments since the nineteenth century.'

Why did infant mortality decrease so rapidly from 1900 to 1945?

66 In the bed was a young woman, wan and dazed. She was holding a week-old baby to her empty breast. It was so pitiful I did not know what to say.

'I thought there were two children.'

'There was three days ago,' the woman said. 'Show her, Jem.' The man got up heavily, and opened the bottom drawer of a rickety chest and there lay a little dead child of about two. I gasped.

He said, 'We be waiting for the parish to come and bury her.' The mother said, 'We couldn't put her upstairs, alone, in the empty room.'

I stood still, sobbing, but the parents shed no tears, nor said a word, except when Jem closed the drawer. 'She were a nice little lass, she were,' he said. 99

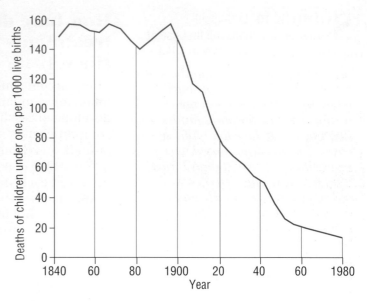

SOURCE 2 Infant mortality 1840–1980

Parents did all they could to protect their children but infant mortality was a normal part of everyone's life in the early twentieth century. In fact in 1901, despite all the progress in science and in public health in the nineteenth century, infant mortality was worse than it had been in 1801. The worst year on record was 1899 when 163 out of every 1,000 babies died before they reached the age of one.

In the twentieth century the picture changed completely as you can see from Source 2.

1. Look at Source 2. When did infant mortality begin to improve?
2. When did it improve most rapidly?
3. Study Source 3. List all the factors leading to high infant mortality.
4. Pick three which you think would be the most difficult problems to solve. Explain your choice.
5. Does Source 3 suggest that ordinary people did or did not understand that germs cause disease?

Diarrhoea caught from germs was the main cause of deaths of young babies. Other infectious diseases (see page 115) were also very serious.

Infant mortality was higher in poor families, who were living in insanitary and badly ventilated housing, or eating a poor diet.

'Infant mortality increases in proportion to adult women taking jobs in factories or farming.'
John Simon 1890

'Cold is a prolific cause of infant mortality.'
Birmingham Medical Officer of Health 1893

'Milk given to children often comes from cows in the most filthy condition. The milkers are filthy and their vessels often dirty.' (Bottle feeding was increasingly popular at this time.)
Parliament's Committee on Physical Deterioration 1904

'Babies are given comforters (dummies) dipped in dirty milk. They fall on the floor. They are never cleaned except on a dirty apron. They are full of germs.'
Newman's report, Infant Mortality

'Overcrowded housing is the most important contribution to the spread of preventable disease.'
Sir Thomas Crawford 1890

'On no account must a baby sleep in bed with its mother because the mother is in danger of rolling over and smothering the baby.'
Health visitor's advice 1910

SOURCE 3 Explanations of infant mortality at the turn of the century

Why did infant mortality decrease?

Sources 4–10 explain various factors which helped reduce infant mortality. First, work through the sources and questions. Then you will write your own account of why things improved.

SOURCE 4 Children queue for a 'farthing breakfast' at the Salvation Army in the East End of London. In the late 1800s such religious organisations took the lead both to help the poor, and to pressurise the government to do something about the problems

SOURCE 5 In 1900 when the army needed recruits for the Boer War, it was found that 38 per cent of volunteers were unfit to be soldiers. The government was so alarmed by the army recruitment problem that it set up a Committee on Physical Deterioration to find out why. These were the main conclusions of the Committee in 1904

Bad health is not inherited. It can be improved by changes in food, hygiene and clothing and by:
a) getting rid of overcrowded housing
b) enforcing building regulations
c) controlling smoke pollution
d) regular medical inspections of school children.
e) setting up day nurseries for the infants of working mothers, run by local councils
f) prohibiting the sale of tobacco to children
The main conclusion of the Committee was:
'The Committee are aware of the enormous sacrifice of infant life due to insufficient or improper feeding. The Committee advocates:
g) the systematic instruction of girls in the process of infant feeding and management.'

6. Some historians think the Committee (Source 5) put an unfair blame on mothers. Do you agree?

The schools taught:
- the importance of hygiene and the danger of diarrhoea for infants
- how flies spread disease from privies and rubbish in the street
- that breast feeding was better than bottle feeding
- that good mothering was a duty women should perform for their king and country.

SOURCE 6 Women at a school for mothers. The first one opened in 1907

7. Look at Source 6. How useful do you think each of the points taught will be in helping reduce infant mortality?

SOURCE 7 Measures taken by the government 1902–30

1902	*Compulsory training for midwives*
1906	*Meals provided for school children*
1907	*All births to be notified to health visitor*
1907	*Schools to provide medical care and checks*
1909	*Overcrowded back-to-back housing banned. Building regulations to be enforced*
1918	*Local authorities to provide health visitors, clinics for pregnant women and infants and day nurseries*
1919	*Local authorities required to build new houses for the working classes*
1930	*Five-year slum clearance programme began*

8. Look at Source 7. Explain how each of these measures from 1902–30 could help reduce infant mortality.

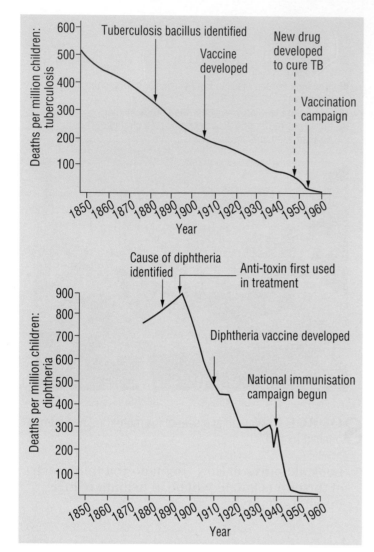

SOURCE 8 Graphs showing the decline in deaths of children from TB and diphtheria, two major killers of young children in the nineteenth century

9. Study Source 8. Which disease was the biggest killer in 1900 and 1940?
10. Did similar factors help reduce deaths from both diseases?

SOURCE 9 Details of housing improvements in the 1930s

In the 1930s the government forced local authorities to rehouse 80 per cent of people living in poor housing. The old houses were demolished. By 1939 700,000 new homes with good sanitation and ventilation had been built by local authorities, many of them on large new housing estates away from the city and town centres.

SOURCE 10 Findings of a survey by Elizabeth Robertson into infant mortality in Preston in the early twentieth century

" *The fall in infant mortality coincided with:*
a) *the replacement of earth privies with water closets*
b) *the introduction of health visitors and qualified midwives*
c) *rise in family incomes at least partly due to a rise in married women's employment*
d) *marked decline in the rate of infectious diseases.* "

11. List the factors shown in Sources 8–10 which are associated with reduced infant mortality. For each one explain whether you think it is more important or less important than educating mothers about hygiene.

The Second World War

During the Second World War health services were reorganised to cope with the high number of casualties from bombing. It gave everyone much better access to health care.

In 1940 a campaign was launched to get all children immunised against diphtheria. You can see the results in Source 8.

Food rationing was introduced together with a healthier eating campaign. The diet of some poorer people improved during the war because the Ministry of Food tried to ensure that rations included the vitamins and calories which many people would not otherwise have had in their diet.

12. Which of the measures taken during the Second World War would have the most major impact on children's health?

■ **TASK**

Write an essay answering the question 'Why did infant mortality decline so rapidly from 1900 to 1945?' You can get a sheet from your teacher to help you structure your essay.

What was the impact of the Second World War on medicine and health in Britain?

SIXTY-FIVE MILLION people died in the Second World War. Millions more were injured both physically and mentally. However, the war triggered a number of important advances in medicine and health. You have already come across the development of penicillin and the continuing improvement in children's health. Source 1 summarises these and other developments.

■ TASK

1. Explain how each development shown in Source 1 improved health. You can get a chart from your teacher to complete.
2. Which of these developments would not have taken place but for the war?

SOURCE 1 The impact of the Second World War

Blood transfusion
This further improved during the Second World War. Blood could be stored for longer. Civilians donated blood.

Surgery
Further advances were made during the Second World War in the use of skin grafts and the treatment of burns.

Diet
Rationing improved some people's diet. Government posters encouraged healthy eating.

Your own vegetables all the year round ...

if you **DIG** FOR **NOW** VICTORY

Hygiene
Government posters educated people about basic health and hygiene.

MINISTRY OF HEALTH says:—
Coughs and sneezes spread diseases
Trap the germs by using your handkerchief
Help to keep the Nation Fighting Fit

Drugs
Penicillin was developed – the first antibiotic.

Disease
The government launched its national diphtheria immunisation campaign.

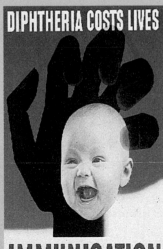

DIPHTHERIA COSTS LIVES
IMMUNISATION COSTS NOTHING
Ask at your local council offices, school or welfare centre

Poverty
Evacuation took 1.5 million urban children out of the cities into rural areas. The experience highlighted for everyone the massive contrast between the living standards of rich and poor. It increased the commitment of the government to fight poverty more seriously after the war.

The National Health Service
With the threat looming of major civilian casualties from German bombing the government reorganised health care. In 1942 William Beveridge, a leading civil servant, proposed that these changes should be preserved in a 'free national health service' for all.

'From cradle to grave' – the National Health Service

THE SECOND WORLD WAR led directly to the setting up of the National Health Service in Britain. You are now going to investigate in detail why the NHS was established and how it changed medicine and health in Britain.

The story starts 40 years earlier at the beginning of the twentieth century.

1911: National Health Insurance introduced

In the early 1900s the government became increasingly aware of the health problems facing ordinary people. Evidence showed that the poor still lived in terrible housing, and that when they were sick they could not afford medical care (see page 165).

In 1911 the government introduced a National Insurance Scheme. Workers and their employer made weekly contributions to a central fund which was then used to give the workers sickness benefit, and free medical care from a panel doctor, if they became ill.

It was limited to those who were employed. This meant that women and children were often not covered by any insurance scheme; nor were the unemployed, the elderly, the mentally ill and the chronically ill.

THE DAWN OF HOPE.

Mr. LLOYD GEORGE'S National Health Insurance Bill provides for the insurance of the Worker in case of Sickness.

Support the Liberal Government
in their policy of
SOCIAL REFORM.

SOURCE 1 A poster produced by the Liberal government

1. Look at Source 1. Who do you think this poster was aimed at?

How did things change in the 1930s?

For many people it became harder to get good medical care during the economic depression of the 1930s. Up to three million people in Britain were unemployed. The government reduced its contribution to health insurance. Many unemployed people could not keep up their contributions and the companies who ran these schemes found that they were not making any profits. In 1934 there were four million insurance policies on which people owed payments. There were alarming statistics to show that in some areas, which were most affected by the depression, infant mortality was climbing again.

The government was, however, unwilling to accept publicly that large portions of the population were suffering, and the government's overall contribution to the nation's health care remained small as you can see from Source 4.

Town	1928	1931	1933
Wigan	93	103	110
Liverpool	94	94	98
St Helens	98	88	116
Bath	47	39	52
Brighton	50	54	47
Oxford	38	44	32

SOURCE 2 The death rate of infants out of 1000 births in selected towns

SOURCE 3 In 1933 the Minister of Health, against the advice of his public health officials and doctors, said:

66 *There is at present no available evidence of any general increase in sickness or mortality as a result of the economic depression or unemployment.* 99

SOURCE 4
Funding for the health services in 1938/9 assessed by C. Webster

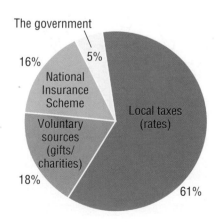

The government 5%
16%
National Insurance Scheme
Voluntary sources (gifts/charities) 18%
Local taxes (rates) 61%

What health care was available to most people?

Despite the National Insurance Scheme many people continued to rely on cheap, easy-to-find remedies or those handed down through families for generations. They relied on neighbours and family for care when they were sick.

SOURCE 5 From an interview with Kathleen Davys, one of a family of thirteen children. She lived in Birmingham. The local doctor charged six pence per visit

66 Headaches, we had vinegar and brown paper; for whooping cough we had camphorated oil rubbed on our chests or goose fat. For mumps we had stockings round our throats and measles we had tea stewed in the teapot by the fire – all different kinds of home cures. They thought they were better than going to the doctor's. Well, they couldn't afford the doctor because sixpence in those days was like looking at a five pound note today. 99

and keep out of the New Hospital!

SOURCE 6 An advert for a healthy drink from a 1930s newspaper. Such remedies continued to sell well in the 1930s

SOURCE 7 Oral history interview describing the 1930s quoted in Gray, *The Worst of Times*, 1986

66 I remember our Brian being born. He was delivered by a doctor up at Oldham, a Scotsman. He got called up and killed in the war, so we never paid for Brian. The doctors were very good. You'd go to the doctor. He had your name and address. And after, you got a bill, and if you couldn't pay it, which very few people could, each doctor had his own collector. The collector used to come round each week and you'd pay sixpence. My wife's father and mother used to say they'd never be straight in their lifetime. The collectors always used to be the same type that were park keepers in them days – they'd be no use today, kids'd throw them in the pond – but they were always wizened little fellers. 99

SOURCE 8 R. Roberts, an interview recorded in the journal *Oral History*, 1984, describing the 1930s

66 She wasn't quite 71 [when she got ill] and she was 77 when she died. She was in bed all that time. It paralysed her all down one side. She could get out of bed ... but she couldn't get back. So my auntie next door took her and she had her in the front room in the bed downstairs and my mother looked to her in the daytime and auntie looked to her at night. 99

SOURCE 9 A pharmacy

SOURCE 10 R. Roberts, an interview with a pharmacist published in *Health, Disease and Medicine in Lancashire 1750–1950*, 1980. He is describing his work in the 1920s

66
Q: Did people ask you for advice?
A: We had to do a bit of diagnosing in our own way and be responsible for it.
Q: Would they for example bring the children in and say 'What is the matter?'
A: Oh my goodness yes.
Q: What sort of things would be the matter?
A: It might be just nettle rash, it might be measles – very often it was measles and teething trouble, a little feverish, constipation or something like that, the usual childish ailments but we had to be very very careful ...
Q: You didn't charge for this advice?
A: Oh dear no. Anything had to be cheap ... 99

2. List the different types of health care shown in Sources 5–10.
3. Does this evidence suggest change or continuity in comparison with earlier centuries?

Why was the National Health Service introduced?

With the outbreak of the Second World War in 1939, the government knew there had to be adequate medical services to cope with large numbers of civilian casualties so it increased its involvement in medical care. By 1942 people were beginning to think about how the system should be organised when the war ended. In that year a leading civil servant, William Beveridge, put forward his ideas about 'a free national health service' as part of a complete rethink of the government's National Insurance Scheme.

O, rare and refreshing Beveridge!

SOURCE 12 The front page and cartoon from the *Daily Mirror*, 2 December 1942

1. Read Source 12. What was the *Beveridge Report* proposing for health care in 1942?
2. How was this different from the system that existed before 1939?
3. In one year over 600,000 copies of the *Beveridge Report* were sold. Why were so many people interested in the changes that it proposed?

Timeline showing the development of the National Health Service

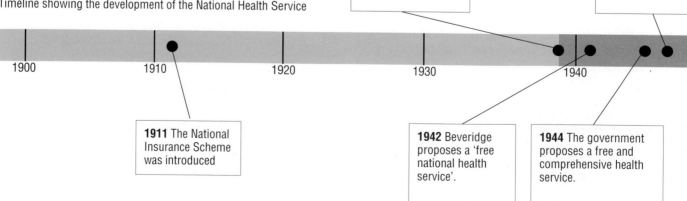

1939 The Emergency Hospital Scheme started – it was funded and run by the government.

1946 National Health Service Act provides for a free and comprehensive health-care system.

1911 The National Insurance Scheme was introduced

1942 Beveridge proposes a 'free national health service'.

1944 The government proposes a free and comprehensive health service.

What was the National Health Service?

By 1944 the system was being planned to be 'comprehensive in two senses – first that it be available to all people, and second, that it cover all necessary forms of health care'. In 1945 a new Labour government was elected, and in 1946 its Bill to introduce a NHS was passed by Parliament.

SOURCE 13
A. The front page of the first leaflet describing the new National Health Service and
B. Diagram showing the services provided by the NHS

A

THE NEW
NATIONAL
HEALTH
SERVICE

Your new National Health Service begins on 5th July. What is it? How do you get it?

It will provide you with all medical, dental, and nursing care. Everyone—rich or poor, man, woman or child—can use it or any part of it. There are no charges, except for a few special items. There are no insurance qualifications. But it is not a "charity". You are all paying for it, mainly as taxpayers, and it will relieve your money worries in time of illness.

B

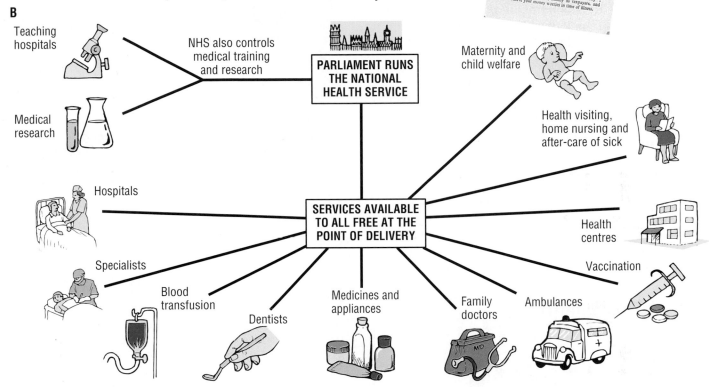

Teaching hospitals

Medical research

NHS also controls medical training and research

PARLIAMENT RUNS THE NATIONAL HEALTH SERVICE

Maternity and child welfare

Health visiting, home nursing and after-care of sick

Hospitals

SERVICES AVAILABLE TO ALL FREE AT THE POINT OF DELIVERY

Health centres

Specialists

Blood transfusion

Dentists

Medicines and appliances

Family doctors

Ambulances

Vaccination

5 July 1948 the first day of the National Health Service:
- the nationalisation of hospitals
- the creation of health centres
- the better distribution of doctors around the country
- a new salary structure for doctors.

1970s Single-issue health-care campaigns begin – for example, against smoking or promoting a healthy diet.

1989 'Working for Patients' produced by the government proposes changes to the NHS with the introduction of competition between hospitals.

1992 'The Health of the Nation' initiative sets the NHS five targets to help prevent and reduce death and illness in the following areas: heart disease; cancer; mental illness; HIV/Aids; and accidents.

1950   1960   1970   1980   1990

1990/91 Hospitals allowed to become Trusts. GPs allowed to become fund holders buying services from hospitals and other services.

Early 1960s A new building programme begins to replace some out-of-date hospitals.

Why did people oppose the NHS?

Most medical changes meet some resistance but the NHS was a major and a sudden change. The minister appointed to introduce it was Aneurin Bevan, an ex-miner from South Wales and a trade-union leader with a reputation for being rebellious and outspoken.

He faced a number of problems.

Local authorities and voluntary organisations

Under the NHS the 3,000 hospitals in Britain would be nationalised. This was opposed by the local authorities and voluntary bodies who currently ran the hospitals.

The cost

Argument raged over the enormous costs involved. Bevan agreed that the NHS was going to be an expensive venture, but he argued that the nation had to afford it and could afford it.

The British Medical Association

The stiffest opposition came from the British Medical Association (BMA), who represented the medical profession. Doctors didn't want to be employed by the government and be told where to work, because they would no longer be able to sell their services. They feared that this would result in a loss of income.

HERE HE COMES, BOYS!

7th August, 1945. Mr. Aneurin Bevan's appointment as Minister of Health is not welcome in certain circles.

SOURCE 14 Cartoon from the *Daily Mirror,* May 1946

How Bevan won

When the BMA ran a survey in late 1946, 54 per cent of its members said they would refuse to co-operate with the NHS, and by January 1948 this had risen to 90 per cent.

However, Bevan had a powerful personality and he won many in the medical profession over to his side. He gained the support of hospital consultants

by promising them a salary and allowing them to treat private patients in NHS hospitals. At the same time, he seemed willing to talk to doctors on the lesser issues. In May 1948 opposition crumbled and when the NHS was finally introduced in July 1948 90 per cent of doctors had enrolled.

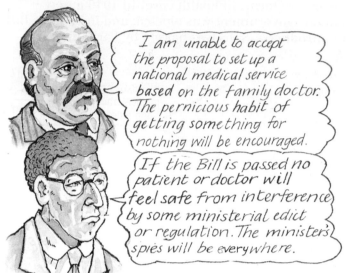

I am unable to accept the proposal to set up a national medical service based on the family doctor. The pernicious habit of getting something for nothing will be encouraged.

If the Bill is passed no patient or doctor will feel safe from interference by some ministerial edict or regulation. The minister's spies will be everywhere.

SOURCE 15 Opposition to the National Health Service

SOURCE 16 From a speech made by Nye Bevan in 1946

❝ *Medical treatment should be made available to rich and poor alike in accordance with medical need and no other criteria. Worry about money in a time of sickness is a serious hindrance to recovery apart from its unnecessary cruelty. The records show that it is the mother in the average family who suffers most from the absence of a full health service. In trying to balance her budget she puts her own needs last… The essence of a satisfactory health service is that the rich and the poor are treated alike, that poverty is not a disability, and wealth is not advantaged.* ❞

■ ACTIVITY

In pairs take the side of either Nye Bevan or a doctor opposed to the National Health Service. Use the information and sources on this page to help you write down the main points on which your argument is based. Try to persuade your partner that you are right.

In class discussion, pick out the most persuasive arguments on each side.

Achievements of the NHS

SOURCE 17 Alice Law recalling 5 July 1948, the first day of the National Health Service

66 *Mother went and got tested for new glasses. Then she went further down the road ... for the chiropodist. She had her feet done. Then she went back to the doctor's because she'd been having trouble with her ears and the doctor said ... he would fix her up with a hearing aid and I remember her saying to the doctor on the way out 'Well, the undertaker's on the way home, I might as well call in there'.* 99

Impact on women

The NHS made women's health a priority and has continued to do so. Women are now four times more likely to consult a doctor than a man. Life expectancy for women has risen from 66 to 78 since 1948. Maternal mortality had been reducing since the development of sulphonamide drugs (see page 155), but under the NHS the rate came down faster still. The NHS also took away the awful worry which women as the main carers in a family often had to bear – helplessly watching the pain or death of a relative for lack of money to do anything about it.

Family doctors

The NHS transformed the role of the family doctor. GPs increasingly work as part of teams offering a whole range of health services.

1. Before the NHS most GPs worked on their own. What are the advantages of working in a team such as in Source 18?

SOURCE 18 Services available through a south London surgery

Problems faced by the NHS

The NHS aimed to provide the best care possible. As medicine has advanced since 1948 the cost of providing that care has increased.

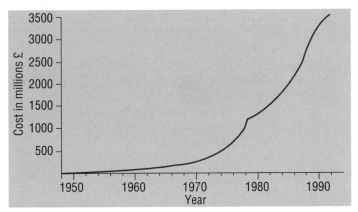

SOURCE 19 The rising cost of the NHS 1948–92

Compromises have had to be made. Prescription charges were introduced in the early 1950s. Charges for other services such as dental treatment were also introduced. In recent years lack of money has left hospital beds unused even though there is a need for them. Some people have even been refused costly services.

However, the fact remains that the NHS costs less than other systems. For example, the USA has a private health care system which costs 12 per cent of national income while the NHS costs just 6 per cent.

■ TASK

Write your own comparison of health services before the NHS with services since 1948. Use the information on the last six pages and your own research. You can also get a sheet from your teacher to help you structure your answer.

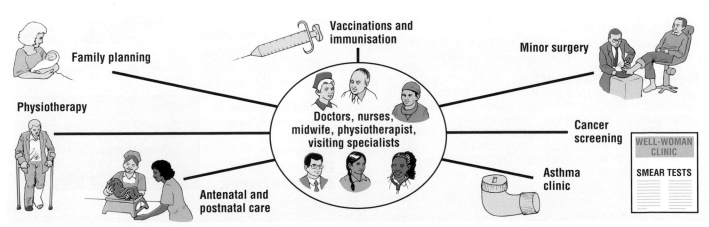

What kills people today?

IN THE LATE twentieth century the dreaded diseases of the nineteenth century no longer cause most deaths. A combination of antibiotics, vaccinations and public health measures has conquered many of them (see Source 1). Instead it is illnesses such as heart disease and cancer which kill most people.

1. Look at Source 2. What do you think is the greatest change between 1919 and 1992? Explain your choice.
2. What things have not changed between 1919 and 1992?

■ ACTIVITY

You have been asked to draw up a three-point plan for reducing either cancer or heart disease. Summarise why:

■ health education
■ more research
■ caring for patients

might help reduce the number of people dying of cancer or heart disease.

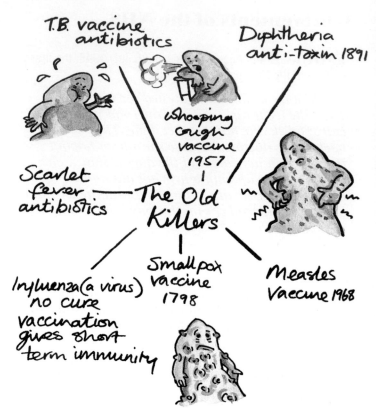

SOURCE 1 How the old killer diseases have been beaten

SOURCE 2 Causes of death in 1919 and 1992

Cancer

Cancer is uncontrolled growth of the cells in one area of the body.

If cancer cells then split off and move into an important organ such as the liver, secondary cancers can grow there. It is often these secondary cancers which cause death.

What causes cancer?
Cancerous growth starts because a change happens to the DNA in a cell. Despite decades of expensive research we still do not know exactly what triggers this change. Skin cancer can be triggered by sunburn; bowel cancer by unhealthy diet; lung cancer by smoking.

Who gets cancer?
It is mostly older people who suffer from cancer. In Britain the most common cancer in men is lung cancer, in women, breast cancer.

How is cancer treated?
The key to tackling cancer is prevention. Cancer can be avoided by having regular check ups; by following a healthy diet and avoiding cancer-causing activities such as smoking.

Once cancer has started, if it is detected early, it can be tackled through radiography (attacking the cancers with X-rays), chemotherapy (chemicals which attack the cancer), surgery or a combination of all these.

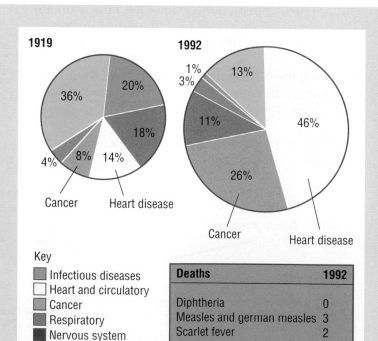

Key

■ Infectious diseases
□ Heart and circulatory
■ Cancer
■ Respiratory
■ Nervous system
■ Injury and poisoning

Deaths	1992
Diphtheria	0
Measles and german measles	3
Scarlet fever	2
Tuberculosis and influenza	418

Why have things changed?

There are a number of explanations why cancer and heart disease have become the big killers of the late twentieth century.

Explanation 1: increased life expectancy

Since 1900 life expectancy in rich countries has increased rapidly. Both cancer and heart disease are diseases of old age. If people had lived to an older age in past periods they also would have suffered from heart disease and cancer just as we do today.

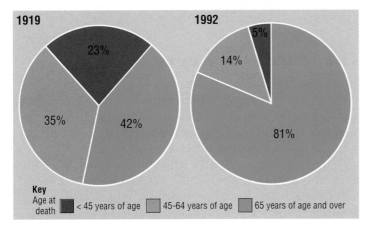

1919

23%

35%   42%

1992

5%

14%

81%

Key
Age at death: ■ < 45 years of age   ■ 45-64 years of age   ■ 65 years of age and over

SOURCE 3   A comparison of age at death of people in Britain in 1919 and 1992

Heart and circulatory diseases

These are diseases which affect the heart or the circulation of the blood. Any disruption of blood supply to important organs of the body can kill very quickly. This can be caused by a heart attack or a **thrombosis** (a blood clot which blocks an artery). If a blood clot reaches the brain and cuts off the supply of oxygen it causes a **stroke**.

What causes heart disease?

Various factors can contribute to heart disease: bad diet (for example, fatty foods can fur up arteries), smoking, stress, alcohol abuse, being overweight, viruses.

Who gets heart disease?

It is mainly older people who suffer from heart disease. It is Britain's biggest killer of both women and men. It is much more common in rich countries than in poor countries.

How is heart disease treated?

Treatment of heart disease usually consists of advice about diet or exercise, drugs to steady the pulse or lower blood pressure.
 Surgery is also increasingly common – to install electronic pacemakers to help the heart keep up a steady beat, or to perform bypass operations to replace damaged or poor arteries taking the blood from the heart. In extreme cases patients can be given a heart transplant (see page 174).

Explanation 2: the victory over other diseases

People simply living longer can't explain the increase on its own. Deaths from cancer and heart disease have increased because diseases such as bronchitis or pneumonia which, in the past, might have killed people, can now be treated by antibiotics. Those who survive into old age are now dying of heart disease and cancer which cannot be cured so easily.

Explanation 3: deaths from cancer and heart disease were underestimated in the past

In the twentieth century diagnosis of disease has improved. Sophisticated scanning machines can now help to spot cancers which in earlier centuries no one would have been able to see until a postmortem was carried out. In the same way, electronic heart monitoring can help detect heart disease which 100 years ago would have been missed by doctors equipped only with a stethoscope. It therefore seems likely that some deaths which were put down to other causes or unknown causes were in fact the result of cancer or heart disease.

Explanation 4: changes in lifestyle

Cancer and heart disease are 'lifestyle diseases'. They are caused by things we do, for example, smoking, unhealthy eating or polluting the environment. This is supported by the rate at which cancer is growing in the developed world. It is growing much faster than life expectancy is.

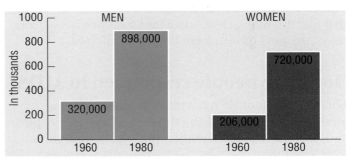

MEN   WOMEN

898,000

720,000

320,000

206,000

In thousands: 0, 200, 400, 600, 800, 1000

1960   1980   1960   1980

SOURCE 4   Increase in number of cancers diagnosed in 28 industrialised countries 1960–80

■ TASK

Explain whether you agree or disagree with the two statements below.

'The increase in cancer and heart disease is a result of the great progress in other areas of medicine and health.'

'The increase in cancer and heart disease is an example of regression – things getting worse – in medicine and health.'

AIDS: the 'charter disease'

AIDS STANDS FOR Acquired Immune Deficiency Syndrome. In a sufferer, a virus, called HIV, destroys the body's immune system to the point where even a common cold can kill. The victim doesn't die of AIDS but of other infections which his or her body can no longer fight. It affects both men and women.

Why has AIDS spread so rapidly?

AIDS is a new disease, yet from a few isolated cases in the early 1980s it has spread rapidly throughout the world. There are now an estimated twelve million sufferers and many thousands of deaths each year.

AIDS cannot be transferred by touch, or through the air. The virus is spread through the blood or body fluids of infected people, for example, through sexual contact or by sharing needles with an infected person. AIDS spreads much more rapidly in societies where sexual activity is freer. For example, in Islamic countries, where stricter rules about sex are followed, it is less of a problem. AIDS is not like the epidemic diseases of the past which could not be avoided. People can protect themselves against AIDS by avoiding unsafe sex or intravenous drug use.

As doctors have tracked the rapid progress of AIDS around the world they have related it to the ease of travel between different countries. It has been called a 'charter' disease because charter flights between the world's capital cities have helped the disease to spread. Just like the Black Death, isolated societies, away from easy transport routes, have been less affected.

How have people responded to AIDS?

The AIDS epidemic has come as a shock to the medical confidence of the developed world. People had become used to the idea that such epidemics were a thing of the past. Governments were very slow in taking action to publicise the risk until AIDS had already become a major problem.

Despite a massive amount of research there is no vaccine or 'magic bullet' which can cure AIDS. Faced by a disease which modern medicine seems unable to control, people have responded in a similar way to the epidemics of earlier centuries. Some have isolated the sufferers – those with AIDS have regularly found that even friends and family deserted them. Some looked for a scapegoat – someone to blame. It was common in Africa – they blamed the Africans; it was common among homosexual men – they blamed their sexual practices. Some even called it a 'gay plague'. Some looked for supernatural explanations – that AIDS was a punishment from God.

Others, of course, set out on a more positive path: caring for the sufferers, educating people about AIDS or finding a scientific explanation for the disease and a cure.

■ TASK 1

Compare AIDS with either the Black Death in the Middle Ages or with cholera in the nineteenth century. Draw up a diagram. On one side list similarities, on the other side list differences.

The search for a cure

It has taken scientists a number of years just to identify the HIV virus which causes AIDS. Even so, modern surveys suggest that most people believe that science *will* find a cure for AIDS. They think it is just a matter of time and money.

Drug companies clearly think the same way. With millions of sufferers who will otherwise die, there will be huge profits for a company which can produce a successful cure. A massive amount of money is therefore being spent on research. In fact, much more money is being put into the search for a cure than into providing facilities to help care for AIDS sufferers and their families, or to educate people about how to avoid AIDS.

Regression?

Seeing AIDS as part of the story of medicine and health through time, some people suggest that AIDS is the beginning of a long period of regression in health. They see whole communities wiped out by the disease in the way that the Black Death wiped out whole villages. Others expect that AIDS will be just a small blip in the story of progress that has characterised the twentieth century. Which view do you favour? No one knows which one is right, because the long-term impact of AIDS is still unknown.

■ TASK 2

1. In what ways have the following factors affected the spread of AIDS: religion, government, communications, science?
2. In what ways might each factor help in the fight against AIDS?

Why has surgery developed so rapidly in recent years?

The story so far

In the late nineteenth century anaesthetics and aseptic surgery allowed surgeons to carry out increasingly complex operations (see pages 134–39). The first successful appendix removal was in the 1880s. The first successful heart operation was in the 1890s. The two world wars saw further advances in blood tranfusion and specialisation of surgeons (see pages 151 and 163).

Improved anaesthetics

Until the 1930s anaesthetics were still breathed in by the patient. This worked, but it was difficult to control the dosage and operations had to be hurried. In the 1930s Helmuth Wesse discovered new anaesthetics and developed a method of injecting them directly into the blood stream. This allowed dosage to be more precisely controlled and operations could now last longer.

Antibiotics

With the discovery and mass production of penicillin during the Second World War the risk of infection during surgery was reduced. This increased the success rate of complex operations considerably. These developments helped lead to rapid progress especially in the area of transplant and replacement surgery as you can see from Source 1.

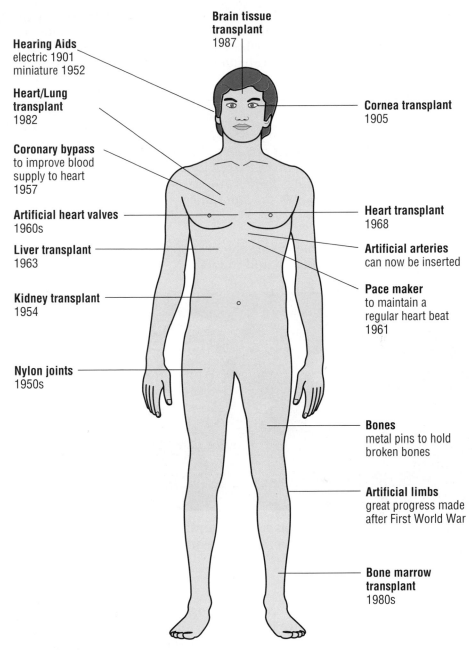

Brain tissue transplant 1987

Hearing Aids electric 1901 miniature 1952

Heart/Lung transplant 1982

Coronary bypass to improve blood supply to heart 1957

Artificial heart valves 1960s

Liver transplant 1963

Kidney transplant 1954

Nylon joints 1950s

Cornea transplant 1905

Heart transplant 1968

Artificial arteries can now be inserted

Pace maker to maintain a regular heart beat 1961

Bones metal pins to hold broken bones

Artificial limbs great progress made after First World War

Bone marrow transplant 1980s

SOURCE 2 The development of transplant and replacement surgery. The dates show when each operation was first performed successfully

SOURCE 1 An athlete taking part in the tennis tournament at the Transplant Games, Manchester, August 1995. This competitor had received a heart transplant five years earlier

Teamwork

Major surgery involves many different skills. This is how Dr Christiaan Barnard described the preparations for the first heart transplant in 1967.

SOURCE 3

Kidney function was checked by measuring urine output … the liver was studied through urine and blood analysis. The heart pattern was plotted by an electrocardiogram. The lungs were X-rayed. Blood chemistry was also checked in the laboratory.

At the operation the specialist surgeon is supported by highly trained anaesthetists and nurses.

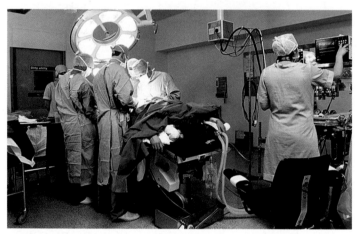

SOURCE 4 A team of surgeons at work. The person on the right is monitoring the life support and anaesthetic equipment

Resources

Major surgery is becoming increasingly costly. The operations themselves involve large teams, and after-care of patients can be long and expensive. Even successful operations may only add a few years to a patient's life. However, such operations are life-saving and, as a result, they capture the public's imagination. Some high-tech surgeons receive attention and money out of all proportion to the number of people who actually benefit. The media treat the pioneers of transplant surgery as heroes just as they treated Pasteur as a hero when he made his breakthroughs in developing new vaccines.

1. Why do you think transplant surgery attracts so much public interest?
2. Do you think that transplant surgery is a good way to use medical resources?

Keyhole surgery

Rummaging about inside someone's body in a pair of rubber gloves with a large knife is not always the most effective way to treat a patient. The patient has to recover from not only the original illness but also a large wound. In recent years, miniaturisation, fibre-optic cables and the use of computers have meant that surgeons can perform operations through very small keyhole incisions.

Keyhole surgery uses an endoscope. This instrument includes all the tools needed to perform an operation.

SOURCE 5 The benefits of keyhole surgery

Micro surgery

Micro surgery is also advancing rapidly. By magnifying the area the surgeon is working on it is possible to rejoin nerves and very small blood vessels. This means that some feeling can be returned to limbs that have been severed and damaged.

3. Draw a timeline from 1800 to the present. Mark on it what you consider to be the major turning points in the development of surgery. You will also need to refer back to pages 134–39, 151 and 163.
4. When has the pace of change been most rapid?
5. How have the following factors influenced change in surgery:

 ■ war
 ■ technology
 ■ individuals
 ■ drug development?

What is alternative medicine?

HIGH-TECH SCIENTIFIC medicine has achieved many things but like other medical developments it faces opposition. Its critics say that doctors do no more than dispense drugs; they treat patients merely as symptoms passing them on an assembly line. The scientific idea that disease can be beaten by finding a cause and then 'zapping' it with a drug so dominates doctors' thinking that they do not look at the patient as a whole.

Alternative medicine is a set of treatments which tries to correct these failings in modern medicine. Three examples of alternative medicine are shown in Source 1. There are many more that could be included. Probably the most important is herbal medicine which uses herbs and plants as medicines just as they have been for thousands of years. No one feature unites all these treatments – they are called alternative medicine simply because they are all alternatives to mainstream, scientific medicine.

Over the last twenty years alternative medicine has become increasingly popular. In the 1990s a government minister was made responsible for alternative medicine. One in seven people in Britain have consulted alternative healers. In a recent poll 75 per cent of the respondents agreed that acupuncture or homeopathy should be available within the NHS. A respected group of doctors support that proposal while others have set up a pressure group, Campaign Against Health Fraud, to expose what they see as the weaknesses of alternative medicine.

1. Write your own ten-word definition of the term alternative medicine.
2. What examples of change and continuity can you find in Source 1?
3. Find out all you can about one of these other forms of alternative medicine: herbalism, osteopathy.
4. There is evidence that alternative medicine works even though scientifically no one can explain why. Are there other examples in history of people using treatments even though they do not know how they work?

SOURCE 1 Three of the more common disciplines of alternative medicine. Alternative medicine is also sometimes known as holistic medicine.

Alternative healers aim to 'treat the person not the disease'. The idea is that each patient is different and therefore needs a personalised response. Healers spend longer with the patient than a doctor can, trying to find out as much about the patient as possible. They suggest changes in lifestyle or diet which might help the patient

Acupuncture

Acupuncture developed in ancient China 4,000 years ago (see page 23).

What is it?
Acupuncture involves the releasing of blocked energy by inserting fine needles on various pressure points of the body. Some modern acupuncture uses needles with a slight electric current. It has been used as an anaesthetic during major surgery.

How does it work?
Acupuncture charts the flow of energy around the human body. When energy paths become blocked or out of balance diseases can occur. Acupuncture allows the energy to flow again – thus relieving pain and stimulating healing.

Homeopathy

Homeopathy was founded in the late 1700s by a German doctor, Samuel Hahnemann.

What is it?
Patients take an extremely diluted amount of a substance which would normally produce symptoms similar to those the patient already has.

How does it work?
Homeo means 'like'. Homeopaths believe that 'like cures like'. They say that the very diluted substance releases a 'vital force' which allows the body to heal itself.

Hypnotherapy

Hypnosis has been practised for hundreds of years.

What is it?
The therapist hypnotises the patient and in that state of hypnosis the patient can be relieved of anxiety, overcome phobias or allergies or even physical conditions such as travel sickness.

How does it work?
It is based on the belief that the patient's own mind can be influenced to bring about his or her healing.

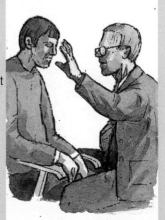

Has public health improved during the twentieth century?

TWO CONCERNS HAVE dominated public health campaigns in the twentieth century – housing and air quality.

Healthier housing

As industrial towns grew in the early nineteenth century, houses were built quickly and sometimes to a very low standard.

Stage 1: Back-to-backs banned

In many cities, to pack in as many houses as possible, and to cut building costs, builders had built back-to-back. These houses were badly ventilated; they had no internal water supply; the only toilets were at the end of the row and there were no gardens.

The surveys of the late 1800s and early 1900s revealed that back-to-back houses were a major cause of ill health. In 1909 they were banned by the government. Local authorities had to submit town-planning schemes to the government for approval. Building standards were established which had to be followed by all builders.

Stage 2: 'Homes for heroes'

The British government had asked working men to lay down their lives in the First World War. In return the government pledged it would do something decisive about the housing problem to ensure that, after the war, soldiers came back to 'homes fit for heroes'. In 1919 a new Housing Act was passed, requiring local authorities to provide good homes for all working-class

people in their area. The government promised to help fund these schemes during the first four years – thus they hoped to speed up the building work by councils.

'Homes for heroes' helped to create a quarter of a million new homes.

Stage 3: 'Slum clearance'

Even a quarter-of-a-million houses were only a small percentage of what was needed. In 1930 the most ambitious step was taken with the beginning of a five-year 'slum clearance' programme. Large areas of bad housing in major cities and towns were labelled improvement areas. The local authorities were forced to rehouse those in the improvement areas. The old housing was rased to the ground.

In the 1930s 700,000 new homes were built by local authorities, many of them on large housing estates away from the city and town centres. The local authorities claimed to have rehoused 80 per cent of slum dwellers in the 1930s. This was an overestimate and it was often the poorest people who remained in some of the worst housing! Many such slums were not demolished until the 1960s when they were largely replaced by high-rise blocks of flats which posed as many problems as the old slums.

■ ACTIVITY

Look at Source 1. Write a detailed description of how the new home is an improvement on the old.

SOURCE 1 Artist's reconstruction of houses in Hereford Street, Brighton. The back-to-back house on the left was demolished after the First World War to make way for the new council house on the right

Cleaner air

Well into the twentieth century air quality in many industrial cities was still appalling (see Source 2).

In 1952 London suffered a terrible smog. Chance weather conditions caused dense, smoke-polluted fog to settle over the city. At least 4,000 people died of respiratory illness brought on by the smog, making it the worst health disaster in the capital since the flu epidemic of 1919. It speeded up action to do something about air pollution.

In 1956 a Clean Air Act was passed to set up smokeless zones in cities and even to control what fuel could be burned by people in their own homes. By 1971 the amount of smoke pollution entering the atmosphere had been reduced by 65 per cent.

1. What factors were important in improving housing and improving air quality?
2. Why do you think neither of these issues was tackled effectively in the nineteenth century?

SOURCE 2 Air pollution in Stoke-on-Trent in the 1920s. The pottery-making town had literally thousands of coal-fired kilns

■ TASK

Study Source 3. It shows how public health concerns have now shifted into wider, even global issues, which cannot be the responsibility of an individual, or even the government of one country. Environmental pressure groups have taken up the campaigning role previously taken by the public health movement.

What do you regard as the three most important priorities for public health today.

1. Almost everyone in Britain has access to fresh water

but is that water clean and is there enough of it?

2. Sewage is disposed of so that it doesn't spread disease in towns and cities

but it sometimes pollutes beaches and kills wildlife

3. There are laws to control waste disposal and rubbish dumping

but toxic waste can still leak into our water supply and some things cannot be disposed of safely.

4. Clean Air Action has stopped factories and coal and coal fires polluting

OFFICIAL Sheffield cleanest industrial city in Europe

but car exhaust fumes create polluted air which can spread from one country to another. Some environmental problems need international solutions.

5. Houses are better built and they have healthier features than they did in 1900

but there are still some people who have no home at all

6. There are laws to enforce safe working conditions

DANGER ASBESTOS KEEP OUT!

but new dangers to health are always emerging.

7. Food must be carefully labelled and hygienically stored

but some people may still have an unhealthy diet

8. Public health may have improved in developed countries

but they are only a small proportion of the world's population. The majority of people are still facing the problems which developed countries faced in the nineteenth century.

SOURCE 3 Public health issues today

Why are people in some countries healthier than in others?

Most of the changes we have described so far in this chapter have only benefited a small minority of the world's population.

■ TASK

Write your own account comparing the problems facing people in developing countries with the problems facing people in nineteenth-century Britain. You will need to refer back to Chapter 4. Make clear which problems are similar, which are different and how they are different.

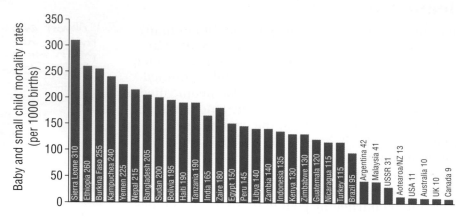

SOURCE 1 Infant mortality in selected countries in 1960

Disease
Diarrhoea spread by infected water is the main cause of infant mortality in developing countries. It kills five million under-fives each year even though it can easily be prevented with a simple and cheap rehydration remedy.

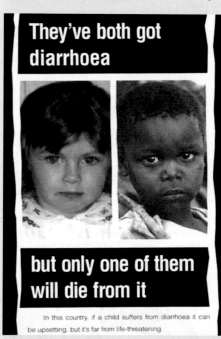

They've both got diarrhoea

but only one of them will die from it

In this country, if a child suffers from diarrhoea it can be upsetting, but it's far from life-threatening.

Infectious diseases cause 40 per cent of all deaths in the developing countries: tuberculosis kills three million and pneumonia two million each year. AIDS is a growing problem in some countries.

Diet
Two-thirds of under-fives are malnourished.

Rich and poor
There are great contrasts between medicine for the rich and the poor. For those who can pay for it there are sophisticated modern hospitals and high-quality treatment; for the poor there may be no health care at all other than nursing in the home, by family members, using herbal remedies.

War
In some countries war has caused massive casualties. It has driven people from their homes into cramped and unhealthy refugee camps. Crops have been destroyed, resulting in famine. Governments have been unable or unwilling to spend money on improving health care.

Communications
In some countries there are very few trained doctors or health workers. Because of poor communications and transport, getting to a health centre can involve many days travel.

Education
Education is still not provided for all children. Many adults cannot read so health education is more difficult.

Unsafe or inappropriate drugs
There is little control of what drugs can be sold. Drugs which would be considered unsafe, or which would be carefully controlled in Britain, are sold over the counter, sometimes with little or no labelling.

Bottle feeding
Bottle feeding is being introduced with all its risks of infection.

SOURCE 2 Health and medicine in developing countries. There are obviously great contrasts between countries and within countries, this diagram simply summarises some of the main problems facing people in developing countries

Twentieth-century medicine: conclusions

■ TASK 1

1. Which of the following can you find examples of from the twentieth century? Medicine:
   a) getting slowly or gradually better
   b) getting better very quickly
   c) staying the same
   d) getting slowly worse
   e) getting rapidly worse.

2. For each example explain how important the following factors were in causing these changes or continuities:

   - war
   - religion
   - government
   - science and technology
   - trade and communications
   - chance
   - individual genius.

3. Do you think that progress in the twentieth century has been faster or slower than progress in the nineteenth century in:
   a) understanding of disease
   b) improving treatments
   c) improving ordinary people's health
   d) public health?

■ TASK 2

Is there a limit to progress?

1. Write your own explanation of each of the problems illustrated in this diagram.
2. Do you think there are other problems associated with the pace of medical progress in the twentieth century?
3. Look back at the graphs showing medical progress on page 55. Draw your own graph showing progress from prehistoric times to the present.
4. How do you expect medicine and health to develop in the next 100 years? Draw a graph to show what you expect to happen and write a paragraph to explain it.

The health jigsaw: AD2000

THIS IS THE last in a series of pictures which show how doctors in each period have tried to help patients towards better health and longer life. The others are on pages 54, 82 and 103. On page 148 you were asked to draw your own version for the nineteenth century.

1. Describe how the changes shown in this picture have helped to improve health.
2. Do you think this picture gives an accurate impression of the state of medical knowledge and skills today? Explain your answer.
3. How significant do you think the contribution of doctors has been to improving medicine and health in the twentieth century? Explain your answer.

chapter 6

CONCLUSIONS: EXPLAINING CHANGE AND CONTINUITY IN MEDICINE AND HEALTH

CONGRATULATIONS! You now know and understand much more than you did a few months ago about the history of medicine and health. This final section will help you to revise the information you have already covered so that you remember it better. It also gives you an opportunity to look at the concepts that are vital to understanding the history of medicine and health.

Pages 182–85 give you an overview of how methods of treatment and explanations of disease have changed over the entire period you have studied.

Finally, **pages 199–210** investigate the different patterns of change that have characterised medicine and health.

Pages 186–198 look at some of the main factors which have led to changes or have prevented change in medicine and health.

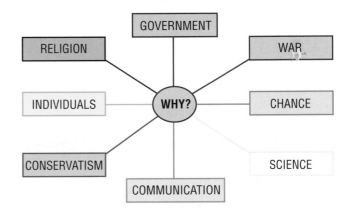

IS THE HISTORY OF MEDICINE AND HEALTH LIKE THIS...?

Things get steadily better

OR LIKE THIS...?

Sometimes things get better, Sometimes they get worse.

How have methods of treatment changed through history?

THIS PAGE SUMMARISES some of the main treatments that have been used across the centuries.

1. Which treatments have been used for the greatest length of time?
2. Why were they used for so long?
3. Which treatments used in earlier times are not used today?
4. Why are they no longer used?
5. Which treatments used today were not used in earlier times?
6. Why were they not used in earlier times?
7. When was the period of greatest change in treatments?

IMMUNISATION

MEDICINES

Herbal remedies

HYGIENE, DIET AND EXERCISE

Personal hygiene

Public health

Diet and exercise

SUPERNATURAL

Spells and charms

Prayers to the gods

Leeches

Bleeding to balance the body's humours

SURGERY

Trephining

Simple surgery

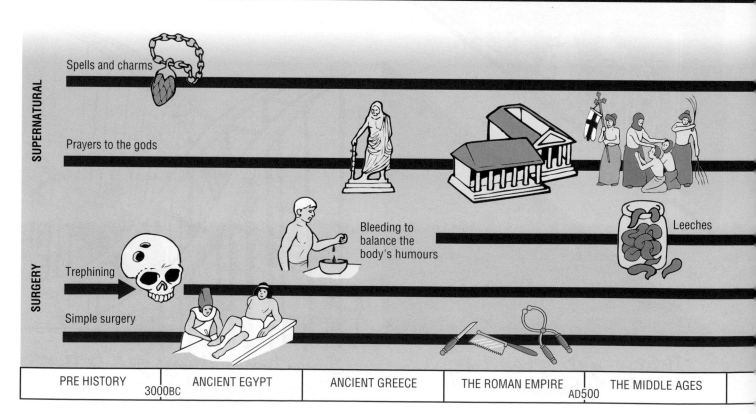

PRE HISTORY		ANCIENT EGYPT	ANCIENT GREECE	THE ROMAN EMPIRE		THE MIDDLE AGES
	3000BC				AD500	

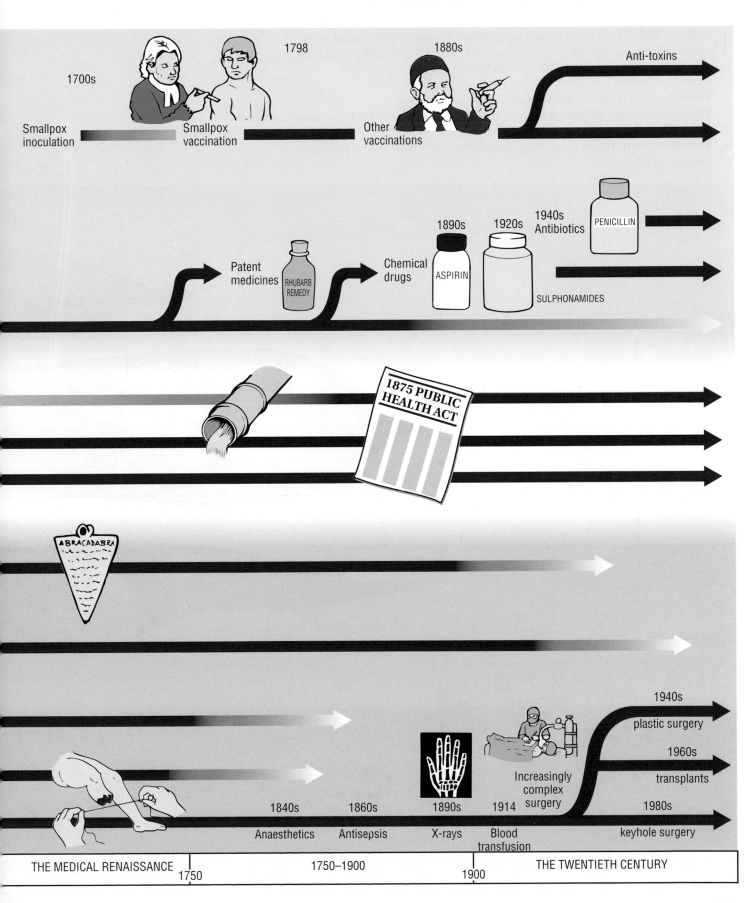

1700s

Smallpox inoculation

1798

Smallpox vaccination

1880s

Other vaccinations

Anti-toxins

Patent medicines

RHUBARB REMEDY

Chemical drugs

1890s

ASPIRIN

1920s

1940s Antibiotics

PENICILLIN

SULPHONAMIDES

1875 PUBLIC HEALTH ACT

ABRACADABRA

1940s

plastic surgery

1960s

transplants

Increasingly complex surgery

1980s

keyhole surgery

1840s

Anaesthetics

1860s

Antisepsis

1890s

X-rays

1914

Blood transfusion

THE MEDICAL RENAISSANCE

1750

1750–1900

1900

THE TWENTIETH CENTURY

183

How has understanding of the causes of disease changed through history?

FOR CENTURIES HEALERS have struggled to understand why people become ill. This page summarises the different explanations for illness and disease that healers have had through history.

1. Which ideas were believed for the longest period?
2. Why were ideas believed for long periods even though they were wrong?
3. When was the most important breakthrough in understanding the causes of disease?

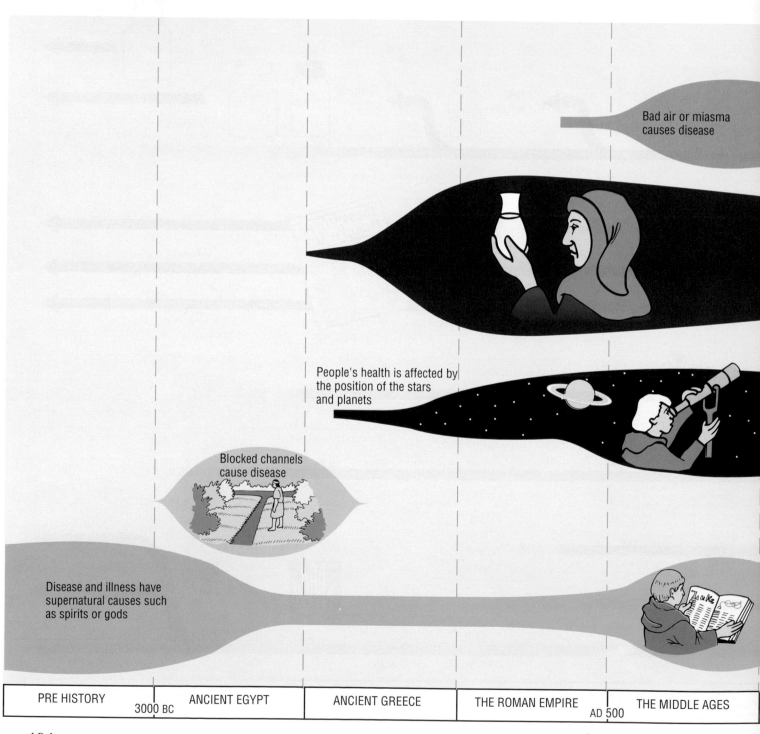

Bad air or miasma causes disease

People's health is affected by the position of the stars and planets

Blocked channels cause disease

Disease and illness have supernatural causes such as spirits or gods

PRE HISTORY		ANCIENT EGYPT	ANCIENT GREECE	THE ROMAN EMPIRE		THE MIDDLE AGES
	3000 BC				AD 500	

Germs cause disease

MEDICAL RENAISSANCE

AD 1750

1750–1900

AD 1900

THE TWENTIETH CENTURY

Why? The factors that have caused change and continuity in medicine and health

WHILE YOU HAVE been working on the history of medicine and health you will have noticed a number of factors cropping up again and again, and if you didn't notice them by yourself some of the questions made sure you did! These factors have included war, religion and the others shown opposite.

These factors are important because our task in history is not just to list or describe the events of the past – it is also to explain why they happened. Therefore, these factors have not kept appearing by accident. They are the causes that have 'made things happen' in the history of medicine. Sometimes they have made things change. Sometimes they have prevented change.

The next eleven pages help you to think about the factors you can see opposite. You begin by studying in detail the impact of three separate factors – governments, religion and war – to see how they affected the development of medicine and health. Then you should examine some of the other important factors more briefly.

However, you must realise from the start that investigating each cause in isolation is misleading because they almost always work together to produce change or continuity. It would be extremely unusual for a single cause by itself to force change or to stop development. So the final aim of this section on factors is to see how these factors worked together.

Our first task is to identify the different factors. Then we must see how these factors worked together

Why did infant mortality go down quickly in the twentieth century?

Science: because of the discovery of germs and the development of vaccinations against killer diseases.

Education: by the 1900s the message about germs was finally getting through to ordinary people.

War led to improved health care.

Religion and individuals helped too. Religious leaders made the government aware of the problems.

Government: healthier housing built by local government.

Then we must see how these factors worked together.

Were any of these reasons linked?

War and government worked together. The Boer War made the government worried about health in the first place. The First World War was what made them do something about housing. The Second World War made them reorganise the health service and try to improve people's diet.

Finally we try to work out which factor or factors were the most important reason for change or continuity

Which reason did you think was most important?

I think war was most important. If it hadn't been for war, no one would have taken action.

Science was most important. If Pasteur hadn't proved his germ theory, then people would never have realised the importance of hygiene, and they would never have developed vaccines.

Look at the factors shown in the picture below.

1. List two ways in which each factor affected the history of medicine.
2. For each factor explain whether it led to change or continuity or both in the history of medicine.
3. Which factors do you think have been the most important in the history of medicine for:
a) causing change
b) maintaining continuity?

Factor 1: Governments

THE SIMPLEST WAY to begin investigating the causes of change and continuity is to study the impact of individual factors. On the next six pages you can investigate three major factors which have affected medicine and health, although they are not in order of importance. You may decide that although we have started with governments they have been less influential than other factors.

SOURCE 1 An announcement by a Roman Emperor

■ TASK

1. List as many examples as you can of governments changing medicine or health for the better. Sources 1–7 will get you started but you can also look at the page references on the timeline.
2. In which periods did governments not try to change medicine or health?
3. What methods have been used by governments to change medicine or health?
4. Have governments ever caused change by themselves or have there always been other factors at work?
5. Describe one example of change where factors worked together.
6. How important have governments been in improving medicine and health? Explain your answer.

SOURCE 2 K. Branigan, *Roman Britain: Life in an Imperial Province*, 1980

66 *In Roman Britain, in towns like Chichester, Leicester and Wroxeter in Shropshire, probably as many as 500 people a day used the public baths, even if they only visited them once a week.*
One of the finest suites of public baths in Britain was at Wroxeter, which also included an outdoor swimming pool and a massive exercise hall. 99

SOURCE 3 From a letter by Edward III to the Mayor of London, 26 September 1371

66 *Edward by the grace of God etc to the mayor and sheriffs of London, greeting. The air in the city has lately been greatly corrupted and infected by the slaughtering of animals in the city, because of the putrefied blood running in the streets and the dumping of entrails in the river Thames, and as a result appalling abominations and stenches have been produced, and sicknesses and other maladies have befallen residents and visitors to the city.* 99

PRE HISTORY	ANCIENT EGYPT	ANCIENT GREECE	THE ROMAN EMPIRE PP. 46–47, 49

3000BC

SOURCE 4 From regulations introduced by the Mayor of London to stop the spread of plague in 1665

" ... *The Government appointed public prayers and days of fasting, to make public confession of sin and implore the mercy of God to avert the dreadful judgement that hung over their heads ...*

in every parish there be one, two or more persons by the name of examiners to enquire and learn what persons be sick. And if they find any person sick of the infection, to give order to the constable that the house be shut up.

to every infected house there be appointed two watchmen, one for every day and the other for the night [so] that no person go in or out of such infected houses. "

SOURCE 6 Measures taken by the government in Britain 1900–45

1902 Midwives Act, compulsory training and the setting of standards.
1906 Education (Provision of Meals) Act, local authorities allowed to provide meals in elementary schools.
1907 Notification of Births Act, so that health visitors could be sure they visited all new babies.
1907 Education (Administrative Provision) Act, medical services provided for children at school.
1911 National Insurance Act, free medical treatment for workers who paid a contribution, but not their families.
1918 Maternal and Child Welfare Act, allowed local authorities to provide free clinics for pregnant women and infants.
1930 Housing Act, slum clearance undertaken.
1940 Diphtheria immunisation campaign.
1940s Funding for the development of penicillin.

SOURCE 7 From a speech by Nye Bevan, the Minister of Health who introduced the NHS in Britain in 1948

" *Medical treatment should be made available to rich and poor alike in accordance with medical need and no other criteria. Worry about money in a time of sickness is a serious hindrance to recovery apart from its unnecessary cruelty. The records show that it is the mother in the average family who suffers most from the absence of a full health service. In trying to balance her budget she puts her own needs last. The essence of a satisfactory health service is that the rich and the poor are treated alike, that poverty is not a disability, and wealth is not advantaged.* "

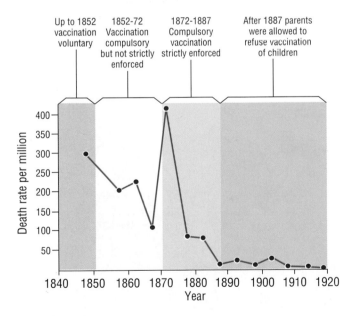

SOURCE 5 Graph showing deaths from smallpox, 1848–1920

THE MIDDLE AGES PP. 61,67	THE MEDICAL RENAISSANCE PP. 97–99	1750–1900 PP. 114, 117, 124, 145–46	THE TWENTIETH CENTURY PP. 158, 160–63, 164–69, 176, 177

500   AD1750   AD1900

Factor 2: Religion

ALL KINDS OF religious beliefs have affected the history of medicine and health, even if today many people would think that belief in spirits or magic is simply superstition.

■ TASK

1. The drawings illustrate five examples of religious beliefs affecting medicine and health. Explain in your own words what each one is.
2. Use Sources 1–5 and the page references on the timeline below to list examples of religion affecting medicine and health.
3. Next to each example write down whether religion caused change or continuity.
4. In which periods did religion have the greatest effect on medicine?

5. Has religion done more to cause change or continuity in medicine? Explain why you think this has happened.
6. How important has religion been in the history of medicine and health:

   ■ very important
   ■ important
   ■ not very important?

   Explain the reasons for your choice.

PRE HISTORY P. 11	ANCIENT EGYPT PP. 17–18, 20	ANCIENT GREECE PP. 24–25	THE ROMAN EMPIRE PP. 40, 42

3000BC

SOURCE 1 A charm made by a mother to protect her child. This was recorded in a collection of Egyptian medical documents, written on papyrus between 1900 and 1500BC

"I have made a charm for my child which will protect him against you, oh evil spirits! This charm is made from evil smelling herbs and from garlic which is harmful to you; from honey which is sweet for men and horrible for spirits, from a fish tail and a rag and a backbone of a perch."

SOURCE 2 From about 600BC temples called Asclepeia were built in quiet places. There the sick bathed, relaxed and slept, and prayed to Asclepius the Greek god of healing

SOURCE 3 Part of a letter from the Prior of the abbey of Christchurch, Canterbury, to the Bishop of London, 28 September 1348

"Terrible is God towards the sons of men ... He often allows plagues, miserable famines, conflicts, wars and other forms of suffering to arise, and uses them to terrify and torment men and so drive out their sins. And thus, indeed, the realm of England, because of the growing pride and corruption of its subjects, and their numberless sins ... is to be oppressed by the pestilences ..."

SOURCE 4 Through most of the Middle Ages the Christian Church banned dissection. Around 1400 it began to allow it

SOURCE 5 Florence Nightingale believed that God had called upon her to become a nurse. Her work had a great influence on nursing

THE MIDDLE AGES PP. 56–57, 64–65, 68, 72, 76–77	THE MEDICAL RENAISSANCE	1750–1900 PP. 126, 136	THE TWENTIETH CENTURY P. 161

500   AD1750   AD1900

Factor 3: War

WHEN YOU WORKED on the previous two factors, governments and religion, you had some questions to structure your work. Can you now work out what questions to ask about the impact of war on medicine – without looking back to the previous pages? Use Sources 1–6 and the page references on the timeline.

SOURCE 1 A scene from the carvings on the Emperor Trajan's column which celebrated his victories over the Dacians. This probably shows medical orderlies at work. Each legion had a doctor and medical orderlies but they rarely held high rank. The military writer Vegetius noted that 'generals believe that daily exercise is better for soldiers than treatment by physicians'. Prevention was better than cure, especially when even leading doctors such as Galen did not know what caused diseases and often had little chance of saving the sick

SOURCE 2 From the writings of Theodoric of Lucca, a thirteenth-century surgeon. His father, Hugh, who was also a famous surgeon in Italy, had travelled to Egypt with a Christian army to fight against the Muslims

❝ The method employed for extracting arrows cannot be described in detail for every day we see new instruments and new methods being invented by clever and ingenious surgeons. ❞

SOURCE 3 In 1536 Ambroise Paré first treated soldiers. He copied the methods of other doctors, using boiling oil on wounds and cauterisation but:

❝ eventually I ran out of oil and I had to use a mixture made of yolks of eggs, oil of roses and turpentine. That night I could not sleep, fearing that the wounded would die or be poisoned because they had not been cauterised. I rose very early to visit them. Beyond my hope, I found those on whom I had used my mixture in little pain, their wounds without inflammation and having rested well. The others whom I had treated with boiling oil, I found feverish, with great pain and swelling around their wounds. I resolved with myself never more to burn thus cruelly poor men wounded with gunshot. ❞

PRE HISTORY	ANCIENT EGYPT	ANCIENT GREECE P. 31	THE ROMAN EMPIRE PP. 37–39, 41, 43

3000BC

SPECIMENS OF MEN IN EACH OF THE FOUR GRADES.

GRADE I.   GRADE II.   GRADE III.   GRADE IV.

SOURCE 4 Photographs of army recruits in the First World War, taken by National Service Medical Boards. The poor physical standard of recruits to the Boer War (1899–1902) had resulted in the rejection of 38 per cent of potential soldiers. In 1914 recruits in the First World War had similar health problems. They suffered from heart complaints, poor sight, inadequate hearing and rotten teeth. This evidence of poor health led to the establishment of the Committee on Physical Deterioration which made far-reaching proposals to improve health

SOURCE 5 Lt Colonel Pulvertaft describes the first use of penicillin by the British Army in 1943

“ We had enormous numbers of infected wounded, terrible burn cases among the crews of the armoured cars. Sulphonamides had absolutely no effect on these cases. The last thing I tried was penicillin … The first man I tried it on was a young New Zealand officer called Newton. He had been in bed for six months with compound fractures of both legs. His sheets were soaked with pus and the heat of Cairo made it smell intolerable. Normally he would have died in a short time. I gave three injections a day of penicillin and studied the effects under the microscope … the thing seemed like a miracle. In ten days' time the leg was cured and in a month's time the young fellow was back on his feet. I had enough penicillin for ten cases. Nine out of ten of them were complete cures. ”

500   AD1750   AD1900

The role of individuals

ANOTHER IMPORTANT FACTOR in the history of medicine is the work of individuals. Some individuals make great discoveries that help to improve people's health. Other individuals had ideas that were used by others for centuries even if they were not correct.

1. Who are the six people shown below?
2. With which breakthrough in medicine and health do you associate each person?
3. On your own copy of the timeline below add the names of these individuals at the appropriate point.
4. Make notes around the timeline to show the significance of all the other individuals shown on it.

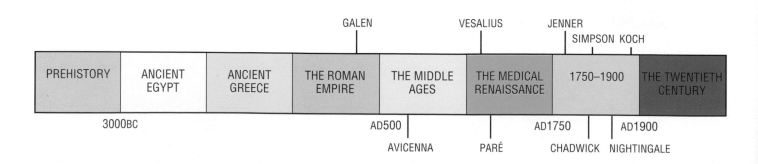

What other factors have affected medicine and health?

THE SOURCES ON this page give you some clues about four other factors:

- chance
- science and technology
- communications
- conservatism.

1. Which factor does each source show?
2. Find one other example of each factor at work using the reference box.
3. Explain whether each factor:
   a) helped to create change
   b) prevented change
   c) did both at different times.
4. These are not the only factors which have been important in the history of medicine and health. Look back through this book and list examples of other factors creating or preventing medical change. You could look at education, industry or another factor which interests you.

Reference box
Page 136, Source 9
Page 91, Source 1
Page 152, Source 4
Page 192, Source 3

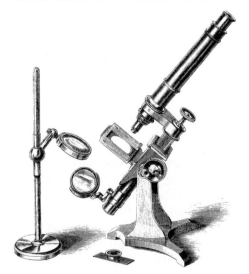

SOURCE 1 The microscope was improved in the 1800s. As a result scientists could study micro-organisms in detail

SOURCE 2 R. Jackson, *Doctors and Diseases in the Roman Empire*, 1988

" … At the same time as knowledge and techniques were spread by the Roman army, fresh information was collected … the mobility that the army provided allowed doctors to learn of and collect new herbs … It is probably fair to say that the Roman army was the single most powerful agency in the spread of Graeco-Roman medicine. "

SOURCE 3 Pasteur's researcher, by chance, used an old batch of bacteria. He found it worked as a vaccine

SOURCE 4 The response of two doctors to the proposals for a National Health Service

How did different factors work together to produce change?

THE FIRST STEP in explaining why an event happened is to identify the causes. Then you need to decide how the causes worked together and which, if any, were the most important. As an example you are going to look again at the medical breakthroughs in the time of the Renaissance between 1400 and 1700: Vesalius's discoveries in anatomy, Paré's work in surgery and Harvey's discovery of the circulation of the blood, which you studied in Chapter 3.

The chart on page 197 identifies five major reasons why these discoveries were made.

Individual genius

The individual scientists and doctors themselves were important. They were highly intelligent and observant people who had original ideas.

War and chance

In the case of Paré (see pages 86–87) war and chance were also an important part of the explanation. Paré was an army doctor who had learned his skills on the battlefield, as had many other surgeons. However, if he had not run out of the hot oil he usually put on wounds he would never have tried his own mixture of eggs, oil of roses and turpentine, which turned out to be both more effective and less painful.

Religious beliefs and attitudes

Changing religious beliefs and attitudes also played a vital part in these discoveries. For the first time in centuries many religious beliefs were being challenged. Even the Pope and the Roman Catholic Church were being criticised and challenged by Protestants who were eager for a purer, simpler kind of Christianity. It seemed as though none of the old ideas were safe.

Science and technology

The loosening of the power of old religious ideas opened the way for science. New scientific methods were applied to solve old problems.

Copernicus, a Polish astronomer, said that the sun did not orbit the earth but that the earth orbited the sun. In medicine, Galen's ideas were being challenged. His theories on anatomy and treatments had been the basis of medicine for over a thousand years but, if the Catholic Church could be challenged,

then why not Galen? When Vesalius discovered through careful scientific observation that Galen's ideas on some parts of anatomy were wrong he was able to say this. Before the new atmosphere brought about by the Renaissance it would have been almost impossible to dare say that Galen was wrong.

Technology was being improved or invented. One improved machine was the water pump which Harvey had in mind when he wrote 'When water is forced through pipes we can see and distinguish the individual compressions of the pump (perhaps at a considerable distance) in the flow of the escaping water. It is the same from the opening of a cut artery …'

Communications

Finally, communications were vital in these discoveries. The greatest invention of the period was the printing press which spread ideas and information far more quickly than had been possible before. New theories reached other scientists and doctors quickly so that they could test and build on the work of Vesalius and others. Printing was especially important for the illustrations of anatomy in Vesalius's work. The detail was captured with a new kind of engraving onto blocks of wood or copper.

These illustrations would also have been impossible without major developments in art. Medieval illustrations often seem unreal compared to the work of Renaissance artists such as Leonardo da Vinci. Da Vinci's work was based on careful observation and even dissection of human bodies because he believed that he needed to study bodies in detail before he could draw them accurately. Other artists copied Da Vinci's methods of research and this meant that Vesalius could find good artists who were able to illustrate his discoveries.

Which of these causes was the most important?

Perhaps it was the change in beliefs and attitudes that created a spirit of enquiry. Without this, it was almost impossible for new ideas to be developed, however clever an individual was, because no one else would take them up. Communications were vital because they spread ideas rapidly. Chance, war, the work of individuals and developments in science could not have had an effect without the changes in beliefs and communications.

■ TASK 1

1. Explain the links shown by three of the arrows in the chart below.
2. Do you think other links should be shown?
3. Which factor or factors do *you* think were most important in causing change between 1400 and 1700?

■ TASK 2

Draw your own similar chart to show how factors worked together to beat the killer diseases of the nineteenth century. You can get a sheet from your teacher to get you started.

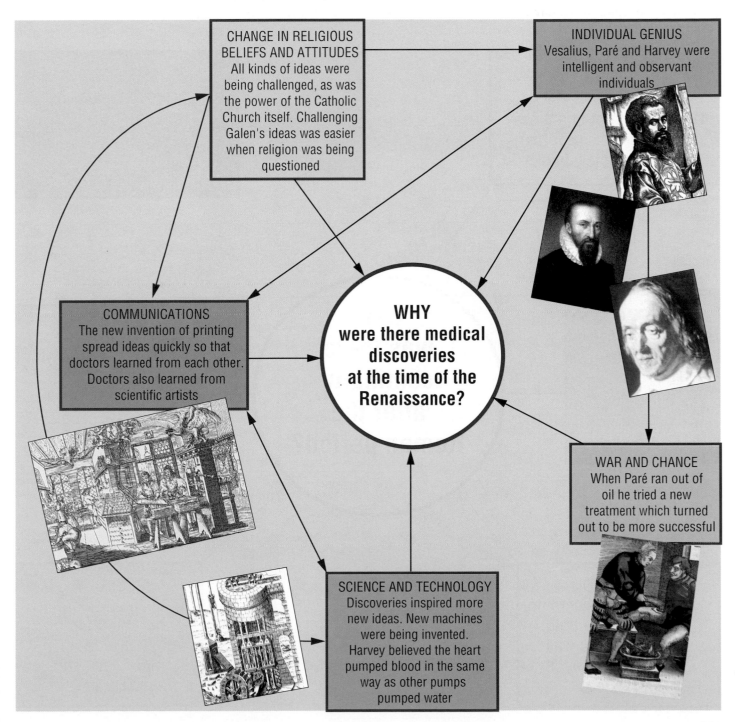

CHANGE IN RELIGIOUS BELIEFS AND ATTITUDES
All kinds of ideas were being challenged, as was the power of the Catholic Church itself. Challenging Galen's ideas was easier when religion was being questioned

INDIVIDUAL GENIUS
Vesalius, Paré and Harvey were intelligent and observant individuals

COMMUNICATIONS
The new invention of printing spread ideas quickly so that doctors learned from each other. Doctors also learned from scientific artists

WHY were there medical discoveries at the time of the Renaissance?

WAR AND CHANCE
When Paré ran out of oil he tried a new treatment which turned out to be more successful

SCIENCE AND TECHNOLOGY
Discoveries inspired more new ideas. New machines were being invented. Harvey believed the heart pumped blood in the same way as other pumps pumped water

How did different factors work together to prevent change?

AFTER THE ROMAN period there was little improvement in medical knowledge in Europe for centuries. For some people, particularly the wealthy, this was actually a time of regression. Health became worse because the Roman public health facilities were destroyed, and some of the methods and skills of the Roman doctors were lost.

In this case the different factors worked together to prevent change. War, for instance, which helped to bring about new medical discoveries in the previous example, had a harmful effect on medical progress during this period.

1. Look back to the chart on page 197. It has arrows showing the links between the factors that caused change. On your own copy of the chart below draw arrows showing how the factors were linked. For example, if you think that war harmed communications you should draw an arrow from war to communications.
2. Choose two of the arrows you have drawn and explain why you have drawn them.
3. Which factors were most important in preventing change?

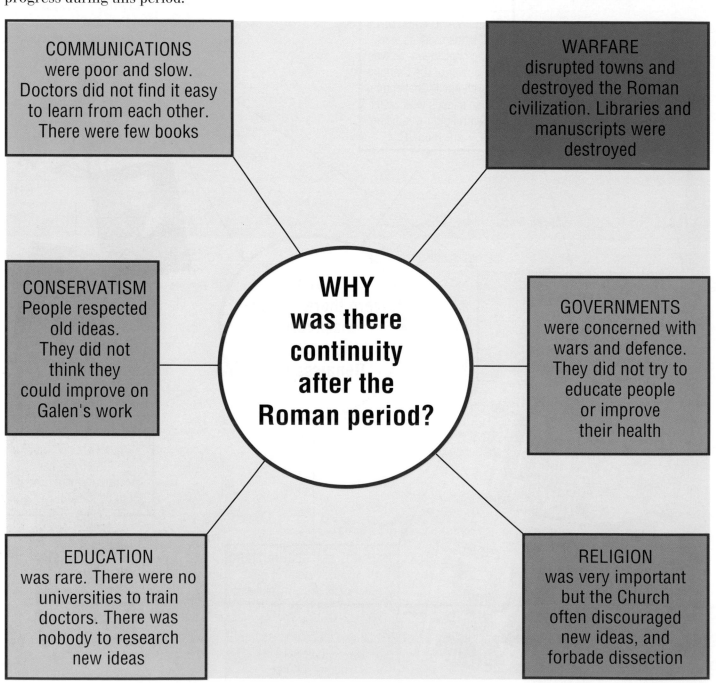

COMMUNICATIONS were poor and slow. Doctors did not find it easy to learn from each other. There were few books

WARFARE disrupted towns and destroyed the Roman civilization. Libraries and manuscripts were destroyed

CONSERVATISM People respected old ideas. They did not think they could improve on Galen's work

WHY was there continuity after the Roman period?

GOVERNMENTS were concerned with wars and defence. They did not try to educate people or improve their health

EDUCATION was rare. There were no universities to train doctors. There was nobody to research new ideas

RELIGION was very important but the Church often discouraged new ideas, and forbade dissection

Patterns of change

EVER SINCE YOU began studying history you have been investigating changes and continuities, and their causes. Now is the time to think in more detail about the pattern of change and continuity in the history of medicine and health.

1. Is this an accurate picture of how life expectancy has changed since prehistoric times? Explain your answer.

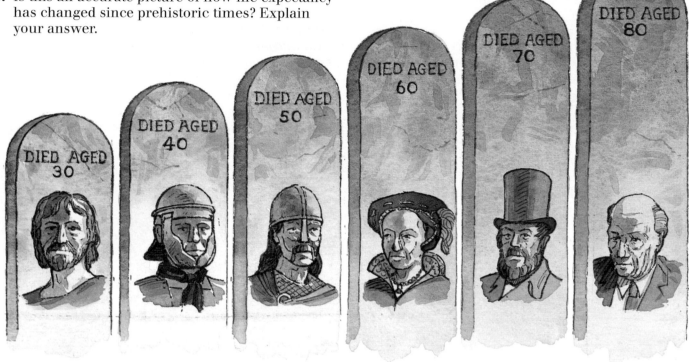

DIED AGED 30

DIED AGED 40

DIED AGED 50

DIED AGED 60

DIED AGED 70

DIED AGED 80

2. Find one more example of each of these patterns of change.

Some aspects of medicine stayed the same for many centuries

At some times there were rapid changes in medicine and health

CHILDREN CLINIC

Sometimes medicine and health grew worse, not better

Continuity: the use of herbs as medicine

IN HISTORY WE often study the things that have changed and try to explain why those changes have happened. However, it is also important to remember that some things have not changed over time and it is just as important to explain these continuities. This page gives you the chance to think about one example of continuity, the use of herbs as medicines.

■ TASK

Use the sources on this page to answer these questions. More evidence can be found on the pages listed on the timeline.

1. What kinds of illnesses were herbs used to treat?
2. Which healers have most used herbs as remedies?
3. 'Herbs have been used as medicines throughout history.' Does the evidence support this statement?
4. Why do you think herbs have been used throughout history as medicines?
5. Can you think of other examples of continuity in the history of health and medicine?

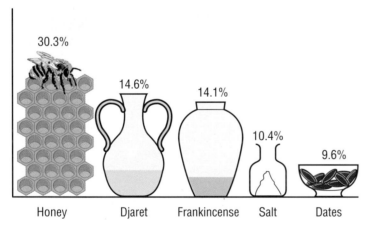

SOURCE 1 These were the most commonly used ingredients in Egyptian medicines recorded in the Ebers Papyrus. Honey, for example, was used in 30.3 per cent of the remedies. Unfortunately historians are not sure what 'djaret' was. Many other ingredients were used including juniper and figs

SOURCE 2 From *Bald's Leechbook*, an Anglo-Saxon compendium of treatments written around 900AD. Bald was the owner of the book and so was probably a doctor

66 Make an eye-salve for a stye: take onion and garlic, equal amounts of both, pound well together, take wine and bull's gall, equal amounts of both, mix with the onion and garlic, then put in a brass vessel, let stand for nine nights in the brass vessel, strain through a cloth and clear well, put in a horn and about night-time put on the stye with a feather; the best remedy. 99

SOURCE 3 From the diary of Parson James Woodforde, 1779

66 May 27 … My maid Nanny was taken very ill this evening with a dizziness in the head and desire to vomit but could not. Her straining to vomit brought on the hiccups which continued very violent till after she got to bed. I gave her a dose of rhubarb going to bed. Ben was also very ill and in the same complaint about noon, but he vomited and was soon better. I gave Ben a good dose of rhubarb also going to bed. 99

SOURCE 4 Some nineteenth-century remedies

*66 For whooping cough – mixtures of dropwort and comfrey.
For diarrhoea – rhubarb, aniseed, marshmallow root – a teaspoonful five or six times a day.
For asthma – the bark of the cranberry shrub, mixed with scull-cap, skunk cabbage, cloves, capsicum, sherry. Take half a wineglass two or three times a day. 99*

PRE HISTORY P. 11	ANCIENT EGYPT PP. 17, 20, 23	ANCIENT GREECE PP. 25, 31	THE ROMAN EMPIRE P. 38	THE MIDDLE AGES PP. 71, 77	THE MEDICAL RENAISSANCE PP. 92–93, 100–101, 102, 104	1750–1900 P. 122	THE TWENTIETH CENTURY PP. 105, 175
	3000BC			AD500		AD1750	AD1900

The leech makes a comeback

NOT ALL CONTINUITIES are straightforward. The leech was used by healers thousands of years ago. It is still used in medicine today. However, for a time the leech almost disappeared from medicine before making a recent dramatic comeback!

Leeches were used for centuries because of the theory of the Four Humours. Healers believed that patients were ill because they had too much of one of the humours in their bodies. One way to make them better was to attach leeches to the patients so that the leeches would suck away the excess blood.

Leeches continued to be used throughout the centuries and even in the nineteenth century they were still widely used to treat illnesses such as whooping cough, skin ailments and mental illnesses. A common treatment for headaches was to attach several leeches to the forehead and leave them to suck blood.

In the twentieth century leeches went out of fashion. They were not scientific enough. Recently, however, they have made a comeback in two different treatments. First, leeches can help patients who have had fingers or ears sewn back on after accidents. Problems have arisen in such cases when the arteries have healed faster than veins so that blood has flowed into the finger along arteries but has not been able to flow out again as quickly along the veins. The result is too much blood in one place and this stops the veins healing at all. Therefore doctors have used leeches on the spot where there is too much blood to suck out the excess and give the veins a chance to heal properly.

Secondly, leeches are helping to save lives with their saliva which contains a substance that stops blood clotting. Scientists can separate out this anti-coagulant and use it to treat people who have blood clots in the brain – the leech's saliva breaks down the blood clot. This treatment is also used to prevent blood clots building up and causing heart attacks.

1. Can you find another example in this book of an ancient treatment which went out of fashion then made a comeback?

SOURCE 1 A medieval man applying leeches to cleanse his blood

SOURCE 2 A doctor applying leeches to a patient in the late 1700s

SOURCE 3 Leech finders hunting for leeches in the nineteenth century

Change and continuity – women's role as midwives

THE HISTORY OF HERBS in medicine has mostly been one of continuity. There have also been continuities in the role played by women as midwives but there have been great changes too.

■ TASK 1

Write your own description of the changes in women's role as midwives from ancient times to the present. Use Sources 1–9.

Include your own analysis of which periods have seen change and which have seen continuity.

■ TASK 2

Did women's role in other branches of medicine, e.g. surgery, undergo similar changes? You can get a sheet from your teacher to help you investigate this.

> **SOURCE 1** Adapted from the works of Hyginus, a Greek writer
>
> 66 *The ancient [Greeks] had no midwives ... for the Athenians had decided that no slave or woman should learn the science of medicine. A certain girl, Hagnodice, as a young woman desired to learn the science of medicine. Because of this desire, she cut her hair, put on male clothing, and entrusted herself to a certain Herophilus for training.* 99
>
> [See page 31.]

SOURCE 2 This drawing of a second-century AD carving shows a Roman midwife and her assistant delivering a baby. Soranus, a Roman medical writer, said that 'we call a midwife faultless if she merely carries out her medical task; whereas we call her the best midwife if she goes further and in addition to her management of cases is well versed in theory [and] ... is trained in all branches of therapy ...'

> **SOURCE 3** M.L. Cameron, *Anglo-Saxon Medicine*, 1993
>
> 66 *I have described the physician as 'he' because there is no evidence that women practised medicine [in the Anglo-Saxon period]. Yet it is most unlikely ... that there were no women practising some form of medicine. Surely there were women midwives and village women gatherers of herbs and wise in their use and women learned in charms ... But there is not a shred of evidence for their existence.* 99

SOURCE 4 Midwives attending a birth. Doctors did not get involved in childbirth in the Middle Ages. By the 1400s midwives in France and Germany had to gain licences, follow apprenticeships and had to keep to rules of behaviour

SOURCE 5 Epitaph for Prudence Potter, Devon, 1689

  “ *Prudence Potter – Her life was spent in the industrious and successful practice of physic, chirurgery and midwifery.* **”**

SOURCE 6

1600s
Midwives were also licensed by the local bishop to supervise the last week of pregnancy and deliver babies. However, if there were complications, the midwife handed her patient over to a physician

1620
Peter Chamberlan invented the obstetric forceps. Anatomical knowledge was needed to use these. Only men could go to university to learn anatomy

1700s
Male doctors began to take over the role of midwives. Female midwives did not disappear, but their status was lowered and they had no way of getting training

SOURCE 7 Stages in the development of training for midwives

1880s *Florence Nightingale, concerned about standards in midwifery, attempts to set up a national training scheme for midwives*

1902 *Parliament passes Midwives Act which set standards for midwifery and made training compulsory*

1918 *Second Midwives Act allowed local authorities to train midwives*

SOURCE 8 Oral history interview quoted in Gray, *The Worst of Times*, 1986

  “ *I remember our Brian being born. He was delivered by a doctor up at Oldham, a Scotsman. He got called up and killed in the war, so we never paid for Brian.* **”**

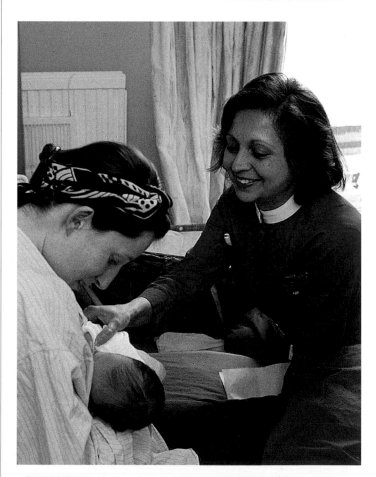

SOURCE 9 A modern midwife. She has had four years training and assists deliveries in hospitals and at home. Complicated births will still often be handed over to a doctor or a surgeon

Progress and regress: the story of public health

■ TASK 1

Sources 1–8 will help you answer the questions below. If you want to add more detail to your answers you can use the timeline as an index.

1. Make a list of the different ways in which governments have protected people's health.
2. In which periods was there progress in providing better public health schemes?
3. In which periods was there regress in the quality of public health care?
4. Look at the three graphs below. Which do you think best summarises the history of public health?

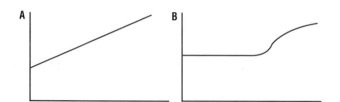

SOURCE 2 A sewer in York built during the Viking period

SOURCE 1 A stone sewer in York built by the Romans

SOURCE 3 A description of public health in fourteenth-century London

66 *By the 1380s there were at least 13 common privies in the city. One on Temple Bridge was built over the Thames.*

Wells and cesspools were often close together. Regulations said that cesspools had to be built two and a half feet from a neighbour's soil if walled with stone, three and a half if walled with earth. 1307 – Thomas Scott was fined for assaulting two citizens who complained when he urinated in a lane instead of using the common privy. 99

PRE HISTORY	ANCIENT EGYPT	ANCIENT GREECE	THE ROMAN EMPIRE PP. 46, 47

3000BC

SOURCE 4 Extract from orders given by the Mayor of London during the plague in 1665

" … every householder do cause the street to be daily prepared before his door, and so to keep it clean swept all the week long. The sweeping and filth of houses be daily carried away by the rakers.

Special care be taken that no stinking fish or unwholesome flesh or musty corn or other corrupt fruits be sold about the city. No hogs, dogs, cats, tame pigeons or conies be suffered to be kept within any part of the city, or any swine to be or stray in the streets or lanes. "

SOURCE 5 A description of the living conditions of Queen Victoria and Prince Albert in the 1850s and 1860s, written by the historian Anthony Wohl

" Although living by the Thames was most scenic, whenever the river rose the lawns were saturated by raw sewage, which habitually floated on the surface of the water. Resigned to this inevitably, they simply had the lawns raked and the filth shovelled back into the river. In drier weather on the other hand, the Thames muck was left high and dry along the banks and gave off an appalling odour. "

SOURCE 6 Slum housing in Glasgow in the 1860s. These houses were badly ventilated and overcrowded. The only toilets were the shared privies which you can see at the end of the yard

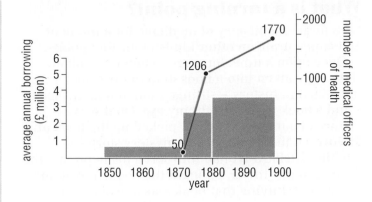

SOURCE 7 Numbers of Medical Officers of Health and average amount borrowed by councils for public health improvements

SOURCE 8 In the twentieth century the government forced local authorities to build better housing

■ TASK 2

Another feature of medicine and health which illustrates progress and regress is the story of hospitals. Use your own research in this book to find out how hospitals have changed. You can also get a sheet from your teacher to help you in your research.

THE MIDDLE AGES PP. 61, 66–67	THE MEDICAL RENAISSANCE	1750–1900 PP. 140–47	THE TWENTIETH CENTURY PP. 161, 164–69, 176–77

D500　　　　　　　　　　　　　　　　　　　　　AD1750　　　　　　　　　AD1900

Turning points: the consequences of germ theory

What is a turning point?

Let's forget the history of medicine for a moment and concentrate on other kinds of turning points.

Once upon a time, long ago, when I was about sixteen I walked into a bookshop in Liverpool. I was interested in history – strange though it might seem – and a book cover caught my eye. On it was a picture of a medieval king. I picked up the book and discovered that it was a true mystery story – whether Richard III had murdered his nephews, the Princes in the Tower. I bought the book, took it home and read it. Buying that book was one of the most important turning points in my life!

Why? Because I became so hooked on the subject of Richard III that I decided I wanted to study more about him at university. The only university that seemed to run a course on him was Leeds so I applied there, got the right grades and a place at Leeds. My life was then set on an entirely different path than if I had stayed at home or gone to a different town because I met my wife in Leeds and we both got jobs in the area. One of those jobs led to my writing a history book for schools and that led to more books until I was asked to co-write a history of medicine and health. So, if you've hated this book, you can blame it all on Richard III and the day I walked into that bookshop. If I hadn't bought that book my life would probably have been very different. Right, now back to the history of medicine!

1. Can you identify turning points from the history of medicine and health:
a) in surgery
b) in women's role as midwives?

■ TASK

1. Explain briefly (in no more than two sentences) why Pasteur's germ theory was a turning point in the history of medicine.
2. Sources 1–7 show consequences of the germ theory. Make a list of all the consequences. There are others suggested by the reference box if you want to draw up a longer list.
3. Divide your list into short- and long-term consequences.
4. Write a longer explanation of why the germ theory was a turning point, using your answers to questions 2 and 3 as the basis. You can get a sheet from your teacher to help you.

Reference box

These references will lead you to other short-term and long-term consequences of germ theory.

Page 130, Source 3
Page 131, Source 5
Page 133, Source 8
Page 138, Source 12
Page 146, Source 21
Page 155, Source 3
Page 156, Source 4
Page 161, Source 6
Page 170, Source 1
Page 173, Source 2
Page 176, Source 1

SOURCE 1 An operation taking place using Lister's carbolic spray

SOURCE 4 Aseptic surgery taking place in a late twentieth-century operating theatre. After germ theory increasingly complex operations inside the body were possible

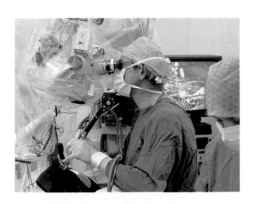

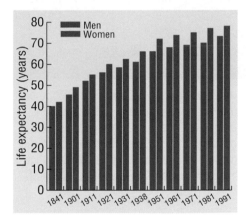

SOURCE 2 Graph showing life expectancy 1841–1991

SOURCE 5 *The Times'* account of Pasteur's triumphant test of his anthrax vaccine, June 1881

" *On 5th May, M. Rossignol's farm and 60 sheep were placed at M. Pasteur's disposal. Ten of the sheep were left untouched in order that they might later serve for a comparison. Of the remaining 50, 25 were marked with a hole in their ear and were inoculated on 5th May with weak virus and on 17th May with stronger virus. On 31st May none of them had lost fat or gaiety or appetite.*

On 31st May the 50 sheep were taken and all inoculated with the strongest virus. M. Pasteur predicted that today, 2nd June, the 25 sheep not inoculated would be dead and that the inoculated animals would show no symptoms of sickness. Today at half past one a number of spectators came together to witness the results. At 2 o'clock, 23 of the sheep which had not been inoculated were dead. The 24th died at 3 o'clock and the 25th an hour later.

The 25 inoculated animals were sound and frolicked and gave signs of perfect health.

The agricultural public now knows that an infallible preventative exists against anthrax. "

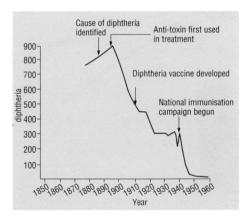

SOURCE 3 Graph showing decline in infant deaths from diphtheria

1880	Typhus
1882	Tuberculosis
1883	Cholera
1884	Tetanus
1886	Pneumonia
1887	Meningitis
1894	Plague
1898	Dysentery

SOURCE 6 Chart showing the dates at which the causes of different diseases were identified

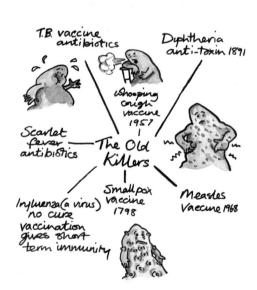

SOURCE 7 How the old killer diseases have been beaten

Patterns of change and continuity: surgery through time

THE LAST EIGHT PAGES have given you the chance to develop your understanding of some key ideas in history, about change and continuity, progress, regress and turning points. You are now going to pull all these ideas together in a study of surgery through time. As before you can use the material on these pages as the basis for your answers but you can also find more information on the pages listed on the timeline.

■ TASK

1. What examples can you find in the history of surgery of
a) continuity
b) progress or regress
c) turning points?
2. Was the pace of change always the same in surgery?
3. Write your own account of the history of surgery. You can base each of your paragraphs on one of these questions:
a) What kind of surgery did doctors perform before the nineteenth century?
b) What helped early doctors to improve their surgery?
c) How did Paré improve surgery?
d) What were the great breakthroughs in surgery in the 1800s?
e) Why were those breakthroughs important?
f) Has surgery changed rapidly in the twentieth century?
g) What were the most important factors in bringing about changes in surgery?
h) What were the most important factors which prevented changes in surgery?
i) What was the most important change in surgery?

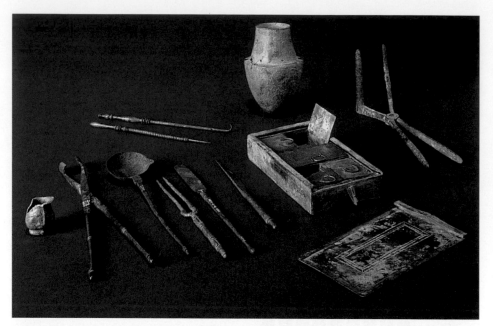

SOURCE 1 A set of Greek surgical instruments. Around 1200BC the development of iron and steel gave doctors stronger and sharper instruments. Greek surgeons developed good techniques for setting broken bones and also, in extreme cases, amputating limbs. However, very few operations were done inside the body. One of the exceptions was the draining of the lungs if a patient had pneumonia, an operation that was frequently and successfully undertaken, thanks to doctors' careful observation of the symptoms and pattern of the illness

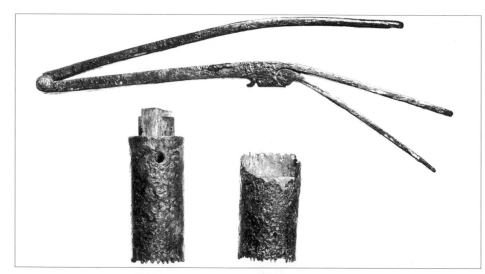

SOURCE 2 Trephining equipment used by surgeons in Roman Britain. Most trephined skulls found in Britain from the Roman period show signs of healing suggesting that this operation was performed successfully. The two crowns have teeth for cutting and the handle was used to rotate them

SOURCE 3 Celsus, *De Medicina*, Book VII

  ... a surgeon should be youthful or at any rate nearer youth than age; with a strong and steady hand which never trembles, and ready to use the left hand as well as the right; with vision sharp and clear, and spirit undaunted; filled with pity, so that he wishes to cure the patient, yet is not moved by his cries, to go too fast, or cut less than is necessary; but he does everything just as if the cries of pain cause him no emotion.

SOURCE 4 Theodoric of Lucca, a thirteenth-century surgeon

  Ancient surgeons and their disciples teach (and almost all modern surgeons follow them) that pus should be generated in wounds. There could be no greater error than this. For pus hinders the work of nature, prolongs the disease, prevents healing and the closing up of wounds ... My father used to heal almost every kind of wound with wine alone and he produced the most beautiful healing without any ointments.

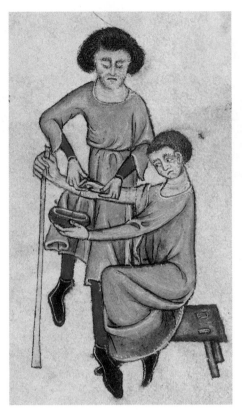

SOURCE 5 A fourteenth-century doctor bleeding a patient

SOURCE 7 Richard Wiseman's description of his treatment of wounds, mid 1600s

  The weapon thus drawn out, cleanse the wound from rags or ought else and permit the wound to bleed accordingly ... if there be hair growing about the wound shave it off, then wipe away the clotted blood with a sponge dipped in red wine, oxycrate or water.

SOURCE 8 Cartoon of a leg amputation in the 1700s. At this time amputation was one of the few operations attempted by surgeons with any success

SOURCE 6 In 1536 Ambroise Paré first treated soldiers. He copied the methods of other doctors, using boiling oil on wounds and cauterisation but:

  eventually I ran out of oil and I had to use a mixture made of yolks of eggs, oil of roses and turpentine. That night I could not sleep, fearing that the wounded would die or be poisoned because they had not been cauterised. I rose very early to visit them. Beyond my hope, I found those on whom I had used my mixture in little pain, their wounds without inflammation and having rested well. The others whom I had treated with boiling oil, I found feverish, with great pain and swelling around their wounds. I resolved with myself never more to burn thus cruelly poor men wounded with gunshot.

THE ROMAN EMPIRE PP. 37–39, 43–45	THE MIDDLE AGES PP. 70, 74	THE MEDICAL RENAISSANCE PP. 84–89, 94–96, 105

AD500   AD1750

SOURCE 9 Eighteenth-century surgical instruments including trephines

SOURCE 10 An account of an operation using ether as an anaesthetic by John Collins Warren, senior surgeon at Massachusetts General Hospital in 1846

66 *The patient was arranged for the operation in a sitting posture, and everything was made ready ... The patient was then made to inhale a fluid from a tube with a glass globe. After four or five minutes he appeared to be asleep, and was thought by Dr Morton to be in a condition for the operation. I made an incision between two or three inches long in the direction of the tumour, and to my great surprise without any starting, crying, or other indication of pain.* 99

	Total amputations	Died	% who died
1864–1866 (without antiseptics)	35	16	45.7
1867–1870 (with antiseptics)	40	6	15.0

SOURCE 11 Figures showing the improvements in Lister's results following the use of carbolic spray

SOURCE 12 *On the New Method of Treating Compound Fractures*, Joseph Lister, 1867

66 *James, aged 11 years, was admitted to the Glasgow Infirmary on August 2nd, 1865, with compound fracture of the left leg caused by the wheel of an empty cart passing over the limb a little below the middle. The wound, an inch and a half long and three quarters of an inch broad, was over the line of the fracture.*

A piece of lint dipped in carbolic acid was laid on the wound, and splints padded with cotton wool were applied. It was left undisturbed for four days and, when examined, it showed no sign of suppuration. For the next four days the wound was dressed with lint soaked with a solution of water and carbolic acid and olive oil which further prevented irritation to the skin. No pus was present, there seemed no danger of suppuration, and at the end of six weeks I found the bones united, and I discarded the splints. The sore was entirely healed ... 99

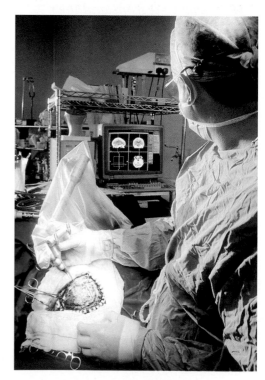

SOURCE 13 A modern surgical team has many technological aids at its disposal, including scanners and electronic monitoring equipment

1750–1900 PP. 134–39	THE TWENTIETH CENTURY PP. 151–53, 173–74

AD1750   AD1900

Glossary

abscess a collection of pus caused by an infection

ague an old-fashioned term for any disease causing a fever

ailment an illness that is not serious

amputation the removal of a limb by surgery

amulet a charm that the wearer believes gives protection from disease

anaesthetic a drug or drugs given to produce unconsciousness before and during surgery

anatomy the science of understanding the structure and make-up of the body

antibiotics a group of drugs used to treat infections caused by bacteria, e.g. penicillin

antisepsis the prevention of infection by stopping the growth of bacteria by the use of antiseptics

antiseptics chemicals used to destroy bacteria and prevent infection

apothecary a pharmacist or chemist

arteries blood vessels that carry blood away from the heart

arthritis the painful swelling of joints

Asclepion temple of the Greek god of healing Asclepius (or Asklepios)

astrology the study of the planets and how they might influence the lives of people

bacterium (pl.bacteria) see **germ**

balm see **salve**

bezoar stone a ball of indigestible material found in goats' stomachs

biochemist a scientist who studies the make-up of living things

Black Death a phrase used in the Middle Ages to describe bubonic plague. (The 'blackness' was caused by bleeding under the skin. Over 50 per cent of all cases were fatal)

bleed/bleeding the treatment of opening a vein or applying leeches to draw blood from the patient. Also means the loss of blood caused by damage to the blood vessels

cauterise using a hot iron to burn body tissue. This seals a wound and stops bleeding

cell the basic unit of life which makes up the bodies of plants, animals and humans. Billions of cells are contained in the human body

cesspool/cesspit a place for collecting and storing sewage

chirurgery/chirurgeons surgery/surgeons

chloroform a liquid whose vapour acts as an anaesthetic and produces unconsciousness

chromosomes thread-like structures in the nuclei of cells that contain genetic information

constipation difficulty clearing the bowels

constitution the physical make-up of a person

consumption/consumptive fever tuberculosis which was observed as the wasting away of the body

contagion the passing of disease from one person to another

contaminated/contamination something that is infected

cordial a non-alcoholic drink

coronary referring to the blood vessels around the heart (coronary thrombosis, a blood clot in the coronary artery)

culture/culturing the growth of micro-organisms in the laboratory

diarrhoea a symptom of a disease, frequent, fluid bowel movements

dissection the cutting up and examination of a body

DNA Deoxyribonucleic acid, the molecule that genes are made of. (see **gene** below)

dropsy an old-fashioned term used to describe fluid collection in the body, often used to account for death

dysentery a severe infection causing frequent, fluid bowel movements

effluvia/effluvial unpleasant smells from waste matter. Blamed for disease in the eighteenth and nineteenth centuries

electron microscope a powerful microscope that uses electrons rather than light to produce a magnified image

embalm the treatment of a dead body to preserve it

endoscope an instrument used to view inside the body

faeces waste material from the stomach and digestive system

flux a watery discharge or diarrhoea

foetus a baby before it is born

gangrene (gas gangrene) the infection of dead tissue causing, in the case of gas gangrene, foul smelling gas

gene part of the nucleus of a cell that determines how our bodies look and work. Genes are passed from parents to children

genetic engineering the investigation of genes and how they can be used to change how the body works

germ a micro-organism that causes disease

germ theory the theory that germs cause disease, often by infection through the air

gonorrhoea a sexually transmitted disease that can be treated with antibiotics

haemorrhage the medical term for bleeding

Health Authority the people controlling NHS health care in the regions

high-tech surgery surgery using the most modern techniques, including computers, new skills and new drugs

Hippocratic Oath the principles by which doctors work, for the best health of the patient and to do no harm, named after Hippocrates who wrote it

immune protected against a disease

immunise the process of giving protection from disease through the body's own immune system

immunity protection against disease through the body's own defences or immune system

incision a cut made with a knife in surgery

infection the formation of disease-causing germs or micro-organisms

infirmary a place where the sick are treated, a hospital

inoculation putting a low dose of a disease into the body to help it fight against a more serious attack of the disease

insulin a hormone (chemical) produced by the pancreas that controls the amount of sugar in the blood

jaundice a sign of a liver disorder that results in the yellowing of the skin

King's Evil see **scrofula**

laissez-faire belief that governments should not interfere in people's lives. It prevented public health schemes getting going in the nineteenth century

leeches a blood-sucking worm used to drain blood from a wound

leper someone suffering from leprosy, an infection that causes damage to the nerves and skin

ligament tough elastic tissue that holds joints of the body together

ligatures a thread used to tie a blood vessel during an operation

lunatic an old-fashioned word for someone who is insane

malady *see* **ailment**

maternity concerning motherhood and looking after children

medical officer a person appointed to look after the public health of an area

melancholy part of the theory of four humours, brought on by excess of gloominess

meningitis inflammation of the brain caused by an infection by micro-oganisms, a virus or bacterium

miasma smells from decomposing material that were believed to cause disease

microbe another name for a micro-organism

micro-organism a tiny single-celled living organism too small to be seen by the naked eye. Disease-causing micro-organisms are called bacteria

osteoarthritis *see* **arthritis**

papyrus early 'paper' made from the papyrus plant

parasites animals that live on or in other animals

penicillin the first antibiotic drug produced from the mould penicillium to treat infections

physic a medicine *or* the skill of healing

physician a doctor of medicine who trained at university

physiology the study of how the body works

plague a serious infectious disease spread to humans by fleas from rats and mice

pneumonia the inflammation of the lungs due to an infection

Poor Law Commission three commissioners who controlled the work of parishes which provided help for the poor. They were influential in public health reforms

poultice a warm dressing made of layers of fabric and moist paste

pre-industrial before the industrial revolution of the eighteenth and nineteenth centuries

prognosis medical judgement about the probable course and result of a disease

public health refers to the well-being of the whole community

pus a pale yellow or green fluid found where there is an infection

putrid decomposing

quack a person who falsely claims to have medical ability or qualifications

quinine the drug treatment for malaria

remedy a drug or treatment that cures or controls the symptoms of a disease

rheumatism a term describing stiffness in muscles or joints

rickets a disease caused by a poor diet resulting in a misshapen skeleton

salve a soothing ointment

sanatorium a place where people who are chronically (very) ill can be cared for

sciatica pain that runs along the sciatic nerve in the leg

scrofula sometimes known as the King's Evil. It is tuberculosis of a gland in the neck. At one time it was believed that being touched by the king could cure the disease

septicaemia blood poisoning caused by the spread of bacteria from an infected area

sinew a tendon or fibrous cord that joins a muscle to a bone

spontaneous generation the theory that decaying matter turns into germs

staphylococci bacteria found on the skin that can cause infection if the bacteria become trapped

sterilise to destroy all living micro-organisms from surfaces and surgical instruments, e.g. on a scalpel before an operation

stye a small pus-filled abscess near the eyelashes caused by infection

sulphonamide an antibacterial drug used to treat bronchitis and pneumonia

supernatural something that cannot be given an ordinary explanation

superstition an unreasonable belief based on ignorance and sometimes fear

suppuration the formation and/or discharge of pus

suture the closing of a cut or wound by the use of stitches (sutures)

syphilis a sexually-transmitted disease that was common from the late fifteenth century until the introduction of penicillin

thalidomide a drug to help morning sickness that was withdrawn in 1961 after it was found to cause limb deformities in babies born to women who had taken it

therapy the treatment of either a physical or mental disease

transfusion the use of blood given by one person to another when a patient has suffered severe blood loss

trephining the drilling of a hole in the skull

tumour a swelling caused by cells reproducing at an increased rate. An abnormal growth of cells which may or may not be cancerous

ulcer an open sore on the skin

unpasteurised food or drink that has not been pasteurised. Pasteurisation is a process of heating which destroys harmful bacteria

vaccination the injection into the body of killed or weakened organisms to give the body resistance against disease

virus a tiny micro-organism, smaller than bacteria, responsible for infections such as colds, flu, polio and chicken pox

wise woman a person believed to be skilled in magic or local customs

witch/witchcraft a person who practises magic and is believed to have dealings with evil spirits

worms an infestation where worms live as parasites in the human body

Index